THE
LIFE OF JESUS CHRIST
FOR THE YOUNG

The Life of Jesus Christ
For the Young

Volume Two

*From the Call of the Apostles
to our Lord's Ascension*

Richard Newton

Solid Ground Christian Books
Birmingham, Alabama USA

Solid Ground Christian Books
2090 Columbiana Rd, Suite 2000
Birmingham, AL 35216
205-443-0311
sgcb@charter.net
http://solid-ground-books.com

The Life of Jesus Christ for the Young
VOLUME TWO: FROM THE CALL OF THE APOSTLES TO THE ASCENSION OF OUR LORD

Richard Newton (1813-1887)

Taken from 1913 edition by George Barrie & Sons, Philadelphia, PA

Solid Ground Classic Reprints

First printing of new edition June 2005

Cover work by Borgo Design, Tuscaloosa, AL
Contact them at nelbrown@comcast.net

Cover painting by William Hole (1846-1917) of the Royal Scottish Academy. Painting entitled "He is not Here, but is Risen" from Luke 23:56; 24:1-9.

ISBN: 1-932474-89-7

CONTENTS

VOLUME III

CHAPTER		PAGE
	MAP OF PALESTINE, ... *Fronts.*	
I	THE APOSTLES CHOSEN	1
II	THE GREAT TEACHER	33
III	CHRIST TEACHING BY PARABLES	61
IV	CHRIST TEACHING BY MIRACLES	93
V	CHRIST TEACHING LIBERALITY	125
VI	CHRIST TEACHING HUMILITY	157
VII	CHRIST AND THE LITTLE CHILDREN	187
VIII	THE TRANSFIGURATION	215
IX	THE LESSONS FROM OLIVET	245
X	THE LORD'S SUPPER	275

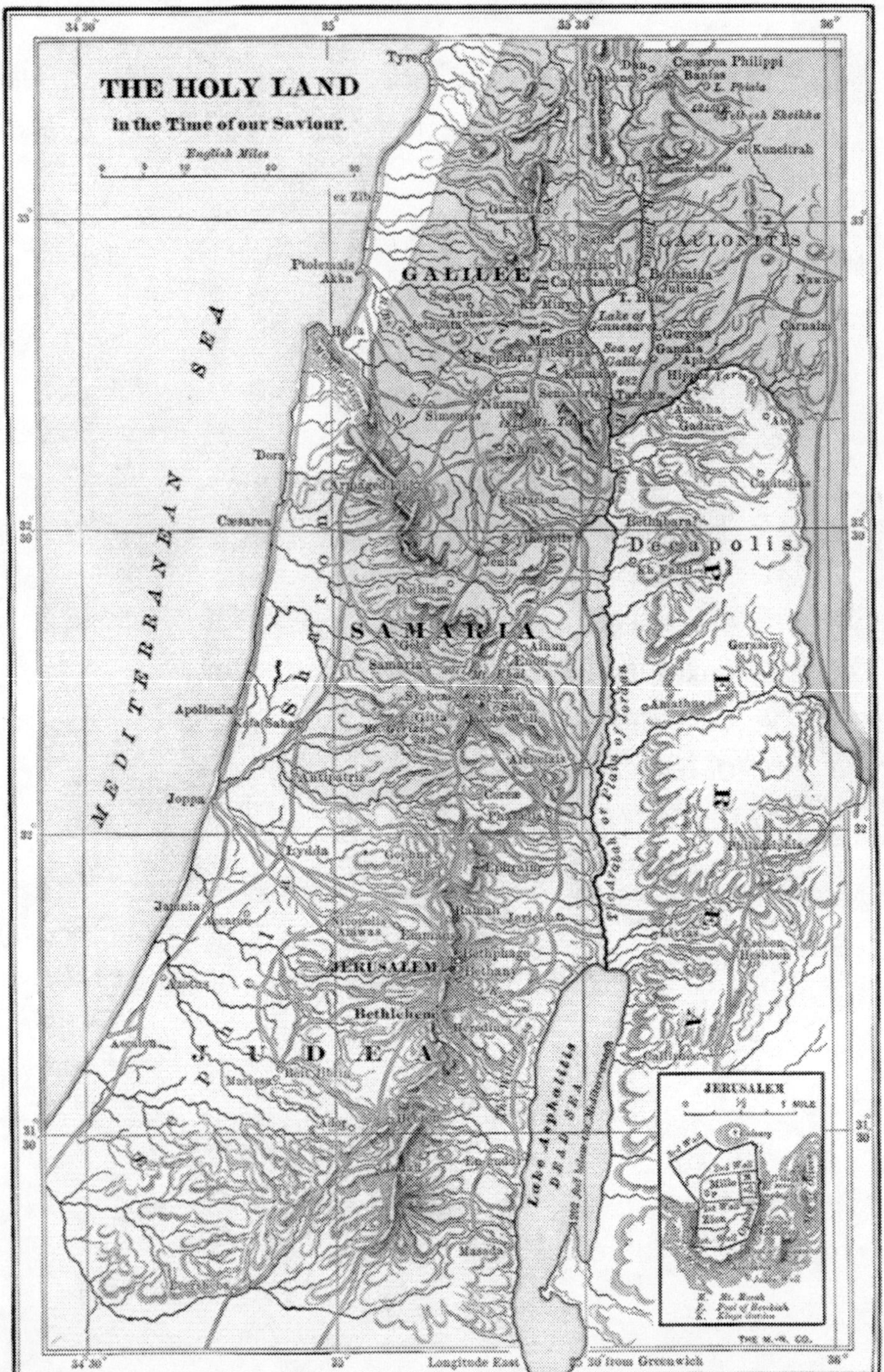
THE HOLY LAND
in the Time of our Saviour.
English Miles
MEDITERRANEAN SEA
GALILEE
GAULONITIS
SAMARIA
JUDÆA
Decapolis
Tyre
Cæsarea Philippi
Banias
el Kuneitrah
Ptolemais
Akka
Capernaum
Chorazin
Bethsaida
Julias
Magdala
Tiberias
Sepphoris
Cana
Nazareth
Simonias
Gergesa
Gamala
Gadara
Dora
Cæsarea
Jezreel
Bethabara
Samaria
Apollonia
Antipatris
Joppa
Lydda
Ephraim
Jericho
Emmaus
Bethphage
Bethany
JERUSALEM
Bethlehem
Jamnia
Ascalon
Amathus
Gerasa
Philadelphia
Heshbon
Lake Asphaltitis
DEAD SEA
Masada
JERUSALEM
Longitude East from Greenwich

THE APOSTLES CHOSEN

AS soon as he returned victorious from the temptation in the wilderness, Jesus entered on the work of his public ministry. We find him, at once, preaching to the people, healing the sick, and doing many wonderful works. The commencement of his ministry is thus described by St. Matt. iv: 23-25. "And Jesus went about all Galilee, teaching in their synagogues, and preaching the gospel of the kingdom, and healing all manner of sickness, and all manner of disease among the people. And his fame went throughout all Syria; and they brought unto him all sick people that were taken with divers diseases and torments, and those which were possessed with devils, and those which were lunatic, and those that had the palsy; and he healed them. And there followed him great multitudes of people from Galilee, and from Decapolis, and from Jerusalem, and from Judea, and from beyond Jordan." What a blessed beginning of the most blessed of all ministries this was! He came to bless our world. He did bless it, as no one else could have done. And here, we see, how he entered on his work.

And one of the first things he did, after thus beginning his ministry, was to gather his disciples round him. The first two that we find named among his disciples are John and Andrew. They had been disciples of John the Baptist. Their master pointed them to Jesus, and said—"Behold the Lamb of God." When they heard this they followed Jesus, and became his disciples. When Andrew met with his brother Simon Peter, he said to him "we have found the Messias—the Christ. And he brought him to Jesus." After this we are told that "Jesus findeth Philip, and saith unto him, Follow me." He was an acquaintance of Andrew and Peter, and lived in the same town with them. He obeyed the call at once and became one of the disciples of Jesus.

Philip had a friend named Nathanael. The next time he met him, he said, "we have found him of whom Moses in the law, and the prophets did write, Jesus of Nazareth, the son of

Joseph." But Nazareth was a despised place, and had a bad reputation. Nathanael had a very poor opinion of the place, and he asked—"Can there any good thing come out of Nazareth?" Philip saith unto him—"Come and see."

And this is what we should say to persons when we wish them to become Christians. There is so much that is lovely and excellent in Jesus that if people will only "come and see," if they will only prove for themselves what a glorious Saviour he is, they will find it impossible to help loving and serving him. Nathanael came to Jesus. And when he heard the wonderful words that Jesus spoke to him he was converted at once, and expressed his wonder by saying—"Rabbi, thou art the Son of God; thou art the King of Israel." We can read all about this in John i: 43-51. Nathanael became a disciple of Jesus, and one of the twelve apostles, and is supposed to be the same one who bears the name of Bartholomew in the different lists of of the apostles.

After this we read of Jesus calling Matthew the publican, who was a tax-gatherer. This is what is meant by his "sitting at the receipt of custom." "Follow me," were the words spoken to him. He obeyed at once; left all and followed Jesus. St. Luke and St. Mark mention this same call, but they give the name of Levi to the person thus called. This is not strange, for it was common among the Jews for persons to have two names. Sometimes they were called by one of these names and sometimes by the other.

Here we have the account of six persons, who became disciples of Jesus; and of the different ways in which they were led to follow him. No doubt many others were led to become his disciples from simply hearing him preach; and from listening to the gracious words that he spoke.

And very soon after he had gathered together a large company of disciples, he made choice of twelve, out of this number, who were to be his apostles. He wished these men to be with him all the time. They were to hear his teaching, and see his miracles, and so be prepared to take his place, and carry on his work when he should return to heaven.

It was necessary for these men to be chosen. When Washington was appointed to conduct our armies during the Revolution, he chose a number of generals to help him. And it is natural for us to think of Washington and his generals. But just as natural it is to think of—Jesus and his apostles.

And this is the subject we have now to consider—*The Apostles Chosen.*

And in considering this subject there are four things of which to speak.

The first, is the condition and character of the men whom Jesus chose as his apostles.

The second, is the work these men were called to do.

The third, is the help that was given them in doing this work; and

The fourth, is the lesson taught us by this subject. Or, to make the points of the subject as short as possible, we may state them thus:

The men. The work. The help. The lesson.

We begin then with speaking of—THE MEN—*or the condition and character of those whom Jesus chose to be his apostles or helpers.*

Now we might have thought that Jesus would have chosen his apostles, or helpers, from among the angels of heaven. They are so wise, and good, and strong, that we wonder why he did not choose them. But he did not. He chose *men* to be his apostles. And what kind of men did he choose? If we had been asked this question beforehand, we should have supposed that he would certainly have chosen the wisest and the most learned men, the richest and greatest men that could be found in the world. But it was not so. Instead of this he chose poor men, unlearned men, men that were not famous at all; and who had not been heard of before. Fishermen, and tax-gatherers, and men occupying very humble positions in life, were those whom Jesus chose to be his apostles.

And one reason, no doubt, why Jesus made choice of men of this character to be his apostles was that when their work was done, no one should be able to say that it was the learning, or wisdom, or riches, or power of men by whom that work was accomplished. The apostle Paul teaches us that this is the way in which God generally acts; and that he does it for the very reason just spoken of. He says, "God hath chosen the foolish things of the world to confound the wise; and God hath chosen the weak things of the world to confound the mighty; and base things of the world, and things which are despised hath God chosen, yea, and things which are not, to bring to nought the things that are; that no flesh should glory in his presence." I. Cor. i: 27-29. The meaning of this passage is that God loves to work by little things. This was the reason why Jesus chose poor, unlearned fishermen to be his apostles. And we see God working in the same way continually.

Look at yonder sun. God made it, and hung it up there in the sky that it might give light to our world. But the light which this sun gives comes to us in tiny little bits, smaller than the point of the finest needle that ever was made. They are so small that hundreds of them can rush right into our eyes, as they are doing all the time, and not hurt them the least. Here we see how God makes use of little things, and does a great work with them.

And then look at yonder ocean. The waves of that ocean are so powerful that they can break in pieces the strongest ships that men have ever built. And yet, when God wishes to keep that mighty ocean in its place, he makes use of little grains of sand for this purpose. Here again we see how God employs little things, and does a great work with them. And we find God working in this way continually. Let us look at one or two illustrations.

"What a Plant Did." A little plant was given to a sick girl. In trying to take care of it, the family made changes in their way of living, which added greatly to their comfort and happiness. First, they cleaned the window, that more light might come in to the leaves of the plant. Then, when not too cold, they opened the window, that fresh air might help the plant to grow; and this did the family good, as well as the plant. Next the clean window made the rest of the room look so untidy that they washed the floor, and cleaned the walls, and arranged the furniture more neatly. This led the father of the family to mend a broken chair or two, which kept him at home several evenings. After this, he took to staying at home with his family in the evenings, instead of spending his time at the tavern; and the money thus saved went to buy comforts for them all. And then, as their home grew more pleasant, the whole family loved it better than ever before, and they grew healthier and happier with their flowers. What a little thing that plant was, and yet it was God's apostle to that family! It did a great work for them in blessing them and making them happy. And *that* was work that an angel would have been glad to do.

"Brought In by a Smile." A London minister said to a friend one day; "Seven persons were received into my church last Sunday, and they were all brought in by a smile."

"Brought in by a smile! Pray what do you mean?"

"Let me explain. Several months ago, as I passed a certain house on my way to church, I saw, held in the arms of its nurse, a beautiful infant; and as it fixed its bright black eyes on me, I smiled, and the dear child returned the smile. The next Sabbath the babe was again before the window. Again I smiled, and the smile was returned, as before. The third Sabbath, as I passed by the window, I threw the little one a kiss. Instantly its hand was extended and a kiss thrown back to me. And so it came to pass that I learned to watch for the baby on my way to church; and as the weeks went by, I noticed that the nurse and the baby were not alone. Other members of the family pressed to the window to see the gentleman who always had a smile for the dear baby—the household pet.

"One Sunday morning, as I passed, two children, a boy and a girl, stood at the window beside the baby. That morning the father and mother had said to those children: 'Get ready for church, for we think that the gentleman who always smiles to the baby is a minister.

When he passes you may follow him, and see where he preaches.'

"The children were quite willing to follow the suggestion of their parents, and after I had passed, the door opened, and the children stepped upon the pavement, and kept near me, till I entered my church, when they followed me, and seats were given them.

"When they returned home, they sought their parents and eagerly exclaimed: 'He is a minister, and we have found his church, and he preached a beautiful sermon this morning. You must go and hear him next Sunday.'

"It was not difficult to persuade the parents to go, and guided by their children they found their way to the church. They, too, were pleased, and other members of the family were induced to come to the house of God. God blessed what they heard to the good of their souls, and seven members of this family have been led to become Christians, and join the church, and, I repeat what I said before: 'they were all brought in by a smile.'"

What a little thing a smile is! And yet, here we see how God made use of so small a thing as this, to make seven persons Christians, and to save their souls forever!

Of the God who can work in this way, it may well be said that he loves to work by little things. It is the way in which he is working continually.

How eagerly, then, we may try to learn and to practise what has been very sweetly expressed in

THE MITE SONG.

"Only a drop in the bucket,
    But every drop will tell,
The bucket would soon be empty,
    Without the drops in the well.

"Only a poor little penny,
    It was all I had to give;
But as pennies make the dollars,
    It may help some cause to live.

"A few little bits of ribbon,
    And some toys—they were not new,
But they made the sick child happy,
    And that made me happy, too.

"Only some out-grown garments;
    They were all I had to spare;
But they'll help to clothe the needy,
    And the poor are everywhere.

"A word now and then of comfort,
    That cost me nothing to say;
But the poor old man died happy,
    And it helped him on the way.

"God loveth the cheerful giver,
  Though the gifts be poor and small;
But what must he think of his children
  Who never give at all?"

God loves to work by little means. We see this when we think of the men whom Jesus chose to be his apostles. The first thing about this subject is—*the men.*

The second thing to speak of, in connection with this subject, is—THE WORK—*they had to do.*

What this work was we find fully stated in the fourteenth chapter of St. Matthew. In this chapter Jesus told the apostles all about the work they were to do for him, and how they were to do it. In the seventh and eighth verses of this chapter we have distinctly stated just what they were to do. "As ye go, preach, saying, The kingdom of heaven is at hand: Heal the sick, cleanse the lepers, raise the dead, cast out devils."

On this occasion Jesus sent his apostles to do the work committed to them, not among the Gentiles, but only among the Jews; or as he calls them—"the lost sheep of the house of Israel," v. 5, 6. But, after his resurrection, and just before he went up to heaven, he enlarged their commission. His parting command to them then was—"*Go ye into all the world, and preach the gospel to every creature.*" St. Mark xvi: 15.

When Jesus, their Master, went to heaven they were to take up and carry on the great work that he had begun. Those twelve men were to begin the work of changing the religion of the world. They were to overturn the idols that had been worshiped for ages. They were to shut up the temples in which those idols had been worshiped. They were to "turn men from darkness to light, and from the power of Satan unto God." Acts xxvi: 18. They were to go up and down the world, everywhere, telling the wondrous story of Jesus and his love. And in doing this work they were to be the means of saving the souls of all who believed their message, and in the end of winning the world back to Jesus, till, according to God's promise, he has "the heathen for his inheritance, and the utmost parts of the earth for his possession." Ps. ii: 8.

This was the grandest and most important work that men were ever called upon to do. The apostles spent their lives in doing this work; and then they left it for others to carry on. The work is not finished yet. And, if we learn to love and serve Jesus, we may help to carry it on. We may be apostles, too, though in a lower sense than that in which the first twelve were apostles. An apostle means—one *sent.* But Jesus *sends* into the vineyard to work for him all who become his loving children. And, in this sense it is true that all who love and serve Jesus are his apostles. He says to each of us—"Go, work to-day, in my vineyard." St. Matt. xxi: 28. And in another place he says—"Let him that heareth, say, Come." Rev. xxii: 17.

And when we are trying to tell people of Jesus and his love, and to bring them to him, then we are helping to carry on the same great work that Jesus gave his apostles to do. Let us look at some examples of persons who have been apostles for God and helped to do the work of apostles.

"Aunt Lucy." I heard the other day of a good old woman in the State of Michigan, known as Aunt Lucy. She is eighty-four years old, and lives all alone, supporting herself principally by carpet-weaving. All that she can save from her earnings, after paying for her necessary expenses, she spends in buying Bibles, which she distributes among the children and the poor of the neighborhood. Thirteen large family Bibles, and fifty small ones, have thus been given away—good, well-bound Bibles.

A neighbor, who has watched this good work very closely, says that two-thirds of the persons to whom Aunt Lucy has given Bibles have afterwards become Christians. In doing this work Aunt Lucy was an apostle.

"The Charcoal Carrier." One Sunday afternoon, in summer, a little girl named Mary, going home from a Sunday-school in the country, sat down to rest under the shade of a tree by the roadside. While sitting there she opened her Bible to read. As she sat reading, a man, well known in that neighborhood as Jacob, the charcoal carrier, came by with his donkey. Jacob used to work in the woods, making charcoal, which he carried away in sacks on his donkey's back, and sold. He was not a Christian man, and was accustomed to work with his donkey as hard on Sunday as on week-days.

When he came by where Mary was sitting, he stopped a moment, and said, in a good-natured way:

"What book is that you are reading, my little maid?"

"It is God's book—the Bible," said Mary.

"Let me hear you read a little in it, if you please," said he, stopping his donkey.

Mary began at the place where the book was open, and read:—"Remember the Sabbath day, to keep it holy. Six days shalt thou labor, and do all thy work."

"There, that's enough," said Jacob, "and now tell me what it means."

"It means," said Mary, "that you mustn't carry charcoal, on Sunday, nor let your donkey carry it."

"Does it?" said Jacob, musing a little. "I tell you what then, I must think over what you have said."

And he *did* think over it. And the result of his thinking was, that instead of going with his donkey to the woods on the next Sunday, he went with his two little girls to the Sunday-school. And the end of it all was that Jacob, the charcoal carrier, became a Christian, and God's blessing rested on him and his family.

Little Mary was doing an apostle's work when she read and explained the Bible to Jacob and was the means of bringing him to Jesus.

"The Use of Fragments." In the Cathedral at Lincoln, England, there is a window of stained glass which was made by an apprentice out of little pieces of glass that had been thrown aside by his master as useless. It is said to be the most beautiful window in the Cathedral. And if, like this apprentice, we carefully gather up, and improve the little bits of time, of knowledge, and of opportunities that we have, we may do work for God more beautiful than that Cathedral window. We may do work like that which the apostles were sent to do. Here are some sweet lines, written by I know not whom, about that beautiful window, made out of the little pieces of glass:

> "Great things are made of fragments small,
>   Small things are germs of great;
> And, of earth's stately temples, all
>   To fragments owe their weight.
>
> "This window, peer of all the rest,
>   Of fragments small is wrought;
> Of fragments that the artist deemed
>   Unworthy of his thought.
>
> "And thus may we, of little things,
>   Kind words and gentle deeds,
> Add wealth or beauty to our lives,
>   Which greater acts exceeds.
>
> "Each victory o'er a sinful thought,
>   Each action, true and pure,
> Is, 'mid our life's engraving, wrought
>   In tints that shall endure."

The second thing about the apostles is, *the work*—they did.

The third thing, for us to notice about the apostles, is—THE HELP—*they received.*

In one place, we are told that Jesus "gave them power against unclean spirits, to cast them out, and to heal all manner of sickness, and all manner of disease." St. Matt. x: 1. In another place we are told, that for their comfort and encouragement in the great work they had to do, Jesus said to them, "Lo, I am with you always, even unto the end of the world." St. Matt. xvviii: 20. And if they only had Jesus with them, no matter what the work was they had to do, they would be sure of having all the help they might need. The apostle Paul understood this very well, for he said, "I can do all things through Christ, which strengtheneth me." Phil. iv: 13.

And then, as if his own presence with them were not enough, Jesus promised that his apostles should have the help of the Holy Spirit in carrying on their work. Just before leaving them to go to heaven, he said to the disciples —"Ye shall receive power, after that the Holy Ghost is come upon you." Acts i: 8. And what this power was we see in the case of the apostle Peter; for the first sermon he preached after the Holy Ghost came upon him, on the day of Pentecost, was the means of converting three thousand souls. Acts ii: 41.

And the same God who gave the apostles all the help they needed, has promised to do the same for you, and me, and for all who try to work for him. There are many promises of this kind in the Bible to which I might refer. But I will only mention one. This is so sweet and precious that it deserves to be written in letters of gold. There is no passage in the Bible that has given me so much comfort and encouragement in trying to work for God as this I refer here to Is. xli: 10. "Fear thou not; for I am with thee; be not dismayed; for I am thy God; I will strengthen thee; yea—I WILL HELP THEE." This promise was not given for prophets and apostles only, but for all God's people to the end of time. You and I, if we are trying to serve God, may take it as ours. God meant it for us. And when we get this promised help from God, we can do any work he has for us to do, and be happy in doing it.

"For Thine is the Power." "I can't do it— it's quite impossible. I've tried five times, and can't get it right"—and Ben Hartley pushed his book and slate away in despair. Ben was a good scholar. He was at the head of his class, and was very anxious to stay there. But the sums he had now to do were very hard. He could not do them, and was afraid of losing his place in the class. Most of the boys had some one at home to help them; but Ben had no one. His father was dead, and his mother, though a good Christian woman, had not been to school much when a girl, and she could not help Ben.

Mrs. Hartley felt sorry for her son's perplexity, and quietly said, "Then, Ben, you don't believe in the Lord's prayer?"

"The Lord's prayer, mother! Why, there's nothing there to help a fellow do his sums."

"O, yes; there is. There is help for every trouble in life in the Lord's prayer, if we only know how to use it. I was trying a long time before I found out what the last part of this prayer really means. I'm no minister, or scholar, Ben, but I'll try and show you. You know that in this prayer we ask God for our daily bread; we ask him to keep us from evil; and to forgive us our sins; and then we say: 'for *thine* is the *kingdom*, and *the power*, and the glory.' It's God's power that we rely on—not our own;

and it often helps me, Ben, when I have something hard to do. I say, 'For *thine* is the power—this is my duty, heavenly Father; but I can't do it myself; give me thy power to help me,' and he does it, Ben, he does it."

Ben sat silent. It seemed almost too familiar a prayer. And yet he remembered when he had to stay home from school because he had no clothes fit to go in, how he prayed to God about it, and the minister's wife brought him a suit the very next day. "But a boy's sums, mother! it seems like such a little thing to ask God about."

"Those sums are not a little thing to you, Ben. Your success at school depends on your knowing how to do them. *That,* is as much to you, as many a greater thing to some one else. Now I care a great deal about that, because I love you. And I know your Father in heaven loves you more than I do. I would gladly help you, if I could; but he *can* help you. His 'is the power;' ask him to help you."

After doing an errand for his mother, Ben picked up his book and slate and went up to his little room. Kneeling down by the bed he repeated the Lord's prayer. When he came to—"thine is the kingdom," he stopped a

moment, and then said, with all his heart—
"'And thine is the power,' heavenly Father. I want power to know how to do these sums. There's no one else to help me. Lord, please give me power, for Jesus' sake, Amen."

Ben waited a moment, and then, still on his knees, he took his slate and tried again. Do you ask me if he succeeded? Remember what Saint James says, "If any man lack wisdom let him ask of God, who giveth to all men liberally, and upbraideth not: *and it shall be given him.*" Jas. i: 5. That is God's promise, and heaven and earth must pass away before one of his promises shall fail. Ben had prayed to God to help him, and God answered his prayer. He tried once more to work out those sums. After thinking over them a little while, he saw the mistake he had made in neglecting one of the rules for working the sums. He corrected this mistake, and then he found they all worked out beautifully. The next day he was head of the class; for he was the only boy who could say that he had done the sum himself, without getting any one at home to help him.

"And yet I was helped, mother," said Ben, "for I am sure my Father in heaven helped me." But that was not what the teacher meant. After this, Ben never forgot the last part of the Lord's prayer. When he needed help he knew where the power was that could help him.

Here was where the apostles got the help they needed in doing the hard work they had to do. And how much help we might get in doing our work if we only make a right use of this "power which belongeth unto God;" and which he is always ready to use in helping us.

The help they received, is the third thing to remember when we think about the apostles and their work.

The last thing to bear in mind when we think of Jesus choosing his twelve apostles, is—THE LESSON —*it teaches us.*

There are many lessons we might learn from this subject; but there is one so much more important than all the rest that we may very well let them go, and think only of this one. When St. Luke tells us about Jesus choosing the twelve apostles, he mentions one very important thing, of which St. Matthew, in his account of it says nothing at all. And it is this thing from which we draw our lesson. In the twelfth verse of the sixth chapter of his gospel, St. Luke says—"And it came to pass in those days, that he (Jesus) went out into a mountain to pray, and *continued all night in prayer to God.*" And after this, the first thing he did, in the morning, was to call his disciples to him, and out of them to choose the twelve, who were to be his apostles. And the lesson we learn from this part of the subject is:

"The Lesson of Prayer." Jesus spent the whole night in prayer to God, before he chose his apostles. How strange this seems to us! And yet it is easy enough to see at least two reasons why he did this. One was because *he loved to pray.* We know how pleasant it is for us to meet, and talk with a person whom we love very much. But prayer is—talking with God—telling him what we want, and asking his help. But Jesus loved his Father in heaven, with a love deeper and stronger than we can understand. This must have made it the most delightful of all things for him to be engaged in prayer, or in talking with his Father in heaven. And, if we really love Jesus, prayer will not be a hard duty to us, but a sweet privilege. We shall love to pray, because, in prayer we are talking to that blessed Saviour, "whom, not having seen, we love." And this was one reason why Jesus spent the whole night in prayer, before choosing his twelve apostles.

But there was another reason why Jesus spent so much time in prayer before performing this important work, and that was to *set us an example*. It was to teach us the very lesson of which we are now speaking—the lesson of prayer. Remember how much power and wisdom Jesus had in himself; and what mighty things he was able to do. And yet, if *He* felt that it was right to pray before engaging in any important work, how much more necessary it is for us to do so!

Let us learn this lesson well. Let it be the rule and habit of our lives to connect prayer with everything we do. This will make us happy in our own souls, and useful to those about us.

How full the Bible is of the wonders that have been wrought by prayer! Just think for a moment of some of them.

Abraham prays, and Lot is delivered from the fiery flood that overwhelmed Sodom and Gomorrah. Gen. xix: 29. Jacob prays, and he wrestles with the angel, and obtains the blessing; his brother Esau's mind is wonderfully turned away from the wrath he had cherished for twenty years. Moses prays and Amalek is discomfited. Joshua prays and Achan is discovered. Hannah prays and Samuel is born. David prays and Ahithophel hangs himself. Elijah prays and a famine of three years comes upon Israel. He prays again, and the rain descends, and the famine ends. Elisha prays, and Jordan is divided. He prays again, and the dead child's soul is brought back from the invisible world. Isaiah and Hezekiah pray, and a hundred and eighty-five thousand Assyrian soldiers are slain in one night by the unseen sword of the angel. These are Bible illustrations of the help God gives to his people in answer to prayer. And the Bible rule for prayer, as given by our Saviour, is, "that men ought *always* to pray," Luke xviii: 1. St. Paul's way of stating it is—"Praying always, with all prayer," Ephes. vi: 18. In another place he says—"Pray without ceasing," I. Thess. v: 17. And even the heathen teach the same rule about prayer. Among the rules of Nineveh, an inscription on a tablet has been found, which, on being translated, proved to contain directions about prayer. It may be entitled:

"An Assyrian Call to Prayer." These are the words of the call:

> " Pray thou! pray thou!
> Before the couch, pray!
> Before the throne, pray!
> Before the canopy, pray!
> Before the building of the lofty head, pray!
> Before the rising of the dawn, pray!
> Before the fire, pray!
> By the tablets and papyri, pray!
> By the side of the river, pray!
> By the side of a ship, or riding in a ship, or leaving the ship, pray!
> At the rising of the sun, or the setting of the sun, pray!
> On coming out of the city, on entering the city, pray!
> On coming out of the great gate, on entering the great gate, pray!
> On coming out of the house, pray! on entering the house, pray!
> In the place of judgment, pray!
> In the temple, pray!"

This is like the Bible rule of—"praying always."

"Praying for a Dinner." Grandma, aren't we going to church this morning?" asked a little girl.

"My child, we have had no breakfast, and have no dinner to eat when we come back," said her grandma.

"But the Lord Jesus can give it to us if we ask him," said the little girl. "Let's ask him." So they kneeled down, and asked that God, "who feedeth the young ravens when they cry," to remember them, and help them.

Then they went to church. They found it very much crowded. An old gentleman took the little girl upon his knee. He was pleased with her quiet behaviour. On parting with her at the close of the service, he slipped a half crown into her hand. "See, Grandma," she said, as soon as they were out of church, "Jesus has sent us our dinner."

But when we ask God to help us, we must always try to help ourselves.

"Working as well as Praying." Two little girls went to the same school; one of them, named Mary, always said her lessons well, the other, named Jane, always failed. One day Jane said, "Mary, how does it happen that you always say your lessons so well?" Mary said she prayed over her lessons, and *that* was the secret of her success.

Jane concluded to try praying. But the next day she failed worse than ever. In tears, she reproached Mary for deceiving her. "But, did you study hard, as well as pray over your lesson?" asked Mary.

"No; I thought if I only prayed, that was all I had to do," replied Jane. "Not at all. God only helps those who try to help themselves. You must study hard as well as pray, if you wish to get your lessons well," was Mary's wise answer. The next day Jane studied, as well as prayed, and she had her lesson perfectly.

The greatest work we can ever do, is to bring a soul to Jesus, or to convert a sinner from the error of his way. Here is an illustration of the way in which this may be done by prayer and effort combined:

"The Coachman and His Prayer." "I was riding once, on the top of a stage-coach," said a Christian gentleman, "when the driver by my side began to swear in a dreadful manner. I lifted up my heart for God's blessing on what I said; and presently, in a quiet way, I asked him this question: 'Driver, do you ever pray?' He seemed displeased at first; but after awhile he replied, '"I sometimes go to church on Sunday; and then I suppose I pray, don't I?"' 'I am afraid you never pray at all; for no man can swear as you do, and yet be in the habit of praying to God.'

"As we rode along he seemed thoughtful. 'Coachman, I wish you would pray now,' I said. '"Why, what a time to pray, Sir, when a man is driving a coach!"' 'Yet, my friend, God will hear you.' '"What shall I pray?"' he asked, in a low voice. 'Pray these words: '"O Lord, grant me thy Holy Spirit, for Christ's sake. Amen."' He hesitated, but in a moment he repeated them; and then, at my request, he said them over a second, and a third time. The end of the journey was reached, and I left him.

"Some months passed away, and we met once more. 'Ah, Sir,' said he, with a smile, 'the prayer you taught me on that coach-box was answered. I saw myself a lost, and ruined sinner; but now, I humbly hope, that through the blood which cleanseth from all sin, and by the power of the Holy Spirit, I am a converted man.'"

And so, when we think of the twelve apostles, appointed by Jesus to preach his gospel, these are the four things for us to remember in connection with them, viz.:—*the men* whom he chose; *the work* they had to do; *the help* given them in doing that work; and *the lesson* we are taught by this subject—the lesson of prayer.

Whatever we have to do, let us do it with all our hearts, and do it as for God, and then we shall be his apostles—his sent ones. Let me put the application of this subject in the form of some earnest, practical lines that I lately met with. The lines only speak of boys, but they apply just as well to girls. They are headed:

DRIVE THE NAIL.

"Drive the nail aright, boys,
    Hit it on the head,
Strike with all your might, boys,
    While the iron's red.

"Lessons you've to learn, boys,
    Study with a will;
They who reach the top, boys,
    First must climb the hill.

"Standing at the foot, boys,
    Gazing at the sky,
How can you get up, boys,
    If you never try?

"Though you stumble oft, boys,
    Never be downcast;
Try and try again, boys,
    You'll succeed at last.

"Ever persevere, boys,
    Tho' your task be hard;
Toil and happy cheer, boys,
    Bring their own reward.

"Never give it up, boys,
    Always say you'll try;
Joy will fill your cup, boys,
    Flowing by and by."

THE GREAT TEACHER

TEACHING was the great business of the life of Christ during the days of his public ministry. He was *sent* to teach and to preach. The speaker in the book of Job was thinking of this Great Teacher when he asked—"*Who teacheth like him?*" Job xxxvi: 22. And it was he who was in the Psalmist's mind when he spoke of the "good, and upright Lord" who would teach sinners, if they were meek, how to walk in his ways. Ps. xxv: 8-9. And he is the Redeemer, of whom the prophet Isaiah was telling when he said—He would "*teach us to profit,* and *would lead us by the way that we should go.*" And thus we know how true was what Nicodemus said of him, that "he was a *teacher sent from God.*" John iii: 2. Thus what was said of Jesus, before he came into our world, would naturally lead us to expect to find him occupied in teaching. And so he *was* occupied, all through the days of his public ministry. St. Matthew tells us that—"Jesus went about all Galilee, *teaching* in their synagogues. Ch. iv: 23. Further on in his gospel he tells us again that "Jesus went about all the cities, and villages, teaching in their synagogues." Ch. ix: 35. When on his trial before Pilate, his enemies brought it as a charge against him that he had been—"*teaching* throughout all Jewry." Luke xxiii: 5. We read in one place that—"the elders of the people came unto him *as he was teaching.*" Matt. xxi: 23. Jesus himself gave this account of his life work to his enemies—"I sat *daily* with you *teaching* in the temple." Matt. xxvi: 55. And so we come now to look at the life of Christ from this point of view—as a Teacher. There never was such a Teacher. We do not wonder at the effect of his teaching of which we read in St. John vii: 46, when the chief priests sent some of their officers to take him prisoner, and bring him unto them; the officers went, and joined the crowd that was listening to his preaching. His words had such a strange effect on them that they could not think of touching him. So they went back to their masters without doing what they had been sent to do. "And when the

chief priests and Pharisees said unto them—
Why have ye not brought him? The officers
answered, *Never man spake like this man.*"
Jesus was indeed—*The Great Teacher.* In this
light we are now to look at him. And as we
do this we shall find that there were *five* great
things about his teaching which made him
different from any other teacher the world has
ever known.

*In the first place Jesus may well be called the
Great Teacher, because of the*—GREAT BLESSINGS—
of which he came to tell.

We find some of these spoken of at the opening of his first great sermon to his disciples, called "The Sermon on the Mount." This is the most wonderful sermon that ever was preached. Jesus began it by telling about some of the great blessings he had brought down from heaven for poor sinful creatures such as we are. The sermon begins in the fifth chapter of St. Matthew, and the first twelve verses of the chapter are occupied in speaking of these blessings. As soon as he opened his mouth and began to speak a stream of blessings flowed out.

It was a beautiful thought, on this subject, which a boy in Sunday-school once had. The teacher had been talking to his class about the beginning of this sermon on the mount. He had spoken of the sweetness of the words of Jesus, when "He opened his mouth and taught" his disciples. "How pleasant it must have been, my dear boys," said he, "to have seen the blessed Saviour, and to have heard him speak!"

A serious-minded little fellow in the class said, "Teacher, don't you think that when Jesus opened his mouth, and began to speak to his disciples, it must have been like taking the stopper out of a scent bottle?" I cannot tell whether this boy had ever read the words of Solomon or not; but he had just the same idea that was in his mind when he said of this "Great Teacher," "thy name is *as ointment poured forth.*" Cant. i: 3. We perceive the fragrance of this ointment as soon as Jesus opens his mouth and begins to speak. If we had been listening to Jesus when he began this sermon, saying:—"Blessed are the poor in spirit; blessed are the meek; blessed are the pure in heart; blessed are the peace-makers"—and so on till he had spoken of *nine* different kinds of blessing, we might have thought that he had nothing but blessings of which to tell. It would have seemed as if his mind, and heart, and lips, and hands were all so filled with blessings that he could do nothing else till he had told about these. And the blessings spoken of here are not all the blessings that Jesus brought. They are only specimens of them. The blessings he has obtained for us are innumerable. David says of them, "If I would declare and speak of them they are more than can be numbered." Ps. xl: 5. And these blessings are not only very numerous, but very *great*. Look at one or two of these blessings that Jesus, the Great Teacher, brings to us. He says, "Blessed are they that mourn, for they shall be comforted." Jesus came to bring comfort to the mourners. Hundreds of years before Christ came the prophet Isaiah had said of him that he would come to *"comfort all that mourn."* Is. lxi: 2. And to show how complete this blessing would be which he was to bring, Jesus said himself— *"As one whom his mother comforteth—so will I comfort you."* Is. lxvi: 13. A young girl was dying. A friend who came in to see her said:

"I trust you have a good hope."

"No," she answered, distinctly; "I am not hoping—I am certain. My salvation was finished on the cross. My soul is saved. Heaven is mine. I am going to Jesus."

What a great blessing it is to have comfort like that!

When Jesus was speaking to the woman of Samaria, as he sat by Jacob's well, he compared the blessing of his grace to the water of that well. Pointing to the well at his side, he said: "Whosoever drinketh of this water will thirst again. But whosoever drinketh of the water that I shall give him, shall never thirst; but the water that I shall give him, shall be *in him, a well of water, springing up unto everlasting life.*" John iv: 13, 14. This is one of the most beautiful illustrations of the blessing Jesus gives that ever was used. It is a great blessing to have a well of clear, cold water in our garden, or near our door. But, only think of having a well of water *in our hearts.* Then, wherever we go, we carry that well with us. We never have to go away from it. No one can separate between us and the water of this well. Other wells dry up and fail. But this is a well that never dries up, and never fails. This well is deep, and its water is all the time "springing up unto everlasting life." How happy they are in whose breasts Jesus opens this well of water!

Coleridge, the English poet, in writing to a young friend, just before his death, said:

"Health is a great blessing; wealth, gained by honest industry, is a great blessing; it is a great blessing to have kind, faithful, loving friends and relatives, *but, the greatest, and best of all blessings is to be a Christian.*"

One of the most able and learned lawyers that England ever had was John Selden. He was so famous for his learning and knowledge that he is always spoken of as "the learned Selden." On his deathbed he said—"I have taken much pains to know everything that was worth knowing among men; but with all my reading and all my knowledge, nothing now remains with me to comfort me at the close of life but these precious words of St. Paul: 'This a faithful saying, and worthy of all acceptation, that Christ Jesus came into the world to save sinners;' to this I cling. In this I rest. This gives me peace, and comfort, and enables me to die happy."

William Wilberforce was another of the great and good men who have been a blessing and an honor to England. When he was on his deathbed, he said to a dear friend:

"Come, let us talk of heaven. Do not weep for me. I am very happy. But I never knew what happiness was till I found Christ as my Saviour. Read the Bible. Let no other book take its place. Through all my trials and perplexities, it has been my comfort. And now it comforts me, and makes me happy."

Here we see "this well of water springing up unto everlasting life." And Jesus, who came to tell us of this water, and to open up this well in our breasts, may well be called, "the Great Teacher," because of the great blessings—of which he tells.

In the second place Jesus may be called "the Great Teacher," because of the—GREAT SIMPLICITY —*of his teachings.*

I do not mean to say that we can understand every thing that Jesus taught. This is not so. He had some things to speak about that are not simple. He said to his disciples, *"I have yet many things to say unto you, but ye cannot bear them now."* John xvi: 12. This means that there are some things about God, and heaven, of which he wished to tell them, but they were too hard for them to understand, although they were full-grown men. And so he did not tell them of these things. But even among the things that Jesus did tell about, there are some which the wisest and most learned men in the world have never been able to understand or explain. Some one has compared the Bible to a river, in which there are some places deep enough for an elephant or a giant to swim in; and other places where the water is shallow enough for a child to wade in. And it is just so with the teachings of Jesus. Some of the most important lessons he taught are so plain and simple that very young people can understand them.

We have a good illustration of this in that sweet invitation which Jesus gave when he said,—*"Come unto me, all ye that labor and are heavy laden, and I will give you rest."* Matt. xi: 28. Very young people know what it is to feel tired and weary from walking, or working too much, or from carrying a heavy burden. And, when they are too tired to do anything else, they know what it is to go to their dear mother and throw themselves into her arms, and find rest there. And, in just the same way, Jesus invites us to come to him when we are tired, or troubled, that our souls may find rest in him. We come to Jesus, when we pray to him; when we tell him all about our troubles; when we ask him to help us; and when we trust in his promises.

"Was there ever gentlest shepherd
   Half so gentle, half so sweet,
As the Saviour, who would have us
   Come and gather round his feet?

"There's a wideness in God's mercy,
   Like the wideness of the sea;
There's a kindness in his justice
   Which is more than liberty.

"There is no place where earth's sorrows
   Are more felt than up in heaven;
There is no place where earth's failings
   Have such kindly judgments given.

"There is plentiful redemption
   In the blood that has been shed;
There is joy for all the members
   In the sorrows of the head.

"If our love were but more simple,
   We should take him at his word;
And our lives would all be sunshine,
   In the sweetness of our Lord."

The prophet Isaiah foretold that when Jesus came, he would teach his doctrines to children just weaned. Chap. xxviii: 9. This shows us that his teaching was to be marked by great plainness and simplicity. And this was just the way in which he did teach when he uttered those loving words:—"*Suffer the little children to come unto me, and forbid them not; for of such is the kingdom of God.*" Mark x: 14. None of the other famous teachers known to the world ever took such interest in children as Jesus did. And none of them ever taught with such great simplicity. What multitudes of young people have been led to love and serve Jesus by thinking of the sweet words he spoke about children!

"The Child's Gospel." A little girl sat still in church listening to the minister. She could not understand what he was saying till he quoted these words of Jesus about the children. But she understood them. She felt that they were words spoken for her. They made her feel very happy. And when she went home she threw her arms around her mother's neck, who had been kept at home by sickness, and said, "O, mother, I have heard the *child's gospel* to-day."

"It's For Me." Little Carrie was a heathen child, about ten years old. After she had been going to the Mission School for some time, her teacher noticed, one day, that she looked sad.

"Carrie, my dear," she said, "why do you look so sad to-day?"

"Because I am thinking."

"And what are you thinking about?"

"O, teacher, I don't know whether Jesus loves me, or not."

"Carrie, what did Jesus say about little children coming to him when he was on earth?"

In a moment the sweet words she had learned in the school were on her lips—"Suffer the little children to come unto me, &c."

"Well, Carrie, for whom did Jesus speak these words?" At once she clapped her hands and exclaimed: "It's not for you, teacher, is it? for you are not a child. No: it's for me! it's for me!"

And so this dear child was drawn to Jesus by the power of his love. And thus, through all the hundreds of years that have passed away since "Jesus was here among men," these same simple words have been drawing the little ones to him.

And so, because of the great simplicity which marked his teaching, Jesus must truly be called —the Great Teacher.

But in the third place there was—GREAT TENDERNESS—*in Jesus, and this was another thing that helped to make him the Great Teacher.*

It was this great tenderness that led him, when he came to be our Teacher and Saviour to take our nature upon him and so become like us. He might have come into our world in the form of a mighty angel, with his face shining like the sun, as he appeared when the disciples saw him on the Mount of Transfiguration. But then we should have been afraid of him. He would not have known how we feel, and could not have felt for us. But instead of this, his tenderness led him to take our nature upon him, that he might be able to put himself in our place, and so to understand just how we feel, and what we need to help and comfort us. This is what the apostle means in Heb. ii: 14, when he says—"Forasmuch as the children were partakers of flesh and blood, he also himself likewise took part of the same." He did this on purpose that he might know, by his own experience, how we are tried and tempted; and so be able to sympathize with us and help us in all our trials.

Here is a little story, very simple, and homely; but yet, one that illustrates very well the point of which we are speaking. It is a story about:

"A Lost Horse Found." A valuable horse was lost, belonging to a farmer in New England. A number of his neighbors turned out to try and find the horse. They searched all through the woods and fields of the surrounding country, but in vain. None of them could find the horse. At last a poor, weak-minded fellow, who was known in that neighborhood as "simple Sam," started to hunt the horse. After awhile he came back, bringing the stray horse with him. The owner of the horse was delighted to see him. He stroked and patted him, and then, turning to the simple-minded man who had found him, he said:

"Well, Sam, how came you to find the horse, when no one else could do it?"

"Wal, you see," said Sam, "I just 'quired whar the horse was seen last; and then I went thar, and sat on a rock; and just axed mysel', if I was a horse, whar would I go, and what would I do? And then I went, and found him." Now, when Sam, in the simplicity of his feeble mind, tried to put himself, as far as he could, in the horse's place, this helped him to find the lost horse, and bring him back to his owner again. And so, to pass from a very little thing to a very great one, when Jesus came down from heaven to seek and to save sinners that were lost, this is just the way in which he acted. He put himself in our place as sinners. As the apostle Paul says: "he who knew no sin, was made sin for us," that he might save us from the dreadful consequences of our sins.

And we see the tenderness of Jesus, not only in taking our nature upon him and becoming man, but in what he did when he lived in this world as a man. *"He went about doing good."* It was his great tenderness that led him to do this. Suppose that you and I could have walked about with Jesus when he was on earth as the apostles did. Just think for a moment what we should have seen. We should have seen him meeting with blind men and opening their eyes that they might see. We should have seen him meeting with deaf men, and unstopping their ears that they might hear. We should have seen him meeting sick people who were taken with divers diseases and torments and healing them. We should have seen him raising the dead; and casting out devils; and speaking words of comfort and encouragement to those who were sad and sorrowful. If we could have looked into his blessed face, we should have seen tenderness there, beaming from his eyes and speaking from every line of his countenance. If we could have listened to his teaching we should have found tenderness running through all that he said. Just take one of his many parables as a sample of his way of teaching—the parable of the lost sheep—and see how full of tenderness it is. The sweet lines of the hymn, about the shepherd seeking his lost sheep, that most of us love to sing, bring out the tenderness of Jesus here very touchingly.

> "There were ninety and nine that safely lay
>   In the shelter of the fold,
> But one was out on the hills away,
>   Far off from the gates of gold—
> Away on the mountains, wild and bare,
> Away from the tender shepherd's care.
>
> "'Lord, Thou hast here Thy ninety and nine;
>   Are they not enough for Thee?'
> But the Shepherd made answer: 'One of mine
>   Has wandered away from me;
> And, although the road be rough and steep,
> I go to the desert to find my sheep.'
>
> "But none of the ransomed ever knew
>   How deep were the waters crossed;
> Nor how dark was the night that the Lord passed through,
>   Ere he found his sheep that was lost.
> Out in the desert he heard its cry—
> Sick and helpless, and ready to die.
>
> "'Lord, whence are those blood-drops all the way
>   That mark out the mountain's track?'
> They were shed for one who had gone astray,
>   Ere the shepherd could bring him back.
> 'Lord, why are Thy hands so rent and torn?'
> They are pierced, to-night, by many a thorn.

"But all through the mountains, thunder-riven,
    And up from the rocky steep,
There rose a cry to the gates of heaven,
    'Rejoice! I have found my sheep!'
And the angels echoed around the throne,
'Rejoice, for the Lord brings back his own.'"

And all that we know of Jesus as "the good Shepherd," demonstrates his great tenderness for his sheep.

But perhaps there was no act in all the life of our blessed Redeemer that showed his tenderness more than taking the little children in his arms, and putting his hands upon them, and blessing them.

To think of the Son of God, who made this world, and all worlds, and whom all the angels of heaven worship, showing so much interest in the little ones; this proves how full of tenderness his heart was.

"I Like Your Jesus." An English lady who had spent six months in Syria, writes: "Going through the places where the Mohammedans live, you continually hear the girls singing our beautiful hymns in Arabic. The attractive power of Christ's love is felt even by the little ones, as we learned from a dear Moslem child, who, when she repeated the text, 'Suffer the little children,' said, 'I like your Jesus, because he loved little children. Our Mohammed did not love little children.'"

And if we all try to imitate the tenderness of Jesus, then, though we may have no money to give, and no great thing to do, yet by being tender, and gentle, and loving, as Jesus was, we shall be able to do good wherever we are.

"Doing Good by Sympathy." A Christian mother used to ask her children every night if they had done any good during the day. One night in answer to this question, her little daughter said: "At school this morning I found little Annie G . . . , who had been absent for some time, crying very hard. I asked her what was the matter? Then she cried more, so that I could not help putting my head on her neck, and crying with her. Her sobs grew less, and presently she told of her little baby brother, whom she loved so much; how sick he had been; and how much pain he had suffered, till he died and was buried. Then she hid her face in her book, and cried, as if her heart would break. I could not help putting my face on the other page of the book, and crying, too, as hard as she did. After awhile she kissed me, and told me I had done her good. But, mother, I don't know how I did her good; *for I only cried with her!*"

Now this little girl was showing the tenderness of Jesus, the Great Teacher. Nothing in the world could have done that poor sorrowing child so much good as to have some one cry with her. Sometimes tears of tenderness are worth more than diamonds. And this is why the Bible tells us to "weep with them that weep." Rom. xii: 15. Jesus did this in the tenderness of his loving heart. And this was one of the things that made him the Great Teacher.

But then there was—GREAT KNOWLEDGE—*in Jesus, and this was another thing that made him great as a teacher.*

If we wish to be good teachers, we must study, and try to understand the things we expect to teach. If a young man wishes to be a minister, he must go through college; and then spend three years in the Divinity School, so that he may understand the great truths of the Bible, which he is to teach the people who hear him. But Jesus never went to college, or to a divinity school. And yet he had greater knowledge about all the things of which he spoke than any other teacher ever had. We are told in the book of Job that "He is *perfect* in knowledge." Job xxxvi: 5. And the apostle Paul tells us that "in him are hid *all the treasures of wisdom and knowledge.*" Col. ii: 3. This is more than can be said of any man, or any angel. If we could take all the knowledge of all the best teachers who ever lived, and give it to one person, it would be as nothing compared to the knowledge which Jesus, "the Great Teacher" had. He knew all about heaven; for that had always been his home before he came into our world. He knew all about God; for, he was "in the bosom of the Father," John i: 18; and, as he tells us himself, had shared his glory with him, "before the world was." John xvii: 5. He knew all about the world we live in, for he made it. John i: 10. He knew all about all other worlds, for he made them, too. John i: 3; Heb. i: 2. He knew all about his disciples and every body else in the world, for he made them all. He saw all they did; he heard all they said; he knew all they thought, or felt. Wise and learned men have been studying, and finding out things for hundreds of years, about geography and natural history—and astronomy; —about light, and heat, and electricity—and steam—and the telegraph, and many other things. Jesus knew all about these things when he was on earth. He could have told about them, if he had seen fit to do so. But he only told us what it is best for us to know, in order that we might be saved; and kept back all the rest. The things that Jesus did teach us when he was here on earth were wonderful; but it is hardly less wonderful to think of the things that he might have taught us, and yet did not. When we think of the great knowledge of Jesus, as a Teacher, we are not surprised that some of those who heard him "wondered at the gracious words" he spake; or that others asked the question: "Whence hath this man this knowledge, having never learned?"

Some one has written these sweet lines about Christ as—*The Great Teacher:*

> " From everything our Saviour saw,
> Lessons of wisdom he could draw;
> The clouds, the colors in the sky;
> The gentle breeze that whispers by;
> The fields all white with waving corn;
> The lilies that the vale adorn;
> The reed that trembles in the wind;
> The tree, where none its fruit could find;
> The sliding sand, the flinty rock,
> That bears unmoved the tempest's shock;
> The thorns that on the earth abound;
> The tender grass that clothes the ground;
> The little birds that fly in air;
> The sheep that need the shepherd's care;
> The pearls that deep in ocean lie;
> The gold that charms the miser's eye;

> The fruitful and the thorny ground;
> The piece of silver lost and found;
> The reaper, with his sheaves returning;
> The gathered tares prepared for burning;
> The wandering sheep brought back with joy;
> The father's welcome for his boy;
> The wedding-feast, prepared in state;
> The foolish virgins' cry, 'too late!'—
> All from his lips some truth proclaim,
> Or learn to tell their Maker's name."

But the difference between Jesus, the Great Teacher, and all other teachers is seen, not only in the greater knowledge he has of the things that he teaches, but in this also, that he knows how to make us understand the lessons he teaches. Here is an incident that illustrates how well Jesus can do this. We may call it:

"The Well Instructed Boy." A minister of the gospel was travelling through the wildest part of Ireland. There he met a shepherd's boy, not more than ten or twelve years old. He was poorly clad, with no covering on his head, and no shoes or stockings on his feet; but he looked bright and happy. He had a New Testament in his hand. "Can you read, my boy?" asked the minister.

"To be sure I can."

"And do you understand what you read?"

"A little."

"Please turn to the third chapter of St. John, and read us a little," said the minister. The boy found the place directly, and in a clear distinct voice, began:

"There was a man of the Pharisees named Nicodemus, a ruler of the Jews; the same came to Jesus by night, and said unto him, Rabbi."

"What does Rabbi mean?"

"It means a master."

"Right; go on."

"We know thou art a teacher come from God; for no man can do these miracles that thou doest, except God be with him."

"What is a *miracle?*"

"It is a *great wonder.* 'Jesus answered and said unto him, verily, verily, I say unto thee.'"

"What does *verily* mean?"

"It means 'indeed.' 'Except a man be born again.'"

"What does that mean?"

"It means a great change, a change of heart."

"Except a man be born again he cannot see the kingdom of God."

"And what is that kingdom?"

He paused a moment, and with a very serious, thoughtful look, placing his hand on his bosom, he said, "It is *something here;*" and then, raising his eyes to heaven, added, *"and something up yonder."* This poor boy had been taking lessons from "the Great Teacher," and he had taught him some of the most important things that we can ever learn. Jesus may well be called "the Great Teacher," because of his great knowledge.

But there is one other thing that Jesus has, which helps to make him "the Great Teacher," and that is—GREAT POWER.

Other teachers can tell us what we ought to learn, and to do, yet they have no power to help us learn, or do what they teach. But Jesus *has* this power. Let us take a single illustration from many of the same kind that occurred while he was on earth. One day he was going about teaching in the streets of Jerusalem. As he went on, he passed by the office of a man who was gathering taxes for the Roman government. The persons who did this were called *publicans*. This man, sitting in his office, was named Matthew. He was busily engaged in receiving the taxes of the people. It was a very profitable business. The men engaged in it generally made a great deal of money. Jesus stopped before the window or door of this office. He beckoned to Matthew, and simply spoke these two words:—"*Follow me.*"

Now, if any other teacher had spoken these words to Matthew, and had tried to make him quit his business and engage in something else, he would have said: "No; I can't leave my office. This is all the means I have of getting a living. The business pays well, and I am not willing to give it up." But when Jesus spoke to him, he did, at once, what he was told to do. We read that "He left all, rose up, and followed him." Matt. ix: 9; Luke v: 28. He became one of the twelve apostles and wrote the gospel which bears his name. But it was the great power which Jesus has over the hearts of men that made Matthew willing to do, at once, what he was told to do.

And the power which Jesus exercised over Matthew, in this case, he still has, and still uses. And when he is pleased to use this power the very worst people feel it, and are made good by it. And Jesus, "the Great Teacher," uses this power sometimes in connection with very simple things. Here is an illustration. We may call it:

"Saved by a Rose." Some time ago, a Christian gentleman was in the habit of visiting one of our prisons. It occurred to him, one day, that it would be a good thing to have a flowering plant in the little yard connected with each cell. He got permission from the officers of the prison to do so. He had a bracket fastened to the wall, in each yard, and a flower pot, with a plant in it, placed on each bracket. One of these prisoners was worse than all the rest. He was the most hardened man that had ever been in that prison. His temper was so violent and obstinate that no one could manage him. The keeper of the prison was afraid of him, and never liked to go near him. He was such a disagreeable-looking man that the name given to him in the prison was "Ugly Greg." A little rose bush was put on the bracket in Ugly Greg's yard, and the effect produced by it is told in these simple lines, which some one has written about it:

> "Ugly Greg was the prisoner's name,
> Ugly in face, and in nature the same;
> Stubborn, sullen, and beetle-browed,
> The hardest case in a hardened crowd.
> The sin-set lines in his face were bent
> Neither by kindness nor punishment;
> He hadn't a friend in the prison there,
> And he grew more ugly and didn't care.

> "But some one—blessings on his name!
> Had caused to be placed in that house of shame,
> To relieve the blank of the white-washed wall,
> Flower-pot brackets, with plants on them all.
> Though it seemed but a useless thing to do,
> Ugly Greg's cell had a flower-pot, too,
> And as he came back at the work-day's close,
> He paused, astonished, before a rose.

The Great Teacher

"'He will smash it in pieces,' the keeper said,
But the lines on his face grew soft instead.
Next morning he watered his plant with care,
And went to his work with a cheerful air;
And, day by day, as the rose-bush grew,
Ugly Greg began changing, too.

"The soft, green leaves unfolded their tips,
And the foul word died on the prisoner's lips;
He talked to the plant, when all alone,
As he would to a friend, in a gentle tone;
And, day by day, and week by week,
As the rose grew taller, so Greg grew meek.

"But, at last they took him away to lie
On a hospital bed, for they knew he must die,
They placed the rose in the sunny light,
Where Greg might watch it, from morn till night,
And the green buds grew, from day to day,
As the sick man faded fast away.

"The lines which sin and pain had traced,
Seemed by the shadowing plant effaced,
Till, came at last, the joyful hour,
When they knew that the bud must burst its flower.
Greg slept, but still one hand caressed
The plant; the other his pale cheek pressed.
The perfumed crimson shed a glow
On the old man's hair, as white as snow;
The nurse came softly—'Look, Greg!' she said,
Ay, the rose had bloomed, but the man was dead."

And the meaning of all this is, not that the rose itself saved this hardened sinner. No; but it led him to think of the lessons of his childhood, when he had been taught about Jesus, "the Rose of Sharon." It led him to think about his sins. It led him to repent of them; to pray to Jesus; to exercise faith in him; and in *this way* he became a changed man, and was saved. And so, though we speak of him as—"a man saved by a rose;" yet it was the power of Jesus, "the Great Teacher," exercised through that rose, which led to this blessed change and saved Greg's soul from death.

And thus we have spoken of five things which help to make up the greatness of Jesus as a Teacher. These are—The Great Blessings—The Great Simplicity—The Great Tenderness—The Great Knowledge—and the Great Power connected with his teachings. Let us seek the grace that will enable us to learn of him, and then we shall find rest for our souls!

CHRIST TEACHING BY PARABLES

WE have spoken of our Saviour as "The Great Teacher," and tried to point out some of the things in his teaching which helped to make him great. And now, it may be well to speak a little of the illustrations which he made use of as a Teacher. These are called—*parables.* Our Saviour's parables were illustrations. This is what is meant by the Greek word from which we get the word parable. It means something *set down by the side of another.* When we teach a lesson we are setting something before the minds of our scholars. But suppose it is a hard lesson and they do not understand it. Then we use an illustration. This is something set down beside the lesson to make it plain. Then this, whatever it be, is a parable.

At the beginning of his ministry, our Saviour did not make much use of parables. But, after he had been preaching for some time, he made a change in his way of teaching, in this respect. He began to use parables very freely. His disciples were surprised at this. On one occasion, after he had used the parable of the Sower, they came to their Master and asked him why he always spake to the people now in parables? We have our Saviour's answer to this question in St. Matt. xiii: 11-18. And it is a remarkable answer. The meaning of it is that he used parables for two reasons: one was to help those who really wished to learn from him to understand what he was teaching. The other was that those who were not willing to be taught might listen to him without understanding what he was saying. These people had heard him when he was teaching without parables. But, instead of thanking him for coming to teach them, and of being willing to do what he wanted them to do, they found fault with his teaching, and would not mind what he said.

Now, there is a great difference between the way in which we are to learn what the Bible teaches us about God and heaven; and the way in which we learn other things. If we want to learn what the Bible teaches us we must be careful that we are having right feelings in our hearts; but if we want to learn other things it does not matter so much what our feelings are. For instance, suppose you have a lesson to learn in geography; no matter how you are feeling, whether you are proud, or humble; whether you are cross, or gentle; yet if you only study hard enough, and long enough, you can learn that lesson. But, if you want to learn one of the lessons that Jesus teaches, no matter how hard, or how long you study it, yet while you are giving way to proud, or angry feelings in your heart, you can never learn that lesson. And the reason is that we cannot learn these lessons unless we have the special help of Jesus, by the Holy Spirit. But this help can never be had while we give way to wrong feelings in our hearts. In learning geography, and other such lessons, we do not need the *special* help of God. We can learn them ourselves, if we only try. But we cannot learn the lessons that Jesus teaches in this way. This is what the Psalmist means when he says:—"The *meek* will he teach his way." Ps. xxv: 9. And this was what our Saviour meant when he said: "If any man will do his will, *he shall know.*" St. John vii: 17. We must be willing to be taught;—and willing to obey; if we wish to understand what Jesus, "The Great Teacher," has to tell us.

Some one has well said that truth, taught by a parable, is like the kernel hid away in a nut. The parable, like the shell of the nut, covers up the kernel. Those who really want the kernel will crack the shell, and get it: but those who are not willing to crack the shell will never get the kernel. The shell of the nut keeps the kernel safe *for* one of these persons, and safe *from* the others.

But, after the time of which we have spoken, Jesus used parables freely. We are told that—"without a parable spake he not unto the people." St. Mark xiii: 34. He used parables among his disciples for two reasons: these were to help them to *understand*, and to remember what he taught them.

We have a great many of the parables of Jesus in the gospels. A full list of them will contain not less than *fifty*. It would be easy enough to make a sermon on each of these parables. But that would make a larger work than this whole LIFE OF CHRIST, on which we are now engaged. It is impossible therefore to speak of all the parables. We can only make selections, or take some specimens of them. We may speak of five different lessons as illustrated by some of the parables of Christ. These are—*The value of religion: Christ's love of sinners: The duty of forgiveness: The duty of kindness: and the effect of good example.*

Well then, we may begin by considering what Jesus taught us of—THE VALUE OF RELIGION—*in his parables.*

The parable of The Treasure Hid in the Field teaches us this truth. We find this parable in St. Matt. xiii: 44. Here Jesus says, "The kingdom of heaven is like unto treasure hid in a field; the which when a man hath found, he hideth, and for joy thereof goeth and selleth all that he hath, and buyeth that field." The words "kingdom of heaven" are used by our Saviour in different senses. Sometimes, as here, they mean the grace of God, or true religion. And what Jesus teaches us by this parable is that true religion is more valuable than anything else in the world.

The next parable, in the forty-fifth and forty-sixth verses of the same chapter, is about The Pearl of Great Price. This teaches the same lesson. It reads thus:—"The kingdom of heaven is like unto a merchantman seeking goodly pearls: who, when he had found one pearl of great price, went and sold all that he had and bought it." By this "pearl of great price" Jesus meant true religion, as he did by the treasure hid in the field in the former parable. And the truth he teaches in both these parables is that religion is more important to us than anything else in the world. Let us look at some incidents that may help to illustrate for us the value of religion.

"Jesus Makes Everything Right." A poor lame boy became a Christian, and in telling what effect this change had upon him, these are the words he used to a person who was visiting him: "Once every thing went wrong at our house; father was wrong, mother was wrong, sister was wrong, and I was wrong; but now, since I have learned to know and love Jesus it is all right. I know why everything went wrong before:—it was because I was wrong myself." And this is true. The first thing that religion does for us is to make us *be* right ourselves, and then to *do* right to others.

"Be." A young lady had been trying to do something very good, but had not succeeded. Her mother said, "Marian, my child, God gives us many things to *do*, but we must not forget that he gives us some things to *be;* and we must learn to *be* what God would have us be, before we can *do* what God would have us do."

"O dear mother, please tell me about *being*, and then I shall know better about doing."

"Well, listen my child, while I remind you of some of the Bible be's: God says:

"*Be*—ye kindly affectioned one to another."
"*Be*—ye also patient."
"*Be*—ye thankful."
"*Be*—ye children in malice."
"*Be*—ye therefore perfect."
"*Be*—courteous."
"*Be*—not wise in your own conceits."
"*Be*—not overcome of evil."

"Thank you, dear mother," said Marian. "I hope I shall have a better day to-morrow; for I see now that *doing* grows out of *being*."

This is a point worth dwelling on, and so I will introduce to your notice here:

A SWARM OF BEES WORTH HIVING.

"Be patient, Be prayerful, Be humble, Be mild,
Be wise as a Solon, Be meek as a child.

"Be studious, Be thoughtful, Be loving, Be kind,
Be sure you make matter subservient to mind.

"Be cautious, Be prudent, Be trustful, Be true,
Be courteous to all men, Be friendly with few.

"Be temperate in argument, pleasure and wine,
Be careful of conduct, of money, of time.

"Be cheerful, Be grateful, Be hopeful, Be firm,
Be peaceful, benevolent, willing to learn;

"Be courageous, Be gentle Be liberal, Be just,
Be aspiring, Be humble, because you are dust.

"Be penitent, circumspect, sound in the faith,
Be active, devoted; Be faithful to death.

"Be honest, Be holy, transparent and pure;
Be dependent, Be Christ-like and you'll be secure."

Here is a swarm of between forty and fifty bees. The religion of Jesus will help us to make these all our own. How great then must the value of religion be! Surely it is worth while for each of us to try and secure it!

I think I never saw a better view of the value of religion than is seen in the following statement of what it does for us. I know not by whom it was written, but it is put in the form of that sacred sign to which we owe all the blessings of salvation—the sign of

THE CROSS.

"Blest they who seek
While in their youth,
With spirit meek,
The way of truth.
To them the sacred scriptures now display
Christ as the only true and living way;
His precious blood on Calvary was given
To make them heirs of endless bliss in Heaven.
And e'en on earth the child of God can trace
The glorious blessings of the Saviour's grace.
For them He bore
His Father's frown;
For them He wore
The thorny Crown;
Nailed to the Cross,
Endured its pain,
That his life's loss
Might be their gain.
Then haste to choose
That better part,
Nor dare refuse
The Lord thy heart,
Lest he declare,—
'I know you not,'
And deep despair
Should be your lot.
Now look to Jesus, who on Calvary died,
And trust on him who there was crucified."

"Leaving it All with Jesus." Annie W . . . was a young Christian. In her fourteenth year she was taken with a severe illness, from which the doctor said she could not recover. When she became too weak to leave the sofa, she would send for one and another of the neighbors to come in to see her, and then she would speak to them of Jesus and his great salvation. One day a poor old woman who was not a Christian, came in to see her.

"You are very ill, my dear," she said to Annie.

"Yes," she replied, "but I shall soon be well."

The poor woman shook her head as she looked at Annie's mother, saying, "Poor dear creature; she cannot possibly get well. No: she will never get over it." Then turning to Annie, she said:

"Don't you know, my dear, that you are going to die?"

"I know I am going to live," she said with a sweet smile. "I shall soon be with Jesus in heaven, and live forever with him."

"Oh, how can you know that, my dear? We must not be *too* sure you know," said the poor woman.

"Oh," said Annie, pointing to a card hanging on the wall, near her bed, on which was printed in large letters the hymn headed—"I leave it all with Jesus." "That's what I do! That's what I do." These are the words of the hymn which gave that dear child so much comfort on her dying bed:

> "I leave it all with Jesus,
>   Then wherefore should I fear?
> I leave it all with Jesus,
>   And he is ever near.
>
> "I leave it all with Jesus,
>   Trust him for what must be;
> I leave it all with Jesus,
>   Who ever thinks of me.
>
> "I bring it all to Jesus,
>   In calm, believing prayer;
> I bring it all to Jesus,
>   And I love to LEAVE it there!
>
> "Each tear, each sigh, each trouble,
>   Each disappointment,—all
> I love to GIVE to Jesus,
>   Who loves to TAKE them all."

And here we have a beautiful illustration of one of the things which Jesus taught us in his parables, namely—*the value of religion.*

Another thing we are taught in these parables is—CHRIST'S LOVE FOR SINNERS.

The parable of the lost sheep teaches us this truth: but as we had occasion to speak of this in our last chapter, when illustrating the tenderness of Christ, as the Great Teacher, we may let that pass now. But the parable of the lost piece of money teaches the same lesson. We have this parable in St. Luke xv: 8th and 9th verses. Here we are told of a woman who had ten pieces of silver, and lost one of them. Then she laid the others aside, and searched diligently for the lost piece till she found it. This woman represents Jesus. The lost piece of money represents our souls lost by sin. The efforts of the woman to find the lost piece represent what Jesus did, when he left heaven, and took our nature upon him, and came as "the Son of man to *seek and to save that which was lost.*" And it was the love of Jesus for poor sinners which led him to do all this for us. And everything connected with the history of Jesus when he was on earth shows the greatness of his love. Think of Bethlehem and its manger; there we see the love of Jesus. Think of Gethsemane with its bloody sweat; there we see the love of Jesus. Think of Calvary with its cross of shame and agony; for *there* we see the love of Jesus.

And the parable of the prodigal son teaches us the same lesson. We read of this in the same chapter, St. Luke xv: 11-32. This son had been disobedient and ungrateful. He had taken the money his father gave him and had gone away and spent it in living very wickedly. And when the money was all spent and he was likely to starve, he went back to his father, hungry and ragged, and asked to be taken in. And instead of scolding and punishing him as he deserved, as soon as his father saw him, he ran, and fell on his neck and kissed him; and took off his rags, and dressed him in good clothes, and made a great feast for him. How beautifully this parable illustrates the love of Christ for sinners!

And when we learn to know and feel the love of Christ for us, it does two blessed things for us.

One is, *it makes us good.* We hear a great deal about *conversion.* This word conversion simply means—*turning.* When a person has been living without trying to serve or please God, and is led to see how wrong it is to live in that way, and then feels an earnest desire to turn around, and live differently, and really does so:—that is conversion. The teaching or preaching of the gospel is the chief means that God employs to convert men. And the thing about the gospel in which this converting power lies is—*the love of Christ.* Here is an illustration of what this means.

"He Loved Me." An English minister of the gospel was traveling in Switzerland one summer. As he passed from place to place, he preached by means of an interpreter in various churches. One Sunday night he preached from the words, "*He loved me, and gave himself for me.*" Gal. ii: 20. Then he went on his way without knowing what effect had followed from his preaching.

One Saturday evening, several weeks after, the minister of this church was sitting in his study. There came a faint knock at his door. He opened it, when, to his great surprise he saw there a young man, who was known as the wickedest young man in that neighborhood, and the leader of others in all sorts of wickedness. He invited him in, gave him a seat, and asked him what he wished. Judge of his surprise when the young man said he wished to inquire if he might come to the sacrament of the Lord's Supper, which was to be celebrated in his church the next day!

"But are you not aware, my young friend," said the minister, "that only those who love Christ, and are trying to serve him, have any right to come to that holy ordinance?"

"I know it, sir," said the young man, "and I am thankful to feel that I am among that number."

"But," asked the astonished pastor, "are you not known in this village as the ringleader in all evil doings?"

"Alas! it is too true that it has been so," he replied, "but thank God all is changed now."

"I am happy indeed to hear it; but pray tell me what led to this great change."

"I was in your church, sir," said he, "some weeks ago, when that English minister preached from the words, 'Who loved me and gave himself for me.' That was the first time I ever understood about the love of Christ. It led to my repentance and conversion; and now I wish to show my love to Jesus by trying to serve and please him."

Here we see how the love of Christ makes us good.

But it *makes us happy*, as well as good. Here is a little story that illustrates this point very well. We may call it:

Maggie's Secret." "Maggie Blake, how can you study so hard, and be so provokingly good?" This question was asked by Jennie Lee, who was one of the largest and wildest girls in the school. Maggie hesitated a moment, whether to tell her secret or not. But, presently she lifted up her eyes, looked her companion bravely in the face, and said—"It's for Jesus' sake, Jennie."

"But do you think he cares?" asked Jennie in a soft, subdued voice,—"do you think he cares how we act?"

"I *know* he does," said Maggie. "And it makes it so pleasant you see, even to study and get hard lessons, when I know he is looking at me, and is pleased to have me working my best for him. He always helps me to get my lessons; and then helps me to say them right. You know I used to be so frightened I could not say them, even when I had learned them well."

"Yes," said Jennie, remembering very well how Maggie had changed in that respect.

"That was before I thought of learning them for Jesus. After that he helped me all along. It makes me like school; and even disagreeable things are pleasant when I think of doing them for him."

Jennie had often watched Maggie, and wondered what made her have such a bright, cheerful, happy look. Now she knew the secret of it. It was doing everything "for Jesus' sake."

She felt she would gladly give everything she had to be as happy as Maggie. She asked Maggie to pray for her, and she began to pray for herself. Then Jesus helped her, and she soon had Maggie's secret for her own. The girls in school wondered at the change which had come over Jennie. But when they heard that she had been confirmed, and had joined the church, they understood it all. They knew she "had been with Jesus;" and that it was learning to know and feel his wonderful love which had made Jennie so good, and so happy.

And so, we see that Jesus was doing a blessed thing for us when he taught the parables which show his love for sinners.

A third thing taught us by some of the parables of Jesus is—THE DUTY OF KINDNESS.

One day, while Jesus was on earth, a young man came to him with the great question, what he should do to obtain eternal life. Jesus referred him to the Ten Commandments; and reducing them to two, he told the young man that these commandments required him to love God with all his heart, and his neighbor as himself; and then said if he would do this he would be saved.

This is perfectly true. Any one would be saved who would do this. But no one ever has done this except our blessed Lord Himself. He "magnified the law and made it honorable" by keeping it perfectly. I suppose that Jesus intended to give this young man some lessons about the commandments of God which would lead him to see that he never could keep them himself; and that he would need some one to keep them for him, and that *this* was the only way in which he, or any one else could be saved. It may have been that the young man did not want to hear any thing more on that subject, and so he gave the conversation a different turn by asking—"who is my neighbor?" when Jesus said he must love his neighbor as himself. And then, in answer to this question Jesus told the parable of the "Good Samaritan." We have this parable in St. Luke x: 30-37.

Here we are told of a certain man who was going down from Jerusalem to Jericho, and fell among thieves. They robbed him; and wounded him; and left him half dead. While he was lying there helpless and suffering, a priest and a Levite came, and looked on him, and passed by on the other side, without giving him any help. Then we are told that a certain Samaritan came by, and when he saw the poor wounded man lying there, although he was a Jew, and the Jews and the Samaritans hated each other very much, yet he pitied him, and went up to him, and bound up his wounds, and set him on his own beast, and carried him to an inn, and told them to take care of him, and said that he would pay all his expenses. Then Jesus asked the question, "Which now, of these three thinkest thou was neighbor to him that fell among thieves? And he said, he that showed mercy on him. Then said Jesus unto him, Go, and do thou likewise."

Thus Jesus taught the duty of kindness. This kindness we must show, not to our friends only, but to our enemies. *Kindness to all* is the duty that Jesus teaches.

Let us look at one or two illustrations of the way in which we should do this.

"The Honey Shield." It is said that wasps and bees will not sting a person whose skin is covered with honey. And so those who are exposed to the sting of these venomous little creatures smear their hands and faces over with honey, and this, we are told, proves the best shield they can have to keep them from getting stung. And the honey here very well represents the kindness which Jesus teaches us to practise. If kindness, gentleness, and forbearance are found running through all our words and actions, we shall have the best shield to protect us from the spiteful stings of wicked people.

"Androcles and the Lion." Most of those who read these pages may have heard this story, but it illustrates the point before us so well that I do not hesitate to use it here.

Androcles was a Roman slave. To escape the cruel treatment of his master he ran away. A lonely cave in the midst of the forest was his home for a while. Returning to his cave one day he met a lion near the mouth of the cave. He was bellowing as if in pain; and on getting nearer to him, he found that he was suffering from a thorn which had run into one of his paws. It was greatly swollen and inflamed, and was causing him much pain. Androcles went up to the suffering beast. He drew out the rankling thorn and thus relieved him of his pain. His nature, savage as it was, felt the power of the kindness thus shown to him. He became attached to the lonely slave, and shared his prey with him while they remained together.

But, after a while the retreat of Androcles was discovered. He was taken and carried back to his master. The lion also was made a prisoner soon after. Androcles was kept in prison for some time; and finally, according to the custom of the Romans, he was condemed to be devoured by wild beasts. The lion to be let loose on Androcles had been kept a long time without food and was very hungry. When the door of his den was opened he rushed out with a tremendous roar. The Colosseum was crowded with spectators. They expected to see the poor slave torn to pieces in a moment. But, to the surprise of everyone, the great monster, hungry as he was, instead of devouring the condemned man, crouched at his feet, and began to fondle him, as a pet dog would do. He recognized in the poor prisoner his friend of the forest and showed that he had not forgotten his kindness. The kindness of Androcles had been like the honey shield to him. It saved his life, first from the savage beast in the forest; and then from the savage men in the city. Let us all put on this shield, and wear it wherever we go. The lesson of kindness which Jesus teaches in this parable, has been very well put by some one in these sweet lines:

THE LESSON OF KINDNESS.

"Think kindly of the erring!
 Thou knowest not the power
With which the dark temptation came
 In some unguarded hour;
Thou knowest not how earnestly
 They struggled, or how well,
Until the hour of weakness came,
 And sadly then they fell.

"Speak kindly to the erring!
 Thou yet may'st lead him back
With holy words, and tones of love,
 From misery's thorny track:
Forget not *thou* hast often sinned
 And sinful yet must be:—
Deal kindly with the erring one
 As God hath dealt with thee!"

The duty of kindness was the third lesson Jesus taught in the parables.

A fourth lesson taught us in some of the parables of Jesus is—THE DUTY OF FORGIVENESS.

The apostle Peter came to Jesus one day, and asked him how often he ought to forgive a brother that offended him; and whether it would be enough to forgive him *seven* times. The answer of Jesus was, "I say not unto thee, until seven times, but until seventy times seven."

St. Matt. 18: 22. Then Jesus spoke the parable of the two debtors. St. Matt. 18: 23-35. One of these owed his master ten thousand talents. If these were talents of silver they would amount to more than fifteen millions of dollars. If they were talents of gold, they would amount to three hundred millions. This would show that his debt was so great that he never could pay it. Then his master freely forgave him. But not long after, he found one of his fellow-servants, who owed him a hundred pence, or about fifteen dollars of our money. The man asked him to forgive him the debt. He would not do it; but put him in prison. When his master heard this he was very angry, and put him in prison, where he should be punished until he had paid all his great debt. And Jesus finished the parable by saying—"*so likewise, shall my heavenly Father do unto you, if ye, from your hearts forgive not every one his brother their trespasses.*" And here we are taught the great duty of forgiveness. And this same duty is taught us in the Lord's Prayer, where he says—"Forgive us our trespasses, as we also forgive those who trespass against us." If we use this prayer without forgiving those who injure us, then, in so using it, we are really asking God *not* to forgive us.

And Jesus *practised* what he *preached*. As he hung bleeding and agonizing on the cross, while his enemies were cruelly mocking his misery, he looked up to heaven, and uttered that wonderful prayer—*Father forgive them; for they know not what they do.*" Here we have the best illustration of forgiveness that the world has ever seen.

"Example of Forgiveness." In a school in Ireland, one boy struck another. The offending boy was brought up to be punished, when the injured boy begged for his pardon. The teacher asked—"Why do you wish to keep him from being flogged?" The ready reply was—"Because I have read in the New Testament that our Lord Jesus Christ said that we must forgive our enemies; and therefore I forgive him, and beg that he may not be punished for my sake."

"Good for Evil." At the foot of a street in New York, stood an Italian organ grinder, with his organ. A number of boys had gathered round him, but they were more anxious to have some fun than to hear music. One of them said to his companions:

"See! I'll hit his hat!"

And sure enough he did. Making up a snow ball, he threw it with so much force that the poor man's hat was knocked into the gutter. A gentleman standing by expected to see him get very angry, and swear at the boy. But, very different from this was the result that followed. The musician stopped; stepped forward and picked up his hat. Then he turned to the rude boy, and gracefully bowing, said:

"And now, I'll play you a tune to make you merry!" There was real Christian forgiveness.

"The Power of the Gospel." Years ago some carpenters moved to the Island of New Zealand, and set up a shop for carrying on their business. They were engaged to build a chapel at one of the Mission Stations. One of these carpenters, a pleasant, kind-hearted man, engaged a native Christian to dig his garden for him. When the work was done the man went to the shop for his pay. Another of the carpenters there, who was a very ill-tempered man, told the native to get out of the shop. "Don't be angry," was the gentle reply; "I have only come to have a little talk with your partner, and to get my wages from him." "But I *am* angry." And then taking hold of the New Zealander by the shoulder, he abused and kicked him in the most cruel manner.

The native made no resistance till the carpenter ceased. Then he jumped up, seized him by the throat, and snatching a small axe from the bench, flourished it threateningly over his head. "Now, you see," said he, "your life is in my hand. You see my arm is strong enough to kill you; and my arm is quite willing, but my heart is not. I have heard the missionaries preach the gospel of forgiveness. You owe your life to the preaching of the gospel. If my heart was as dark now as it was before the gospel was preached here, I should strike off your head in an instant!"

Then he released the carpenter withot injuring him and accepted from him a blanket as an apology for the insult. How faithfully this man was practising the duty of forgiveness which Jesus taught!

The only other thing of which we shall now speak, as taught by our Saviour in the parables, is
—THE INFLUENCE OF GOOD EXAMPLE.

The parable which teaches this lesson is that of the lighted candle. It is one of the shortest of our Lord's parables, and yet the truth it teaches is very important. We first find this parable in the sermon on the mount. These are the words in which it is given: "Neither do men light a candle and put it under a bushel, but on a candlestick; and it giveth light unto all that are in the house. Let your light so shine before men, that they may see your good works, and glorify your Father which is in heaven." Matt. v: 15. This parable is so important that we find it repeated in three other places. Mark iv: 21, Luke viii: 16, and xi: 33.

We find the same idea taught by one of England's greatest writers. Looking at a candle shining through a window, he says:

> "How far yon little candle throws its beam!
> So shines a good deed in a naughty world."

And the lesson we are here taught is that we should always set a good example by doing what we know to be right, and then, like a candle shining in a dark place, we shall be useful wherever we go. Let us look at one or two incidents that illustrate this.

"A Boy's Influence." Two families lived in one house. In each of these families there was a little boy about the same age. These boys slept together. One of them had a good pious mother. She had trained him to kneel down every night, before getting into bed, and say his prayer in an audible voice, and to repeat a text of scripture which she had taught him. Now the first time he slept with the other little boy, who never said any prayers, he was tempted to jump into bed, as his companion did, without kneeling down to pray. But he was a brave and noble boy. He said to himself—"I am not afraid to do what my mother taught me. I am not ashamed for anybody to know that I pray to God. I'll do as I have been taught to do." He did so. He let his light shine. And see what followed from its shining!

The little boy who had never been taught to pray learned his companion's prayer, and the verse he repeated, by hearing them, and he never forgot them. He grew up to be an earnest Christian man. When he lay on his deathbed, quite an aged man, he sent for the friend, whose prayer he had learned, to come and see him, and told him that it was his little prayer, so faithfully said every night when they were boys, which led him to become a Christian. He repeated the prayer and the verse, word for word, and with his dying lips thanked his friend for letting his light shine as he did, for *that* had saved his soul.

Here is another illustration of a Christian letting his light shine and the good that was done by it. We may call it:

"The Shilling Bible, and what Came of It." Some years ago a Christian gentleman went on a visit for three days to the house of a rich lady who lived at the west end of London. After tea, on the first evening of his arrival, he called one of the servants, and telling her that in the hurry of leaving home he had forgotten to bring a Bible with him, he requested her to ask the lady of the house to be kind enough to lend him one.

Now that house was beautifully furnished. There were splendid pictures on the walls, and elegantly bound volumes in the library and on the tables in the parlor; but there was not a Bible in the house. The lady felt ashamed to own that she had no Bible. So she gave the servant a shilling and told her to go to the book store round the corner and buy a Bible. The Bible was bought and given to the gentleman. He used it during his visit, and then went home, little knowing how much good that shilling Bible was to do.

When he was gone the lady at whose house he had been staying said to herself:

"How strange it is that an intelligent gentleman like my friend could not bear to go for three days without reading the Bible, while I never read it at all, and don't know what it teaches. I am curious to know what there is in this book to make it so attractive. I mean to begin and read it through." She began to read it at first out of simple curiosity. But, as she went on reading she became deeply interested in it. It showed her what a sinner she was in living without God in the world. It led her to pray earnestly for the pardon of her sins; and the end of it was that she became a Christian. Then she desired that her children should know and love the Saviour too. She prayed for them. She talked with them, and taught them the precious truths contained in that blessed book. And the result was that, one by one, they were all led to Jesus and became Christians. And so *that whole family were saved by means of that shilling Bible.*

When that gentleman asked for the use of a Bible in the house where he was visiting, he was setting a good example. He was putting his candle on a candlestick and letting it shine. And the result that followed gives us a good illustration of the meaning of our Saviour's words when he said:—"Let your light so shine before men, that they may see your good works and glorify your Father which is in heaven."

And so, when we remember the parables that Jesus taught, among other things illustrated by them, we can think of these,—*the value of religion;—Christ's love for sinners;—the duty of kindness;—the duty of forgiveness;—the influence of a good example.*

I know not how to finish this subject better than in the words of the hymn:

"Father of mercies! in thy word,
What endless glory shines!
Forever be thy name adored
For these celestial lines.
O, may these heavenly pages be
My ever dear delight;
And still new beauties may I see,
And still increasing light."

CHRIST TEACHING BY MIRACLES

WE have seen how many valuable lessons our Saviour taught while on earth by the parables which he used. But we teach by our lives, as well as by our lips. It has passed into a proverb, and we all admit the truth of it, that "Actions speak louder than words." If our words and our actions contradict each other, people will believe our actions sooner than our words. But when both agree together, then the effect is very great. This was true with our blessed Lord. There was an entire agreement between what he said, and what he did. His words and his actions, the teaching of his lips, and the teaching of his life—were in perfect harmony. He practised what he preached.

But then, in addition to the every day common actions of the life of Christ, there were actions in it that were very uncommon. He was daily performing miracles, and doing many mighty and wonderful works. And the prophets before him, and apostles after him, performed miracles too; yet there were two things in which the miracles of Christ differed from those performed by others. One was as to the *number* of them. He did a greater number of wonderful things than anyone else ever did. Indeed if we take the miracles that were done by Moses, by Elijah and Elisha, in the Old Testament, and those that were done by the apostles in the New Testament and put them all together we shall find that they would not equal, in number, the miracles of Christ. There are between thirty and forty of the mighty works wrought by our Saviour mentioned in the gospels. And these, as St. John says, are only a small portion of them. Ch. xxi: 25.

The other thing in which the miracles of Christ are different from those performed by other persons, is *the way in which they were done.* The prophets and apostles did their mighty works in the name of God, or of Christ. Thus when Peter and John healed the lame man at the gate of the temple they said:—"*In the name of Jesus Christ of Nazareth,* rise up and walk." Acts iii: 6. But Jesus had all the power in himself by which those wonderful things were done. He could say to the leper, —"*I will;* be thou clean." He could say to the sick man:—"Take up thy bed and walk." When speaking of his death and resurrection, he could very well say that it was his own power which would control it all. His life was in his own hands. It was true, as he said, "No man taketh it from me; but I lay it down of myself. I have power to lay it down and I have power to take it again." John x: 18. And it was the same with all his other mighty works. He had all the power in himself that was needed to do them.

And these miracles of Christ were the proofs that he was the Messiah, the great Saviour, of whom the prophets had spoken. This was what Nicodemus meant when he said to Jesus: —"We know that thou art a teacher come from God: for no man can do these miracles that thou doest, except God be with him." John iii: 2. And Jesus himself referred to his miracles as the proof that God had sent him. John v: 36; x: 25.

And this was what he meant by the message which he sent to John the Baptist, when his disciples came to Jesus, saying, "Are thou he that should come, or look we for another?

Jesus answered and said unto them, Go, and show John again those things which ye do hear and see; the blind receive their sight; and the lame walk; the lepers are cleansed; and the deaf hear; the dead are raised up; and the poor have the gospel preached unto them." Matt. xi: 2-6. These were the very things which the prophets had foretold that Christ would do when he came. Is. xxix: 18. xxxv: 4-6. xlii: 7.

It is clear from these passages that all the miracles performed by our Lord were intended to teach this lesson, that he was the great Saviour of whom the prophets had spoken. But then, in addition to this, these wonderful works of Jesus were made use of by him to show that he has power to do everything for his people that they may need to have him do.

It is impossible for us to speak of all the miracles of Christ. We can only make selections from them, as we did with the parables in the last chapter. In looking at these we may see Jesus teaching us that he has power to do *four* things for his people.

In the first place some of the miracles of Christ teach us that he has great power to—HELP.

We see this in the account given us of the miraculous draught of fishes. Luke v: 1-11.

Peter was a fisherman before he became a disciple of Jesus. And James and John, the sons of Zebedee, were partners with him in the same business. On one occasion they had been busy all night throwing out and hauling in their nets, but without catching a single fish. Early the next morning, Jesus was walking along the shore of the lake, near where their boats were. He knew how tired and discouraged they were, and how much they needed help; and he wished to show them what wonderful power he had to help in time of need. So he told them to cast their net on the other side of the ship. They did so; and immediately their nets were full; and they had more fish than they could well manage. Here we are taught that even in the depths of the sea nothing can be hid from the all-seeing eye of our divine Saviour. He knows where everything is that his people can need; and he has the power to bring it to them.

And then, by his miracle of walking on the sea Jesus taught the same lesson. We have an account of this miracle in three places. Matt. xix: 22-33. Mark vi: 45-52. John vi: 14-21.

At the close of a busy day, in which he had been teaching the people and feeding them by miracle, Jesus told his disciples to go on board a vessel and cross over to the other side of the lake. Then he sent the multitude away, and went up into the mountain to pray to his Father in heaven whom he loved so much. It proved to be a stormy night. The wind was dead ahead; and the sea was very rough. The disciples were having a hard time of it. Tired of rowing, and making little progress, there was no prospect of their getting to land before morning. But, dark as the night was, Jesus saw them. It is true as David says, that—*"The darkness and the light are both alike to thee."* Ps. cxxxix: 12. He saw they needed help and he resolved to give it to them. But there was no boat at hand for him to go in. True: but he needed none. He could walk on the water as well as on the land. He steps from the sandy shore to the surface of the storm-tossed sea. He walks safely over its troubled waters. The disciples see him. Supposing it to be a spirit, they are alarmed, and cry out in their fear. But presently the cheering voice of their Master comes to them, saying: *"It is I. Be not afraid."* He steps on board. The wind ceases, and immediately, without another stroke of the oars, the mighty power of Jesus brings them "in safety to the haven where they would be." Other miracles might be referred to as teaching the same lesson. But these are sufficient. And Jesus has the same power to help now that he had then.

Here are some illustrations of the strange way in which he sometimes helps his people in their times of need.

"The Dead Raven." A poor weaver in Edinburgh lost his situation one winter, on account of business being so dull. He begged earnestly of his employer to let him have work; but he said it was impossible. Well said he, "I'm sure the Lord will help." When he came home and told his wife the sad news she was greatly distressed. He tried to comfort her with the assurance—"The Lord will help." But as he could get no work, their money was soon gone; and the day came at last, when there was neither food nor fuel left in the house. The last morsel of bread was eaten one morning at breakfast. "What shall we do for dinner?" asked his wife.

"The Lord will help"—was still his reply. And see how the help came. Soon after breakfast, his wife opened the front window, to dust off the sill. Just then a rude boy, who was passing, threw a dead raven in through the window. It fell at the feet of the pious weaver. As he threw the bird in, the boy cried out in mockery, "There, old saint, is something for you to eat." The weaver took up the dead raven, saying as he did so:—"Poor creature! you must have died of hunger!"

But when he felt its crop to see whether it was empty, he noticed something hard in it. And wishing to know what had caused its death, he took a knife and cut open its throat. How great was his astonishment on doing this, to find a small diamond bracelet fall into his hand! His wife gazed at it in amazement. "Didn't I tell you," he asked, in grateful gladness, "that the Lord will help?"

He went to the nearest jeweler's, and telling how he had found the precious jewels, borrowed some money on them. On making inquiry about it, it turned out that the bracelet belonged to the wife of the good weaver's late employer. It had suddenly disappeared from her chamber. One of the servants had been charged with stealing it, and had been dismissed. On hearing how the bracelet had disappeared, and how strangely it had fallen into the hands of his late worthy workman, the gentleman was very much touched; and not only rewarded him liberally for returning it—but took him back into his employ, and said he should never want work again so long as he had any to give.

How willing, and how able our glorious Saviour is to help those who trust in him!

"The Sailor Boy's Belief." One night there was a terrible storm at sea. All at once a ship, which was tossing on the waves, keeled over on her beam ends. "She'll never right again!" exclaimed the captain. "We shall all be lost!"

"Not at all, sir!" cried a pious sailor boy who was near the captain. "What's to hinder it?" asked the captain. "Why you see, sir," said the boy, "they are praying at this very moment in the Bethel ship at Glasgow for all sailors in danger: and I feel sure that God will hear their prayers: Now see, sir, if he don't!"

These words were hardly out of the boy's mouth, before a great wave struck the ship, and set her right up again. And then a shout of praise, louder than the howling of the storm, went up to God from the deck of that saved ship.

And so, in the miracles that he performed, one thing that Jesus taught was his power to help.

In the next place, among the miracles of Christ, we find some that were performed in order to teach us his power to—COMFORT.

One day, a great multitude of people waited on Jesus from morning till evening, to listen to his preaching. They were so anxious to hear that even when hungry they would not go away to get food. As the evening came on, the disciples asked their master to send the people away to get something to eat. But Jesus told them to give the people food. They said they had only five loaves and two fishes. Jesus told them to make the people sit down on the grass. And when they were seated he took the loaves and blessed, and brake them, and gave them to the disciples, and they gave them to the people. And great as that multitude was the supply did not fail. This was wonderful! Those loaves were very small. They were not bigger than a good-sized roll. The whole of the five loaves and two fishes would not have been enough to make a meal for a dozen men. And yet they were made sufficient to feed more than five thousand hungry people. How strange this was! The mighty power of Jesus did it. We are not told just *where*, in the interesting scene, this wonder-working power was put forth. It

Christ Teaching by Miracles

may have been that as Jesus brake the loaves and gave the pieces to the disciples, the part left in his hands grew out at once, to the same size that it was before. Or the broken pieces may have increased and multiplied while the disciples were engaged in distributing them. It is most likely that the miracle took place in immediate connection with Jesus himself. The power that did it was his: and in his hands, we may suppose that the wonderful work was done. As fast as he broke the loaves they increased, till all the people were fed. This was indeed not *one* miracle, but a multitude of miracles, all performed at once. The hungry multitude ate till all were satisfied: and yet the fragments left filled twelve baskets. Five thousand men were fed, and then there was twelve times as much food left as there was before they began to eat. All this was done to satisfy that hungry crowd, and to teach them, and us, what power this glorious Saviour has to comfort those who are in need or trouble.

And when he healed the daughter of the Syrophœnician woman, as we read in St. Matt. xii: 21-28; when he healed the lunatic child, as we read in St. Matt. xvii: 14-21; and when he raised Lazarus from the dead, after he had lain four days in the grave, as we read in St. John xi: 1-54, he was working miracles to show his power to comfort those in trouble.

And we see him using his power still to comfort persons who are in distress. Here are some illustrations of the way in which he does this:

"Shining in Every Window." A Christian lady, who spent much time in visiting among the poor, went one day to see a poor young girl, who was kept at home by a broken limb. Her room was on the north side of the house. It did not look pleasant without or cheerful within. "Poor girl!" she said to herself, "what a dreary time she must have!" On entering her room she said:

"I am sorry, my friend, that your room is not on the other side of the house, where the sun could shine upon you. You never can have any sunshine here."

"Oh, you are mistaken," she said: "the sunshine pours in at every window, and through every crack."

The lady looked surprised.

"I mean Jesus, 'the Sun of righteousness,' shines in here, and makes everything bright to me."

Here we see Jesus showing his power to comfort.

"Ice in Summer." Some years ago a Christian merchant, in one of our eastern cities, failed in business, and lost everything he had. After talking over their affairs with his wife, who was a good Christian woman, they concluded to move out to the west and begin life again there. He bought some land on the wide rolling prairie, built a log cabin, and began to cultivate his farm. In the midst of the second summer, hard work and exposure to the sun brought on an attack of sickness, and a raging fever set in. They were twelve miles away from the nearest town. One of the neighbors went there and came back with a doctor. He examined the case very carefully, and left some medicine with them, and told them what to do. He said it was a very dangerous attack. If they could only get some ice to apply to the burning brow of the sick man, he thought he might get over it; but, without that, there was very little prospect of his recovery.

As soon as the doctor was gone, the sorrowful wife gathered her family and friends round the bedside of her sick husband, and kneeled down with them in prayer. She told God what the doctor had said, and prayed very earnestly that he who has the power to do everything, would send them some ice.

When the prayer was over, some of the neighbors whispered to each other that the poor distressed woman must be losing her mind. "The idea of getting ice here," they said, "when everybody knows there isn't a bit of ice in all the country! It would be contrary to all the laws of nature to have ice in summer."

The wife of the sick man heard their remarks, but they did not shake her faith in God, and in the power of prayer. Silently, but earnestly, her heart breathed forth the cry for ice.

As the day wore on, heavy clouds began to gather in the western sky. They rolled in darkness over the heavens. The distant thunder was heard to mutter. Nearer and louder it was heard. The lightning began to flash. Presently the storm burst in its fury. It came first in rain, and then in hail. The hail-stones came in lumps of ice as big as eggs. They lay thick in the furrows of the field. The thankful wife went out, and soon came in rejoicing with a bucket full of ice. It was applied in bags to her husband's head. The fever broke, and he was restored to life and health.

This grateful woman never troubled herself with any questions about whether it was a miracle or not. She only knew that she had prayed for ice in summer, and that the ice had come. And her faith was stronger than ever that the gracious Saviour, who did so many miracles when he was on earth, has just the same power now to comfort his people when they are in trouble.

In the third place, we see Jesus performing miracles to teach us what power he has to— ENCOURAGE—*his people.*

We have an account in St. Luke xiii: 10-17, of the miracle he performed on the woman who had "a spirit of infirmity." This means that she was a cripple. Her body was bound down, so that she had no power to straighten herself or to stand upright. She had been in this condition we are told for *eighteen* years. How hard to bear—and how discouraging this trial must have been to her! No doctor could give her any relief, and she had made up her mind, no doubt, that there was no relief for her till death came. But when Jesus saw her, he pitied her. A miracle of healing was performed upon her. He laid his loving hand upon her bent and crippled body, and in a moment her disease was removed. She stood straight up, and glorified God. What encouragement that must have given to her!

One day, when Jesus was at Capernaum, the tax-gatherers came to Peter to get the tribute, or tax-money, that was due to the Roman government, for himself and his master. But, it happened so that neither of them had money enough with which to pay that tax. Peter went into the presence of Jesus to speak to him about this matter. But Jesus knowing what was in his mind, before Peter had time to say anything on the subject, told him what to do. He directed him to take his fishing-line and go to the lake, and cast in his line, and catch the first fish that should bite; and said that in its mouth he would find a piece of money with which he might pay the tribute that was due for them both.

Peter went. He threw in his line. He soon caught a fish. He looked into the fish's mouth, and lo! there was a piece of money called a stater. It was worth about sixty cents of our money, and was just enough to pay the tribute for two persons. How wonderful this was! If Jesus made this piece of money in the mouth of the fish, at the time when Peter caught it, how wonderful his *power* must be! And if, without making it then, he knew that *that* one fish, the only one in the sea, probably, that had such a piece of money in its mouth, would be the first to bite at Peter's line, then how wonderful his *knowledge* must be!

Peter would not be likely to forget that day's fishing as long as he lived. And when he thought of the illustration it afforded of the wonderful power and the wonderful knowledge of the master whom he was serving, what encouragement that would give him in his work!

And Jesus is constantly doing things to encourage those who are trying to serve him.

Let us look at some of the ways in which this is done. Our first illustration is from the life of Washington Allston, the great American painter. We may call it:

"Praying for Bread." Many years ago Mr. Allston was considered one of the greatest artists in this country. At the time to which our story refers, he was living in London. Then he was so poor that he and his wife had not a morsel of bread to eat; nor a penny left with which to buy any. In great discouragement he went into his studio, locked the door, and throwing himself on his knees, he told the Lord his trouble, and prayed earnestly for relief.

While he was still upon his knees, a knock was heard at the door. He arose and opened the door. A stranger stood there.

"I wish to see Mr. Allston," said he.

"I am Mr. Allston," replied Mr. A.

"Pray tell me, sir, who has purchased your fine painting of the 'Angel Uriel,' which won the prize at the exhibition of the Royal Academy?"

"That painting has not been sold," said Mr. A.

"Where is it to be found?"

"In this very room," said the artist, bringing a painting from the corner, and wiping off the dust.

"What is the price of it?" asked the gentleman.

"I have done fixing a price on it," said Mr. A., "for I have always asked more than people were willing to give."

"Will four hundred pounds be enough for it?" was the next question.

"That is more than I ever asked."

"Then the painting is mine," said the stranger, who introduced himself as the Marquis of Stafford; and from that day he became one of Mr. Allston's warmest friends.

What a lesson of encouragement the great painter learned that day, when he asked for bread, and while he was asking, received help that followed him all his days!

"The Hushed Tempest." A minister of the gospel in Canada gives this account of a lesson of encouragement to trust God in trouble, which he once received.

"It was in the year 1853, about the middle of the winter that we had a succession of snow-storms, followed by high winds, and severe cold. I was getting ready to haul my supply of wood for the rest of the winter. I had engaged a man to go out the day before and cut the wood and have it ready to haul. I borrowed a sled and two horses from a neighbor and started early in the morning to haul the wood. Just as I reached the place, it began to snow hard. The wind blew such a gale that it was impossible to go on with the work. What was I to do? If it kept on snowing, I knew the roads would be impassable by the next day. Besides, that was the only day on which I could get the help of the man or the team. Unless I secured the wood that day it would not be in my power to get the fuel we needed for the rest of the winter. I thought of that sweet promise, 'Call on me, in the day of trouble, and I will deliver thee.' Ps. i: 15.

"I kneeled down amid the drifting snow, and said, 'O, my God, this is a day of trouble to me. Lord help me. The elements are subject to thy will: Thou holdest the winds in thy hands. If thou wilt speak the word, there will be a great calm. O Lord, for the sake of my helpless little ones, let this snow lie still, and give me the opportunity of doing what I came to do, and what it is so necessary to do to-day, for Jesus' sake. Amen!'

"I do not think it was more than fifteen minutes from the time I began to pray, before there was a visible change. The wind became more moderate; the sky was calm; in less than half an hour all was still; and a more pleasant time for wood-hauling than we had that day I never saw, nor desire to see. While I live, I never shall forget the lesson of encouragement to trust in God that was taught me on that day." And this was one of the lessons Jesus taught us by his miracles.

In the fourth place, among the miracles of Jesus we see some that were intended to teach us his power to—PROTECT—*his people.*

And there is no lesson that we more need to be taught than this; because we are exposed to many dangers, from which we are too weak to protect ourselves.

One day, Jesus went into the house of the apostle Peter, and found the family in great distress, because the mother of Peter's wife was very ill and in danger of dying. We judge from the history that she was the head of the family. Her death would have been a great loss to them all, and yet it seemed as if no human power could protect them from that loss. But Jesus performed a miracle to save them from this threatened danger. He went into the room where she lay. He put his healing hands upon her, and at once she was well. Immediately she rose up from that sick bed, and took her place in the family and waited on Jesus.

On another occasion he was crossing the sea of Galilee with his disciples. Weary with the work of love in which he had been engaged, he laid down in the hinder part of the ship and fell asleep. While he was lying there a sudden storm burst upon the sea. The wind howled in its fury. The angry waves rose in their might and dashed against the vessel in hissing foam. The ship was full of water, and in danger of sinking. The terrified disciples came to their sleeping Master with the earnest cry:—"Lord save us: we perish." He heard their cry. He rose at once. Quietly he took his stand by the side of the storm-tossed vessel. He rebuked the winds, and said unto the sea:—"Peace: be still." They recognized their Master's voice and obeyed. "The wind ceased, and immediately there was a great calm."

As long as those disciples lived they never would forget the lesson he taught them by that miracle of his power to protect in danger.

And then many of the miracles of our Saviour were performed for the purpose of showing what power he had to protect his people from Satan, and the evil spirits that serve him. It pleased God to allow these evil spirits to have more power over men during the time when Jesus was on earth than they had before, or than they have now. We often read in the gospels of men who were "possessed of devils." This means that the evil spirits entered into the bodies of these men, and used them as their own; just as you, or I, might go into an empty house, and use it as if it belonged to us. But Jesus performed a number of miracles to show that he was able to control those spirits; to cast them out of the bodies of men and to protect

Christ Teaching by Miracles

his people from their power. We have an account of one of these miracles in St. Matt. viii: 28, 34; of another in St. Mark v: 1-20; and of another in St. Luke viii: 26-39.

The Bible speaks of Satan "going about, like a roaring lion, seeking whom he may devour." I. Peter v: 8. But he is a chained lion: and Jesus holds the chain. If we are trying to love and serve Jesus, we need not be afraid of this roaring lion. He cannot touch us till our Saviour gives him permission; and he will not let him hurt us. We see this illustrated in Job's case. Satan wanted very much to injure Job in some way. But he could not do it. And the reason of it was, as he said himself, that God had "put an hedge about him, and about his house, and about all that he had on every side." Job i: 10. This hedge, or fence, means the power which Jesus exercises to protect his people from the harm that Satan desires to do to them. In this way he protected Job. And in this way he protects all who love and serve him.

Let us take an illustration or two to show how he is doing this continually.

"Providential Deliverance." One of the best men, and one of the most useful ministers in London, during the last century, was the Rev.

John Newton. Before entering the ministry he held an office under the government. One of the duties of this office was for him to visit and inspect the vessels of the navy as they lay at anchor in the river Thames. One day he was going out to visit a man-of-war that lay there. He was a very punctual man. When he had an engagement he was always ready at the very moment. But when he reached the dock on this occasion the boat which was to take him off to the man-of-war was not there. He was obliged to wait five, ten, fifteen minutes before the boat came. This displeased him very much. But the hand of God was in this delay. For, just as the boat was leaving the dock, a spark fell into the powder magazine on board the man-of-war. An explosion took place. The huge vessel was blown to pieces, and all the men on board of her were killed. That delay of a quarter of an hour saved Mr. Newton's life. In this way that gracious Saviour whom he served protected him from the danger to which he was exposed.

"Willie's Heroism." One summer afternoon a teacher told her geography class that they might close their books and rest a little, while she told them a story. The story was about

William Tell, the famous hero of Switzerland. She told the scholars how a wicked governor placed an apple on the head of Tell's little boy and then compelled the father to take his bow and arrow and shoot the apple from the head of his son. He was very unwilling to do it, for he was afraid the arrow might miss and kill his child. But the brave boy stood firm, and cried out—"Shoot, father! I am not afraid." He took a steady aim; fired, and knocked the apple off without hurting his son.

Just as the teacher was telling this story a sudden storm burst from the sky. There was a flash of lightning, and a loud crash of thunder. Some of the children screamed, and began to cry and ran to the teacher for protection. But a little boy named Willie Hawthorne, kept his seat and went on quietly studying his lesson.

When the storm was over the teacher said:

"Willie why were you not afraid like the other children?"

"Because," said he, "I knew the lightning was only an arrow in my Heavenly Father's hand, and why should I be afraid?"

How well Willie had learned the lesson which Jesus taught his disciples when he performed so many miracles to show what power he has to protect his people from danger!

Here is just one other story to illustrate this truth. We may call it:

"The Widow's Tree." Some years ago a violent storm, with wind and thunder, swept through the valley of Yellow Creek, in Indiana County, Georgia. For more than a mile in width trees were uprooted, houses, barns, and fences were thrown down, and ruin and desolation was spread all over the land.

In the centre of the region over which this hurricane swept stood a small cabin. It was occupied by an aged Christian widow, with her only son. The terrible wind struck a large tree in front of her humble dwelling, twisting and dashing it about. If the tree should fall it would crush her home, and probably kill herself and son. The storm howled and raged, and the big trees were falling on every hand. In the midst of all the danger the widow knelt in prayer, and asked God to spare that tree, and protect her home, and save her own life, and that of her son. Her prayer was heard. And when the storm was over, the widow's tree was spared, and strange as it may seem, was the only one left amidst that scene of desolation. There it stood, as if on purpose to show what power our loving Saviour has to protect from danger those who trust in him!

But, in the last place, we see that Jesus performed some of his miracles for the purpose of teaching us that he has power to—PARDON.

A man was brought him, one day, who was sick of the palsy. His limbs were helpless. He was not able to come to Jesus himself, so his friends carried him on a bed. At this time Jesus was preaching in the yard, or court, connected with some rich man's house. In those eastern countries the houses were not built as ours are, with a yard back of them. There is a square yard in the centre, and the house is built round the four sides of this square. This open space is generally used as a garden. It has a fountain playing in it, and a covering of cloth or mats spread over it to keep off the sun. It was in one of these open courts that Jesus was preaching on this occasion. A great crowd had gathered round him, so that the friends of the palsied man could not get near him with the bed on which the sufferer lay. Then they concluded to carry him up to the top of the house, and lower him down inside. This would not be easy to do with us. But the eastern houses are not so high as ours. And then they have flat roofs, and a flight of steps leading from the ground, on the outside, to the top of the house. This made it very easy to get up. When they were on the roof they removed the covering from the inner court, and let down the bed, with the sick man on it, directly in front of our Saviour. When he saw him he pitied him, and said, "Son, be of good cheer; thy sins be forgiven thee." The people were surprised at this. The Pharisees said among themselves "This man blasphemeth." Jesus knew their thoughts and told them it was as easy for him to heal the souls of men, as it was to heal their bodies. And then, to show them that he had power on earth to forgive sins, he said to the sick man—"Arise, take up thy bed, and go unto thine house. And he arose, and went to his house." Matt. ix: 1-8. Certainly the object Jesus had in view, in performing this miracle, was to prove that he had power to forgive sins; or to pardon.

And when he healed the leper it was to teach us the same great truth. This disease was not only like all other diseases, the result of sin; but, unlike most other diseases, it was a type, or figure of sin. It affected the body as sin affects the soul. And then, leprosy was a disease which none but God could cure; just as sin is an offence which none but God our Saviour can pardon. And so Jesus performed the miracle of healing the palsied man and the lepers in order to teach his disciples the great lesson that he "had power on earth to forgive sins."

And he has the same power still. Here are some illustrations of the way in which he exercises this power now.

"No Pardon but From Jesus." There was a heathen man in India once, who felt that he was a sinner, and longed to obtain pardon. The priests had sent him to their most famous temples, all over the country, but he could get no pardon, and find no peace. He had fasted till he was about worn to a skeleton, and had done many painful things—but pardon and peace he could not find. At last he was told to put pebbles in his shoes and travel to a distant temple, and make an offering there; and he would find peace. He went. He made the offering; but still he found no relief from the burden of his sins.

Sad, and sorrowful, he was returning home with the pebbles still in his shoes. Wearied with his journey, he halted one day in the shade of a grove, by the wayside, where a company of people was gathered round a stranger who was addressing them. It was a Christian missionary preaching the gospel. The heathen listened with great interest. The missionary was preaching from the words:—"The blood of Jesus Christ cleanseth from all sin." He showed what power Jesus had to forgive sins and how able and willing he is to save all who come unto him. The heart of the poor heathen was drawn to this loving and glorious Saviour. He took off his shoes and threw away the pebbles, saying "This is the Saviour I have long sought in vain. Thank God! I have found salvation!"

Here is one more illustration of the way in which Jesus pardons our sins, and of the effect which that pardon has on those who receive it. We may call it:

"Pardon and Peace." An officer who held a high position under the government of his country, and was a favorite with the king, was once brought before the judge and charged with a great crime. He took his place at the bar with the greatest coolness, and looked at the judge and jury and the great crowd of spectators as calmly as if he were at home, surrounded by his own family.

The trial began. The witnesses were called up, and gave clear evidence that he was guilty. Still he remained as calm and unmoved as ever. There was not the least sign of fear visible on his countenance; on the contrary, his face wore a pleasant smile.

At last the jury came in, and while the crowd in the court-room held their breath, declared that the prisoner was guilty. In an instant every eye was turned upon the prisoner to see what effect this sentence would have upon him. But just then, he put his hand in his bosom, drew out a paper, and laid it on the table. It was a pardon, a full, free pardon of all his offences, given him by the king, and sealed with the royal signet. This was the secret of his peace. This was what gave him such calmness and confidence in his dreadful position as a condemned prisoner.

And so Jesus gives his people pardon in such promises as these: "Though your sins be as scarlet, they shall be white as snow: though they be red like crimson, they shall be as wool." Is. i: 16. "Let them return unto the Lord, for he will *abundantly pardon.*" Is. lv: 7. "All that believe are justified from *all* things." Acts xiii: 39. These promises are like the king's pardon which the officer had received. Faith in these promises brings pardon, and the pardon brings peace. And so, by what he is doing now, as well as by the miracles he performed when on earth, we are taught the precious truth, that —"The Son of man hath power to forgive sins."

Then when we think of the wonderful miracles that Jesus did, let us always remember the illustrations they afford of the power he had to *help—to comfort—to encourage—to protect—and to pardon.*

Let us seek to secure all these blessings to ourselves, and then we shall find that what Jesus taught by his miracles will be very profitable teaching to us!

CHRIST TEACHING LIBERALITY

IF WE should attempt to mention all the parables which Jesus spoke, and the miracles which he performed, and the many other lessons which he taught, it would make a long list. As we have done before we can only take one or two specimens of these general lessons which Jesus taught.

We have one of these in the title to our present chapter, which is—*Christ Teaching Liberality*. This was a very important lesson for Jesus to teach. One of the sad effects of sin upon our nature is to make it selfish, and covetous. We are tempted to love money more than we ought to do. We are not so willing to part with it as we should be. And we never can be good and true Christians unless we overcome the selfishness of our sinful hearts, and not only learn to give, but to give liberally. The Bible teaches us that God not only expects his people to give, but, as St. Paul says, in one place, to give "*cheerfully.*" II. Cor. ix: 7.

And this is the lesson Jesus taught when he said to his disciples,—"Give, and it shall be given unto you; good measure, pressed down, and shaken together, and running over, shall men give into your bosoms." St. Luke vi: 38.

And when we come to consider these words of Jesus, there are three things to engage our attention. *The first of these is the*—LESSON OF LIBERALITY—*here set before us.*

The second is—THE PROOF—*that this lesson is taught all through the Bible.*

And the third is—THE ILLUSTRATIONS—*of this lesson.*

And then, when put into its shortest form, our present subject may be thus expressed—*the lesson of liberality; its proofs; and its illustrations.*

And the lesson which Jesus here taught is all wrapped up in this little word—"*Give.*" Here we learn what the will of Jesus is on this subject. This is not simply the expression of his opinion. It is not merely his advice; no, but it is his *command.* He is speaking here as our Master —our King—our God. He *commands* us to— give. And when we remember how he said to his disciples, "If ye love me, *keep my commandments*," we see plainly, that we have no right to consider ourselves as his disciples if we are neglecting this or any other of his plain commands.

And this command about giving is not intended for any *one* class of persons among the followers of Christ, but for *all* of them. It is not a command designed for kings, or princes, or rich men only, but for the poor as well. It is not a command for grown persons alone, but for children also. As soon as we begin to *get*, God expects us to begin to *give*.

Jesus says nothing here about *how much* he expects us to give. But, from other places in the Bible, we learn that he expects us to give *at least one-tenth* of all that we have. If we have a thousand dollars he expects us to give one hundred out of the thousand. If we have a hundred he expects us to give ten. If we have ten dollars we must give one of them to God. If we have only one dollar we must give ten cents of it to Him. If we have but ten cents we must give one of them. If we have no money to give, God expects us to give kind words, and kind actions, our sympathy and love.

Jesus does not tell us here *how often* we are to give, but simply—give. This means that we are to learn the lesson and form the habit of giving. His command is—give. And in giving us this command he is only asking us to imitate his own example. *He is giving all the time.* The apostle Paul tells us that Jesus is "exalted to the right hand of the Father to—give." He never tires of giving. "He giveth to all life, breath, and all things." And if we have not the Spirit of Christ in this respect, "we are none of his."

This, then, is the lesson of liberality that Jesus taught when he said—"give." And that *giving is God's rule for getting* is what we are taught by our Saviour, when he said—"*Give, and it shall be given unto you.*"

And now, having seen what this lesson of liberality is, which Jesus taught, *let us look at some of the Scripture proofs of it.* The same lesson is taught in other places in the Bible. Let us see what is said about it in some of these places.

In Ps. xli: 1 David says—"Blessed is he that considereth the poor: the Lord will deliver him in time of trouble." Considering the poor here, means being kind to them, and giving them such things as they need. And the blessing promised to those who do this means that God will reward them by giving to them good things in great abundance. And, if this is so, then we have proof here that "giving is God's rule for getting."

We have another proof that "giving is God's rule for getting," in Prov. iii: 9, 10. Here Solomon says—"Honor the Lord with thy substance, and with the first-fruits of all thine increase: So shall thy barns be filled with plenty, and thy presses shall burst out with new wine."

When the Jewish farmers gathered in their harvests they were required to make an offering to God, of what had been gathered, before they used any part of it for themselves; and the offerings thus made were called "the first-fruits." God considered himself honored by his people when they did this, because they were keeping his commandments and doing what he wished them to do. And the meaning of this command, when we apply it to ourselves, is that we should give something to the cause of God from all the money, or property we have, and from all the gain, or increase that we make to the same. This is the Bible rule—the will or command of God for all his people. And then, in the other part of this passage we have the promise of God to all who do this. "So shall thy barns be filled with plenty, and thy presses shall burst out with new wine."

This means that they shall be rich and prosperous. And so we see that this passage from the book of Proverbs, teaches the same lesson of liberality that our Saviour taught when he said—"*Give and it shall be given unto you.*" It proves that "giving is God's rule for getting."

And Solomon teaches the same, again, when he says, "The liberal soul shall be made fat; and he that watereth shall be watered also himself." Prov. xi: 25.

A "liberal soul" means a person who is in the habit of giving; and to be "made fat" means to be prospered and happy. If you undertake to water a garden, you are *giving* to the thirsty plants that which they need to make them grow and thrive; and when it is promised that the person who does this shall "be watered also himself," the meaning is that he shall have given to him all that is most important to supply his wants, and make him happy. And this, we see, is only teaching what our Saviour taught when he said, "Give, and it shall be given unto you." It furnishes us with another proof that "giving is God's rule for getting."

In the nineteenth chapter of Proverbs and seventeenth verse we have a very clear proof of the lesson we are now considering. Here we find it said: *"He that hath pity upon the poor, lendeth unto the Lord; and that which he hath given will he pay him again."* Having pity on the poor, as here spoken of, means giving them such things as they need. Whatever we use in this way God looks upon as so much money lent unto him; and we have his solemn promise that when we lend anything to him, in this way, "He will pay us again." And when he pays again what has been lent to him, it is always with interest. He pays back four, or five, or ten times as much as was lent to him. This proves that "giving is God's rule for getting."

One other passage is all that need be referred to in order to prove that the lesson of liberality which our Saviour taught is the same lesson which the Bible teaches everywhere. In Eccles. xi: 1, God says, *"Cast thy bread upon the waters; for thou shalt find it after many days."*

If we should see a man standing on the end of a wharf and throwing bread upon the waters, we should think that he was a foolish man, who was wasting his bread, or only feeding the fishes with it. But suppose that you and I were travelling through Egypt—the land of the celebrated pyramids and other great wonders. The famous river Nile is there. During our visit the inundation of that river takes place. It overflows its banks, and spreads its water over all the level plains that border on the river. This takes place every year. And when the fields are all overflowed with water, the farmers go out in boats, and scatter their grain over the surface of the water. The grain sinks to the bottom. The sediment in the water settles down on the grain, and covers it with mud. By and by the waters flow back into the river. The fields become dry. The grain springs up and grows. The mud that covered it is like rich manure, and makes it grow very plentifully, and yield a rich harvest. And here we see the meaning of this passage. God makes use of this Egyptian custom to teach us the lesson of liberality that we are now considering. He tells us that the money which we give to the poor, or use to do good with, is like the grain which the Egyptian farmer casts upon the water, and which will surely yield a rich harvest by and by.

This teaches us the lesson of liberality. And when we think of all these passages, we see very clearly that the Bible teaches the same lesson which Jesus taught when he said to his disciples, "Give, and it shall be given unto you." And what we learn, both from the teaching of Christ, and from the different passages referred to, is—that "giving is God's rule for getting."

And now, having seen some of the Bible. proofs for this lesson of liberality, or for this rule about giving and getting, *let us go on to speak of some of the illustrations of this rule.* These are very numerous.

And we may draw our illustrations from three sources, viz.:—*from the Bible; from nature; and from everyday life.*

There are two illustrations of which we may speak from the Bible. We find one of these in the history of the prophet Elijah. You remember that there was a great famine in the land of Israel during the lifetime of this prophet. For more than three years there was not a drop of rain all through the land. The fields, the vineyards, and gardens dried up, and withered, and yielded no fruit. During the first part of the time when this famine was prevailing, God sent Elijah to "the brook Cherith, that is before

Jordan." I. Kings xvii: 7-17. There the ravens brought him food, and he drank of the water of the brook.

But after awhile the brook dried up. Then God told him to go to the city of Zarephath, or Sarepta, on the coast of the Mediterranean Sea, and that he had commanded a widow woman there to sustain him. He did not tell him the name of the woman; nor the street she lived in; nor the number of her house. Elijah went. When he came near the place he met a woman, picking up some sticks of wood. I suppose God told him that this was the woman he was to stay with. Elijah spoke to her, and asked her if she would please give him a drink of water. When she was going to get it, he called to her again, and said he was hungry, and asked her to bring him a piece of bread. Then she told him that there was not a morsel of bread in her house. All she had in the world was a handful of meal in a barrel, and a little oil in a cruse, and that she was gathering a few sticks, that she might go and bake the last cake for herself and her son, that they might eat it and die. And Elijah said, "Fear not; go, and do as thou hast said; but make me thereof a little cake first, and bring it unto me, and after make for thee, and for thy son. For thus saith the Lord God of Israel, The barrel of meal shall not waste, neither shall the cruse of oil fail, until the day that the Lord sendeth rain upon the earth."

This was a hard thing to ask a mother to do. It was asking her to take the last morsel of bread she had, and that she needed for herself and for her hungry boy, and give it to a stranger. Yet she did it; because she believed God. I seem to see her turning the meal barrel up, to get the meal all out. Then she pours out the oil from the cruse, and drains out the last drop. She mixes the meal and the olive oil together, as is the custom in that country still, and makes a cake which can soon be baked. She takes it to the man of God, who eats it thankfully, and is refreshed. Then she returns to the empty barrel and cruse, and finds as much in them as she had lately taken out. She prepares some bread for herself and her son, and they eat it thankfully as bread sent from heaven. The next day it is the same, and the day after, and so on through all the days of the famine. We are not told how long it was after Elijah went to the widow's house before the days of the famine were over. But suppose we make a calculation about it. The famine lasted for three years. Now let us suppose, that the first half of this time was spent by the prophet at the brook Cherith. Then his stay at the widow's house must have been at least eighteen months. And, if this miracle of increasing the meal and the oil was repeated only once a day, there would be for the first twelve months, or for the year, three hundred and sixty-five miracles; and for the six months, or the half year, one hundred and eighty-two more; and adding these together we have the surprising number of *five hundred and forty-seven* miracles, that were performed to reward this good widow for the kindness she showed to the prophet Elijah, when she gave him a piece of bread, and a drink of water! What an illustration we have here of the truth we are considering, that *giving is God's rule for getting.*

But the best illustration of this subject to be found in the Bible is given in our Saviour's own experience. He not only *preached* the lesson of liberality, but *practised* it. He is himself the greatest giver ever heard of. In becoming our Redeemer he showed himself the Prince of givers. He gave—not silver and gold; not all the wealth of the world, or of ten thousand worlds like ours; but "He gave *Himself* for us."

He can say indeed, to each of us, in the language of the hymn:

> "I gave my life for thee,
>   My precious blood I shed,
> That thou might'st ransomed be,
>   And quickened from the dead."

And what is the result of this glorious giving to Jesus himself? St. Paul answers this question when he says, "Wherefore God also hath highly exalted him; and given him a name which is above every name; that at the name of Jesus every knee should bow, of things in heaven, and things in earth, and things under the earth; And that every tongue should confess that Jesus Christ is Lord, to the glory of God the Father." Phil. ii: 9-11. Because of what he gave "for us men, and for our salvation," he will be loved and praised and honored in heaven, on the earth, and through all the universe, above all other beings, for ever and ever. What a glorious illustration we have here of the truth of this statement, that "giving is God's rule for getting." These are some of the illustrations of this lesson of liberality that we find in the Bible.

And now, let us look at some illustrations of this subject, that we have in nature.

Solomon suggests one of these when he says, "*There is that scattereth, and yet increaseth.*" Prov. xi: 26. He is evidently speaking here of a farmer sowing his fields with grain.

Now suppose that we had never seen a man sowing; and that we knew nothing at all about the growth of grain, or how wonderfully the seed sown in the spring is increased and multiplied when the harvest is reaped. Then, the first time we saw a farmer sowing his fields, we should have been ready to say, "What a foolish man that is! He is taking that precious grain by the handful, and deliberately throwing it away."

Of course, we should have expected that the grain thus thrown away, or scattered over the ground, would all be lost. But, if we could have come back to visit that farmer when he was gathering in his harvest, how surprised we should have been! Then we should have learned that for every handful of grain that the farmer had scattered, or, as we thought, thrown away, in the spring, when he was sowing, he had gained forty or fifty handfuls when he reaped in his harvest. Then we should have understood what Solomon meant when he said, "There is that scattereth, and yet increaseth."

And we should have here a good illustration of our Saviour's lesson of liberality, when he said, "Give, and it shall be given unto you;" and of the Bible truth we are now studying, that "giving is God's rule for getting."

Yonder is the great ocean; it is one of the grandest of nature's works. And the ocean gives us a good illustration of the lesson of liberality which our Saviour taught. The waters of the ocean are spread out for thousands of miles. As the sun shines on the surface of the ocean, it makes the water warm, and turns it into vapor, like the steam that comes from the boiling kettle. This vapor rises into the air, and helps to form the clouds that are floating there. These clouds sail over the land, and pour out the water that is in them, in refreshing and fertilizing showers of rain. This rain makes the rills start from the sides of the mountains. The rills run down into the rivers, and the rivers flow back into the sea again. In this way the ocean is a great giver. It has been giving away its water for hundreds and thousands of years, ever since the day when God made it.

Now, let us suppose that the ocean could think, or speak; and that it had power to control its own motions. And suppose that the ocean should say:—"Well, I think I have been giving away water long enough. I am going to turn over a new leaf. The sun may shine as much as it pleases. I won't let another drop of water go out from my surface. I am tired of giving, and I mean to stop doing it, any longer." Let us pause for a moment here, and see what the effect of this would be upon the ocean itself.

We know that all the water in the ocean is salt water. But when the sun takes water from the ocean, in the form of vapor, it is always taken out as fresh water. It leaves the salt behind it. Then the water on the surface of the ocean, from which this vapor has been taken, has more salt in it than the water underneath it. This makes it heavier than the other water. The consequence of this, is that this heavier water, on the top of the ocean, sinks to the bottom; and at the same time the lighter water at the bottom rises to the top. And so a constant change is taking place all over the ocean. The water from the top is sinking to the bottom, and the water from the bottom is rising to the top. And this is one of the means which God employs to keep the waters of the ocean always pure and wholesome. But if the ocean should stop giving away its water, as it has always been doing, then this constant change of its waters would cease. The ocean would be left still and stagnant. It would become a great mass of corruption; and the breezes from the ocean, that now carry health and life to those who breathe them, would carry only disease and death. And the thousands of people who now love the ocean and seek its shores every summer, to get strong and well by breathing the air that sweeps over its surface, and by bathing in its foaming surf, would all be afraid of the ocean; and would keep as far away from its shores as they could. And so we see how the ocean stands before us as a grand illustration of the lesson of liberality which our Saviour taught when he said, "Give, and it shall be given unto you." The ocean gives away its water continually, and, in return for this, God gives it freshness and purity, and makes it a blessing to the world. And so the ocean illustrates the truth of the lesson we are now studying, that "giving is God's rule for getting."

And yonder is the great sun, shining up in the sky. We do not know as much about the sun as we do about the ocean, because it is so far away from us. The ocean is very near us. We can walk along its shores, and plunge into its waters, and sail over its surface. We can study out all about the laws that govern it, and what the effect of those laws is upon it. But it is very different with the sun. It is about ninety millions of miles away from us. This is too far off for us to know much about it. And yet, we know enough about the sun to get from it a good illustration of God's rule about giving and getting. The sun, like the ocean, is a great giver. It is giving away light all the time. It was made for this purpose; and for this purpose it is preserved. If the sun should stop giving, and should try to keep all its light and heat for itself, the effect would be its ruin. By ceasing to give it would be burnt up and destroyed. And so, when we see the sower sowing his seed, or the reaper gathering in his harvest; when we look upon the ocean, and see the clouds formed from its waters, as they go sailing through the sky; or when we see the sun rising in the morning, going forth again to his appointed work of giving light to a dark world; let us remember that these are nature's illustrations of the lesson of liberality which Jesus taught when he said, "Give, and it shall be given unto you." They all help to show how true it is, that "giving is God's rule of getting."

And now we may go on to look for our illustrations of this subject from everyday life.

If we are only watchful we shall meet with illustrations of this kind continually. It would not be difficult to fill a volume with them. Here are a few out of many that might be given.

"The Travellers in the Snow." Two travellers were on a journey in a sleigh during a very severe winter. It was snowing fast as they drove along. One of the travellers was a liberal, generous-hearted man, who believed in giving; and was always ready to share whatever he had with others. His companion was a selfish ungenerous man. He did *not* believe in giving; and liked to keep whatever he had for himself. As they drove along, they saw something covered up in the snow that looked like the figure of a man. "Look there," said the generous man to his friend, "that must be some poor fellow overcome by the cold. Let's stop and see what we can do for him."

"You can get out, if you like," was his reply, "but it's too cold for me. I intend to stay where I am;" and he wrapped his furs closely round him.

The other traveller threw aside his furs and jumped out of the sleigh. He found it was a poor man, who had sunk down in the snow a short time before, overcome by the cold. He shook the snow from him, and began to rub his hands and face and feet. He kept on rubbing for a good while. At last the man began to get warm again and was saved from death. Then the generous-hearted traveller helped him into the sleigh, and shared his wrappings with him. The exertion he had made in doing this kind act put him all in a glow of warmth. He made the rest of the journey in comfort. But when they stopped at the end of their journey, the selfish man, who was not willing to do anything for the help of another, had his fingers, and toes, and nose, and ears frozen. This illustrates the lesson of liberality; and shows that "giving is God's rule for getting."

Here we see the truth of the lines which someone has written:

> "Numb and weary on the mountan
>   Wouldst thou sleep amidst the snow?
> Chafe the frozen form beside thee,
>   And together both shall glow.
> Art thou stricken in life's battle?
>   Many wounded round thee moan;
> Lavish on their wounds thy balsams,
>   And that balm shall heal thine own."

"The Officer and the Soldier." In one of the terrible battles in Virginia, during the late war, a Union officer fell wounded in front of the Confederate breastwork, which had been attacked. His wounds brought on a raging fever, and he lay on the ground crying piteously for water. A kind-hearted Confederate soldier heard the touching cry, and leaping over the fortifications, with his canteen in his hand, he crawled up to the poor fellow and gave him a drink of water. O, what a comfort this was to the wounded man! His heart was filled with gratitude towards this generous and noble soldier. He pulled out his gold watch from his pocket, and cheerfully offered it to his benefactor; but he refused to take it. Then he asked the soldier's name and residence. He said his name was James Moore, and that he lived in Burke County, North Carolina. Then they parted. This noble soldier afterwards lost a limb in one of the Virginia battles, and returned to his home as a cripple.

The officer recovered from his wounds; but he never forgot the kindness of that Confederate soldier. And when the war was over, and he was engaged in his business again, he wrote to James Moore, telling him that he intended to send him the sum of ten thousand dollars in four quarterly installments of twenty-five hundred dollars each; and that he wished him to receive the same in token of the heartfelt gratitude with which his generous kindness on the battle-field was remembered. Certainly these were two noble men. It is hard to tell which was the more noble of the two. But when the crippled soldier thought of the drink of water which he gave to the wounded officer, and of the ten thousand dollars which he received for the same, he must have felt how true our Saviour's words were, when he said: "Give, and it shall be given unto you." And he must have felt sure of the lesson we are now considering, that "Giving is God's rule for getting."

"The Secret of Success." Some time ago a Christian gentleman was visiting a large paper mill that belonged to a friend of his, who was a very rich man. The owner of the mill took him all through it, and showed him the machinery, and told him how the paper was made. When they were through the visitor said to his friend, "I have one question to ask you; and if you will answer it, I shall feel very much obliged to you. I am told that you started in life very poor, and now you are one of the richest men in this part of the country. My question is *this:* will you please tell me the *secret* of your success in business?"

"I don't know that there is any great secret about it," said his friend, "but I will tell you all I know. I got a situation, and began to work for my own living when I was only sixteen years old. My wages, at first, were to be forty dollars a year, with my board and lodging. My clothing and all my other expenses were to come out of the forty dollars. I then made a solemn promise to the Lord that *one-tenth* of my wages, or four dollars out of the forty, should be faithfully laid aside to be given to the poor, or to some religious work. This promise I kept religiously, and after laying aside one-tenth to give away, at the end of the year, besides meeting my expenses, I had more than a tenth left for myself. I then made a vow that whatever it might please God to give me, I would never give *less* than one-tenth of my income to him. This vow I have faithfully kept from that day to this. If there be any secret to my success—*this is it.* Whatever I receive during the year, I feel sure that I am richer on nine-tenths of it, with God's blessing, than I should be on the whole of it, without that blessing. I believe that God has blessed me, and made my business prosper. And I am sure that anyone who will make the trial of this secret of success, will find it work as it has done in my case."

This man was certainly proving the truth of our Saviour's words, when he said—"Give, and it shall be given unto you." And his experience shows most satisfactorily that "giving is God's rule for getting."

"The Steamboat Captain and the Soldier." During the late war there was a steamboat, one day, in front of a flourishing town on the Ohio River. The captain, who had charge of her was the owner of the boat. The steam was up; and the captain was about to start on a trip some miles down the river with an excursion party, who had chartered the boat for the occasion. While waiting for the party to come on board, a poor wounded soldier came up to the captain. He said he was suffering from severe sickness, as well as from his wounds. He had been in the hospital. The doctor had told him he could not live long; and he was very anxious to get home, and see his mother again, before he died; and he wished to know if the captain would give him a passage down the river on his boat. On hearing where his home was, the captain said that the party who had chartered his boat were going near that place; and he told the poor soldier that he would gladly take him to his home.

But, when the excursion party came on board, and saw the soldier, with his soiled and worn clothes, and his ugly-looking wounds, they were not willing to let him go; and asked the captain to put him ashore. The captain told the soldier's sad story, and pleaded his cause very earnestly. He said he would place him on the lower deck and put a screen round his bed, so that they could not see him. But the young people refused. They said as they had hired the boat, it belonged to them for the day, and they were not willing to have such a miserable-looking object on board their boat; and that if the captain did not put him off, they would hire another boat, and he would lose the twenty dollars they had agreed to give him for the day's excursion.

The good captain made one more appeal to them. He asked them to put themselves in the poor soldier's place, and then to think how they would like to be treated. But still they refused to let the soldier go. Then the noble-hearted captain said: "Well, ladies and gentlemen, whether you hire my boat or not, I intend to take this soldier home to-day."

The party did hire another boat. The captain lost his twenty dollars. But, when he returned the poor dying soldier to the arms of his loving mother, he felt that the tears of gratitude with which she thanked him were worth more than the money he had lost. The gentle mother dressed the wounds of her poor suffering boy; and nursed and cared for him, as none but a mother knows how to do. But she could not save his life. He died after a few days; and the last words he spoke, as his loving parents stood weeping at his bedside were—"Don't forget the good captain." And he was not forgotten. For after the soldier's funeral was over, his father went up the river to the town where the captain lived. He found him out. He thanked him again for his kindness in bringing home his dying boy; and made him a present that was worth four or five times the twenty dollars he had lost for the hire of his boat.

But this was not the end of it. For not long after this, the captain and his wife were taken suddenly ill with a fatal disease that was prevailing in that region of the country. They both died; leaving two little orphan children, with no one to take care of them. The soldier's father heard of it; and he went at once and asked that he might be permitted to take the two helpless little ones and adopt them as his own children. He took them home; and was a father and a friend to them as long as he lived.

How beautifully our Saviour's words—"Give, and it shall be given unto you," are illustrated in this story! How clearly we see here, that "Giving is God's rule for getting!"

I have just one other illustration before closing this subject. We may call it:

"The Miser and the Hungry Children." In a village in England were two little motherless girls who lived in a small cottage. Sally, the elder, was about eight years old and her sister Mary was six. They were very poor. Their father was a laboring man, and he found great difficulty in supporting himself and his children.

Once, in the midst of winter, these two little girls were left alone all day, as their father had gone out to work. They had their breakfast in the morning with their father, before he left. But they had no dinner, nor anything to eat during the rest of the day. About the middle of the afternoon, Mary said to her sister; "Sally, I'm very hungry. Is there anything in the closet that we can get to eat?"

"No," said Sally; "I've looked all through the closet; but there isn't a crust of bread, or a cold potato; nor anything to eat. I wish there was something; for I'm hungry too."

"O, dear! what shall we do?" cried Mary; "I'm too hungry to wait till father comes home!"

"Mary," said her sister, "suppose we ask our Father in heaven to give us something to eat? Let us kneel down, and say the Lord's Prayer. When we come to that part about 'daily bread' we'll say it over three times, and then wait, and see if God will send us some."

Mary agreed to this. They both kneeled down, and Sally began: "Our Father, who art in heaven; hallowed be thy name; thy kingdom come; thy will be done on earth, as it is in heaven: give us this day our daily bread; give us this day our daily bread; give us this day our daily bread." Then they waited quietly, to see if anything would come.

And now, while this was going on inside of that little cottage, let me tell you what was taking place outside.

Not far from this cottage lived an old man who was a miser. He had a good deal of money, but he never gave any of it to others;

and never would spend a penny for himself, if he could possibly help it. But, on that afternoon, he had left home to go to the baker's and buy a loaf of bread. He got the loaf, and, as it was a stormy afternoon, he put it under his coat before starting to walk home. Now, it happened, that just as he was passing the cottage in which the little girls were, a strong blast of wind blew the rain in his face, and he stepped into the porch of the cottage and crouched down in the corner, to shelter himself from the wind and rain. In this position his ear was brought quite close to the keyhole of the door. He heard what the little girls had said about being hungry. He heard their proposal to pray to the Father in heaven to give them bread. He heard the thrice repeated prayer—"give us this day our daily bread." And then came the silence, when the little ones waited, and watched for the bread. This had a strange effect on the miser. His hard, selfish heart, which had never felt a generous feeling for anyone, warmed up, and grew suddenly soft in tenderness towards these helpless, hungry little ones. Tears moistened his eyes. He put his thumb on the latch of the door. The latch was gently lifted and the door opened. He took the loaf from under his coat and threw it into the room. The little girls, still waiting and watching on their knees, saw the loaf go bouncing over the floor. They jumped up on their feet, and clapped their hands for joy.

"O, Sally," said little Mary, "how good God is to answer our prayer so soon! Did He send an angel from heaven to bring us this bread?"

"I don't know who brought it," answered Sally, "but I am sure that God sent it."

And how about the miser? For the first time in his life he had given to the poor. Did the promise fail which says, "Give, and it shall be given unto you?" No; God's promises *never* fail. He went to the bakery and bought another loaf for himself, and then he went home with different feelings from what he had ever had before. The warm, soft feeling that came into his hard heart when he gave the loaf to those children did not pass away. It grew upon him. He had found so much pleasure in doing that one kind act that he went on and did more. And God blessed him in doing it. He began to pray to that God who had answered the prayer of those little girls for bread in such a strange way. He read the Bible. He went to church. He became a Christian; and some time after, he died a happy Christian death. But before he died, as he was the owner of the cottage in which the little girls lived, he gave it to their father. What a beautiful illustration we have here of our Saviour's words—"Give, and it shall be given unto you!" This miser gave *a loaf of bread* to these hungry children and God gave him *the grace that made him a Christian!* And as we think of this we may well say that "giving *is* God's rule for getting."

And thus we have considered the lesson of liberality which our Saviour taught; the proofs of that lesson found in the Bible; and the illustrations of it from the Bible, from nature, and from everyday life. The three things to be remembered from this subject are *the lesson—the proofs—the illustrations.*

I will quote here, in finishing, three verses which teach the same lesson that our Saviour taught when he spoke the words from which I have tried to draw the lesson of liberality. The title at the head of them is taken from Solomon's words in one of the passages from the book of Proverbs, which we have already used.

"THERE IS THAT SCATTERETH AND YET INCREASETH."

"Is thy cruse of comfort wasting?
   Rise, and share it with another;
And through all the years of famine,
   It shall serve thee and thy brother.
God himself will fill thy storehouse,
   Or thy handful still renew:
Scanty fare for *one* will often
   Make a royal feast for *two*.

"For the heart grows rich in giving;
   All its wealth is living grain:
Seeds which mildew in the garner,
   Scattered, fill with gold the plain.
Is thy burden hard and heavy?
   Do thy steps drag wearily?
Help to bear thy brother's burden,—
   God will bear both it and thee.

"Is thy heart a well left empty?
   None but God its void can fill;
Nothing but a ceaseless fountain
   Can this ceaseless longing still.
Is the heart a living power?
   Self-entwined its strength sinks low;
It can only live in loving,
   And by serving love will grow."

CHRIST TEACHING HUMILITY

DURING the earthly life of our blessed Saviour, we see how everything connected with it teaches the lesson of humility. This is pointed out in the beautiful collect in The Book of Common Prayer for the first Sunday in Advent. Here we are taught to say:—"Almighty God, give us grace to cast away the works of darkness, and put upon us the armor of light, now in the time of this mortal life, in which thy Son Jesus Christ came to visit us in—great *humility.*"

If Jesus had come into our world as an angel, it would have been an act of humility. If he had come as a great and mighty king, it would have been an act of humility. But when he was born in a stable, and cradled in a manger; when he could say of himself, "the foxes have holes, and the birds of the air have nests, but the Son of man hath not where to lay his head;"

when there never was an acre, or a foot of ground that he called his own, although he made the world and all things in it; when he sailed in a borrowed boat, and was buried in a borrowed tomb; how well it might be said that he was teaching humility all the days of his life on earth! Yet he did not think that *this* was enough. And so he gave his disciples a special lesson on this subject.

We have an account of this lesson in St. John xiii: 4-15. It is taught us in these words:—"He riseth from supper, and laid aside his garments; and took a towel and girdled himself. After that he poureth water into a bason, and began to wash his disciples' feet, and to wipe them with the towel wherewith he was girded." Then occurs the incident about the objection which Peter made to letting Jesus wash his feet, and the way in which that objection was overcome. And then the story goes on thus:—"So after he had washed their feet, and had taken his garments, and was set down again, he said unto them, 'Know ye what I have done unto you? Ye call me Master, and Lord; and ye say well; for so I am. If I then, your Lord and Master, have washed your feet; ye ought also to wash one another's feet. For I have given you an example, that ye should do as I have done to you.'"

This was a very surprising scene. How astonished the angels must have been when they looked upon it! They had known Jesus in heaven, before he took upon him our nature, and came into this fallen world. They had seen him in "the glory which he had with the Father, before the world was." They had worshipped him in the midst of all that glory. And then, when they saw him, girded with a towel and washing the feet of poor sinful men whom he came from heaven to save, how surprising it must have seemed to them! And when Jesus told his disciples that his object in doing this was to set them an example, that they should do as he had done to them, he did not mean that they should literally make a practice of washing each other's feet; but that they should show the same humility to others that he had shown to them, by being willing to do anything, however humble it might be, in order to promote their comfort and happiness. It is not the act itself, here spoken of, that Jesus teaches us to do; but the spirit of humility in which the act was performed that he teaches us to cultivate. We might go through the form of washing the feet of other persons, and yet feel proud and haughty all the time we were doing it. Then we should not be following the example of Jesus at all. When Jesus washed his disciples' feet, what he wished to teach them, and us, and all his people, is how earnestly he desires us to learn this lesson of humility. And when we think of the wondrous scene which took place on that occasion, the one thought it should impress on our minds, above all others is—*the importance of humility.*

And if any one asks what is meant by humility? No better answer can be given to this question than we find in Romans xii: 3, where St. Paul tells us "not to think of ourselves more highly than we ought to think, but to think soberly." Pride is "thinking of ourselves more highly than we ought to think." Humility is—*not* "thinking of ourselves more highly than we ought to think." And humility is the lesson we are now to study. This is the lesson that Jesus wishes all who love him to learn. It is easy to speak of *five* reasons why we should learn this lesson.

And the first reason for learning it is—the COMMAND—*of Jesus.*

When he had finished washing his disciples' feet, he told them that "they should do as he had done to them." This was his command to his disciples, and to us, to learn the lesson of humility. And this is not the only place in which Jesus taught this lesson. He gave some of his beautiful parables to teach humility. We find one of these in St. Luke xiv: 7-12.

On one occasion when he saw the people all pressing forward to get the best seats for themselves at a feast, he took the opportunity of giving his disciples a lesson about humility. He told them, when they were bidden to a wedding feast, not to take the highest seats; because some more honorable person might be bidden, and when the master of the feast came in he might say to them 'let this man have that seat, and you go and take a lower seat'; then they would feel mortified, and ashamed. And then he gave his disciples this command: "When thou art bidden, go and sit down in the lowest room," or seat; "that when he that bade thee cometh, he may say unto thee, Friend, go up higher: then shalt thou have worship"—or honor—"in the presence of them that sit at meat with thee." Here we have Jesus repeating his command to all his people to learn and practise the lesson of humility.

And then we have another of our Saviour's parables in which he taught this same lesson of humility, and that is the parable of the Pharisee and the Publican. We find it in St. Luke xviii: 10-15. The parable reads thus: "Two men went up into the temple to pray; the one a Pharisee, and the other a publican. The Pharisee stood and prayed thus with himself, 'God, I thank thee, that I am not as other men are, extortioners, unjust, adulterers, or even as this publican. I fast twice in the week, I give tithes of all that I possess.'" Here we have a picture of a proud man. He pretended to pray, but asked for nothing, because he did not feel his need of anything. And so his pretended prayer brought him no blessing.

And then in the rest of the parable we have our Saviour's description of a man who was learning the lesson of humility, and of the blessing which it brought to him.

Here is a story told by one of our missionaries of the way in which this parable brought a heathen man to Christ.

"That's Me." A poor Hottentot in Southern Africa lived with a Dutch farmer, who was a

Christ Teaching Humility 163

good Christian man, and kept up family prayer in his home. One day, at their family worship he read this parable. He began, "Two men went up into the temple to pray." The poor savage, who had been led to feel himself a sinner, and was anxious for the salvation of his soul, looked earnestly at the reader, and whispered to himself, "Now I'll learn how to pray." The farmer read on, "God, I thank Thee that I am not as other men are." "No, I am not," whispered the Hottentot, "but I'm worse." Again the farmer read, "I fast twice in the week; I give tithes of all that I possess." "I don't do that. I don't pray in that way. What shall I do?" said the distressed savage.

The good man read on till he came to the publican, "standing afar off." "That's where I am," said the Hottentot. "Would not lift up so much as his eyes unto heaven," read the farmer. "That's me," cried his hearer. "But smote upon his breast saying, God be merciful to me a sinner." "That's me; that's my prayer," cried the poor creature, and smiting on his dark breast, he prayed for himself in the words of the parable,—"God be merciful to me a sinner!" And he went on offering this prayer till the loving Saviour heard and answered him, and he went down to his house a saved and happy man.

Thus we see how this poor man learned the lesson of humility which Jesus taught, and how much good it did to him.

And it is Jesus who is speaking to us and commanding us to learn this lesson of humility, when we read, in other passages of Scripture, such words as these:—"Put on therefore—humbleness of mind, meekness, long-suffering." Col. iii: 12. "Humble yourself therefore in the sight of God." James iv: 10. "Be clothed with humility." I. Pet. v: 5. In all these places we have Jesus repeating his command to us to learn the lesson of humility. And this command is urged thus earnestly upon us because it is so important.

When St. Augustine, one of the celebrated fathers of the early Church, was asked—What is the first important thing in the Christian religion? his reply was—"Humility." "What is the second?" "Humility." "And what is the third?"—the reply still was—"Humility."

And if this be true, we need not wonder that Jesus should have been so earnest in teaching this lesson; or that he should have urged so strongly on his disciples to learn it.

The *command* of Christ is the first reason why we should learn the lesson of humility.

But the second reason why we should learn this lesson is, because of the—EXAMPLE—*of Christ.*

There are many persons "who say and do not." There are some ministers who preach very well, but they do not *practise* what they preach. Such persons may well be compared to finger-boards. They point out the way to others, but they do not walk in it themselves. But this was not the case with our blessed Saviour. He practised everything that he preached. And when he gave us his command to learn this lesson of humility, he gave us, at the same time, his example to show us *how* to do it.

He was illustrating this command by his example when he washed his disciples' feet. And this was only one out of many things in which he set us this example. When he chose to be born of poor parents, he was giving an example of humility. When he lived at Nazareth till he was thirty years of age, working with his reputed father as a carpenter, and during the latter part of the time, as is supposed, laboring for the support of his mother, he was giving an example of humility. When he said, "The Son of man came not to be ministered unto, but to minister," Matt. xx: 28; and again—"I am among you as he that serveth," Luke xxii: 27, he was giving an example of humility. When he borrowed an ass to make his triumphal entrance into Jerusalem; though he could say in truth, "every beast of the forest is mine, and the cattle upon a thousand hills;"—(Ps. l: 10), he was setting an example of humility. When he hid himself away from the people because he saw that they wanted to take him by force and make him king, he was giving a lesson of humility. When he allowed himself to be taken prisoner, though he knew that if he had asked his Father in heaven, he would, at once, have sent "more than twelve legions of angels" to deliver him, he was giving an example of humility. When he kept silence, at the bar of the high-priest, of Herod, of Pontius Pilate, like "a lamb dumb before her shearers," while his enemies were charging him falsely with all kinds of wickedness; when he allowed the Roman soldiers to scourge him with rods, till his back was all bleeding; to put a crown of thorns upon his head; to array him in a purple robe in mockery of his being a king; to smite him with the palms of their hands, and spit upon him; and then to nail him to the cross, and put him to the most shameful of all deaths —as if he were a wicked man, who did not deserve to live—he was giving the most wonderful example of humility that ever was heard of. Jesus, the Lord of glory hanging on the shameful cross!—O, this was an example of humility that must have filled the angels of heaven with surprise, and wonder!

And when we think of all that Jesus did and suffered, to set us an example of humility, it should make us ashamed of being proud; and anxious, above all things, to learn this lesson which he did so much to teach us.

"Imitating Christ's Humility." I think I never heard of a more beautiful instance of persons learning to imitate the humility of Christ, than is told of some Moravian Missionaries. These good men had heard the story of the unhappy slaves in the West Indies. Those poor creatures were wearing out their lives in hard bondage. They had very little comfort in this life, and no knowledge of that gracious Saviour who alone can secure, for sinful creatures, such as we are, a better portion in the life to come. These missionaries offered to go out to the West Indies, and teach those slaves about Jesus, and the great salvation that is to be found in him. But they were told that the owners of the slaves would not let them go to school or to church. They would not allow them to take time enough from their work to learn anything about the salvation of their souls. There was only one way in which those poor slaves could be taught anything about Jesus and his love, and that was, for those who wished to teach them, to go and be slaves on the plantations, to work, and toil, if need be, under the lash, so that they could get right beside them and then tell them about the way of salvation that is in Christ Jesus. This was a hard thing to undertake. But those good missionaries said they were willing to do it. And they not only *said* it, but *did* it. They left their homes, and went to the West Indies. They worked on the plantations as slaves. And working thus, by the side of the slaves, they got close to their hearts. The slaves heard them. Their hearts were touched because these teachers of the gospel had humbled themselves to their condition. While they were teaching the commands of Christ, they were illustrating and following his example. How beautiful this was! How grand! How glorious!

And yet Christ's own example was still more glorious. He laid aside the glory of his

Godhead, and came down from heaven to earth, that he might get by our side. He laid himself beside us that we might feel the throbbings of his bosom and the embrace of his loving arms; and he draws us close to himself, while he whispers in our ears the sweet words, "God so loved the world that he gave his only begotten Son, that whosoever believeth in him should not perish, but have everlasting life."

And so, when we think of the example of Christ, we should strive to learn the lesson of humility which he taught.

A third reason why we should learn this lesson of humility is because of the—COMFORT—*that is found in it.*

Just think for a moment what God says on this subject, in Is. lvii: 15. These are his words: —"Thus saith the high and mighty One that inhabiteth eternity, whose name is Holy; I dwell in the high and holy place, with him also that is of a contrite and humble spirit, to revive the spirit of the humble, and to revive the heart of the contrite ones." Here, the same loving Saviour who gave us the command to learn the lesson of humility promises to give comfort to all who learn this lesson. And the way in which he secures this comfort to them is by coming and dwelling in their hearts. And who can tell what a comfort it is for a poor pardoned sinner to have Jesus—the Lord of heaven and earth—dwelling in his heart? It is his presence in heaven which makes those who dwell there feel so happy. This is what David taught, when he looked up to him, and said—"In thy presence is fulness of joy." Ps. 16: 11. And when that presence is felt, here on earth, it gives comfort and joy, as certainly as it does in heaven. It was the presence of Jesus which enabled Paul and Silas to sing at midnight, for very joyfulness, in the prison at Philippi, though their feet were fastened in the stocks, and their backs were torn and bleeding from the cruel scourging which they had suffered. And it was this presence of Christ in the hearts of his people that good John Newton was speaking of, in one of his sweet hymns, when he said:

> "While blest with a sense of his love
> A palace a toy would appear;
> And prisons would palaces prove,
> If Jesus would dwell with me there."

But it is only those who learn the lesson of humility that Jesus will dwell with. He says himself, "If any man love me, he will keep my words; and My Father will love him; and we will come unto him, and make our abode with him." St. John xiv: 23. And among the words of Christ which we must keep, if we wish him to dwell in our hearts, are those in which he commands the lesson of humility. It is only the humble with whom he will dwell. For "every one that is proud in heart is an abomination unto the Lord." Prov. xvi: 5.

The reason why so many people are unhappy in this world is that they do not learn the lesson of humility.

"Learn to Stoop." The story is told of some celebrated man—I think it was Dr. Franklin—who had a friend visiting him on one occasion. When the gentleman was about to leave, the doctor accompanied him to the front door. In going through the entry there was a low beam across it, which made it necessary to stoop, in order to avoid being struck by it. As they approached it the doctor stooped himself, and called out to his friend to do the same. He did not heed the caution, and received a severe thump on his head as the result of his neglect. In bidding him good-bye, the doctor said—"Learn to stoop, my friend; and it will save you from many a hard knock, as you go on through life." This illustrates the comfort which comes from learning the lesson of humility. It is those who are unwilling to stoop; or to be anything, or nothing, as God wants them to be, who have no comfort.

"The Fable of the Oak and the Violet." In a large garden there grew a fine oak tree, with its wide-spreading branches, and at its foot there grew a sweet and modest violet. The oak one day looked down in scorn upon the violet, and said: "You, poor little thing, will soon be dead and withered; for you have no strength, no size, and are of no good to anyone. But I am large and strong; I shall still live for ages, and then I shall be made into a large ship to sail on the ocean, or into coffins to hold the dust of princes."

"Yes," answered the violet, in its humility, "God has given *you* strength, and *me* sweetness. I offer him back my fragrance, and am thankful. I hope to die fragrantly, as I have lived fragrantly, but we are both only what God made us, and both where God placed us."

Not long after the oak was struck by lightning and shivered to splinters. Its end was to be burned. But the violet was gently gathered by the hand of a Christian lady, who carefully pressed it, and kept it for years, in the leaves of her Bible to refresh herself with its fragrance.

Here we see illustrated the difference between pride and humility.

"The Secret of Comfort." Some years ago there was a boy who had been lame from his birth. He was a bright intelligent boy, but he was not a Christian. As he grew up, with no other prospect before him but that of being a cripple all his days, he was very unhappy. As he sat by his window, propped up in his chair, and saw the boys playing in the street, he would say to himself: "Why has God made me thus? Why have I not limbs to run and jump with like other boys?"

These thoughts filled him with distress, and caused him to shed many bitter tears.

One day a Christian friend, who was visiting him, gave him a book and requested him to read it. He did so; and it led to his becoming a Christian. His heart was renewed; the burden of his sin was removed; and the love of God was shed abroad in his heart by the Holy Ghost. He learned the lesson of humble submission to the will of God. After this, as he looked out, and saw the young people happy at their sports; or, as he gazed on the green earth and the beautiful sky, and knew that he must remain a helpless cripple as long as he lived, he yet could say, with the utmost cheerfulness:—"It's all right. My Father in heaven has done it. I love him. He loves me. I know he is making all things work together for my good." He had learned the lesson we are now considering, and we see what comfort it gave him. And the thought of the comfort which this lesson gives, should be a good reason with us all for learning it.

A fourth reason why we should learn the lesson of humility is because of the—USEFULNESS—*connected with it.*

Jesus tells us, by his apostle, that "God resisteth the proud, but giveth grace to the humble." St. James iv: 6. If we have the grace of God we can be useful in many ways, but, without that grace we cannot be useful at all. And this is what our Saviour taught his disciples, when he said to them—"without me ye can do nothing." St. John xv: 5. By the words "without *me*" he meant without my help, or without my grace; or without the help of my grace. And it was of this grace that St. Paul was speaking when he said—"I can do all things through Christ who strengtheneth me." Phil. iv: 13.

And we could not possibly have a stronger reason for trying to learn the lesson of humility than this, that our receiving the grace of God, and consequently our usefulness, depends upon it. God will not give us his grace to enable us to be truly good and to make ourselves useful, unless we learn this lesson. And unless we have the grace of God, we cannot be useful. Like barren fig-trees we shall be useless cumberers of the ground.

Now let us look at one or two illustrations which show us how pride hinders the usefulness of men, while humility helps it.

"The Fisherman's Mistake." An English gentleman was spending his summer holidays in Scotland. He concluded to try his hand at fishing for trout in one of the neighboring streams. He bought one of the handsomest fishing rods he could find, with line and reel, and artificial flies, and everything necessary to make a perfect outfit for a fisherman. He went to the trout stream, and toiled all day, but never caught a single fish.

Towards the close of the day he saw a ragged little farmer boy, with a bean pole for a rod, and the simplest possible sort of a line, who was nipping the fish out of the water about as fast as he could throw his line in. He watched the boy in amazement for awhile, and then asked him how it was that one, with so fine a rod and line, could catch no fish, while he with his poor outfit was catching so many. The boy's prompt reply was:—"Ye'll no catch ony fish Sir, as lang as ye dinna keep yersel' oot o' sicht."

The gentleman was proud of his handsome rod and line, and was showing it off all the time. His pride hindered his usefulness as a fisherman. The farmer's boy had nothing to show off; so he kept himself out of sight, and thus his humility helped his usefulness in fishing.

"The Thames' Tunnel Teaching Humility." Most strangers who visit the great city of London go to see the famous tunnel under the river Thames. This is a large, substantial road that has been built, in the form of an arch, directly under the bed of the river. It is one of the most wonderful works that human skill ever succeeded in making. The man who planned and built it was made one of the nobility of England. His name was Sir Isambard Brunel. He was so humble that he was willing to learn a lesson from a tiny little ship worm. These worms bore small round holes through the solid timbers of our ships.

One day Mr. Brunel visited a ship-yard. An old ship was on the dry-dock getting repaired.

A quantity of worm-eaten timber had been taken out from her sides. He picked up one of these pieces of timber, and saw a worm at work, boring its way through. If he had been a proud man, he might have thrown the timber aside, and said—"Get away you poor little worm. I am a great master builder. You can't teach me anything." And if he had done so that famous tunnel under the Thames would probably never have been built. But Mr. Brunel had learned the lesson of humility. He was willing to learn from anything that God had made, however insignificant it might be. So he sat down and watched the worm at its work. He studied carefully the form of the hole it was boring. The thought occurred to him how strong a tunnel would be, that was made in the shape of this hole! And when he was asked whether it would be possible to build a tunnel under the Thames, he said he thought it could be done. He undertook to build it. He succeeded in the work. But, in accomplishing the great undertaking that little ship-worm was his teacher.

And now, if any of my young friends who may read this book should ever visit London, and go to see the great tunnel, as they gaze in wonder at it, let them remember Sir I. Brunel, and that little ship-worm; and then, let them say to themselves: "This mighty tunnel is an illustration of the truth that humility helps to make us useful."

"George Washington and His Humility." Here is a story connected with the great and good Washington—"the Father of his country," which illustrates very well this part of our subject.

During the war of the American Revolution, the commander of a little squad of soldiers was superintending their operations as they were trying to raise a heavy piece of timber to the top of some military works which they were engaged in repairing. It was hard work to get the timber up, and so the commander, who was a proud man and thought himself of great importance, kept calling out to them from time to time, "Push away, boys! There she goes! Heave ho!"

While this was going on, an officer on horseback, but not in military dress, rode by. He asked the commander why he did not take hold, and give the men a little help. He looked at the stranger in great astonishment, and then, with all the pride of an emperor, said:

"Sir, I'd have you know that I am a corporal!"

"You are—are you?" replied the officer, "I was not aware of that," and then taking off his hat, and making a low bow, said, "I ask your pardon Mr. Corporal."

After this he got off his horse, and throwing aside his coat, he took hold and helped the men at their work till they got the timber into its place. By this time the perspiration stood in drops upon his forehead. He took out his handkerchief and wiped his brow. Then turning to the commander he said:

"Mr. Corporal, when you have another such job on hand, and have not men enough to do it, send for your Commander-in-chief, and I will come and help you again."

It was General Washington who did and said this. The Corporal was thunderstruck! The great Washington, though honored above all men on the continent, was humble enough to put his hand and shoulder to the timber, that he might help the humblest of his soldiers, who were struggling for the defence of their country, to bear the burdens appointed to them.

This is an excellent illustration of the truth we are now considering. And certainly we should all try to learn the lesson of humility which Jesus taught, when we see how it helps to make us useful.

And then there is one other reason why we should learn this lesson, and that is because of the —BLESSING—*that attends it.*

Mary, the Mother of Jesus, in her noble song about the birth of her wonderful Son, said that God "filleth the hungry with good things, and sendeth the rich empty away." By the "*hungry*" she meant the *humble*, and by the "*rich*" the *proud*. And the "good things" with which God fills them mean the blessings He bestows on the humble. Our Saviour taught the same truth when he said, "he that humbleth himself shall be exalted." Luke xiv: 11. Being exalted here means being honored and blessed. These passages teach very clearly the truth of which we are now speaking. They show us that we must learn the lesson of humility if we hope to have God's blessing rest upon us. And it is not more true that two and two make four, than it is that God's blessing *does* attend and follow those who learn the lesson of humility.

How many illustrations of this truth we find in the Bible! Moses had learned the lesson of humility before God sent him on his great mission, which has given him a name and a place among the most famous men of the world.

Gideon had learned the lesson of humility before God made choice of him to be the deliverer of his people Israel from the hands of their enemies; and then, for years to be their honored ruler. John the Baptist was so humble that he said of himself that he was not worthy to stoop down and unloose the latchet of our Saviour's shoe; and yet Jesus said of him that he was one of the greatest men that ever had been born.

The apostle Paul was so humble that he considered himself "less than the least of all saints," and "the chief of sinners;" and yet God honored and blessed him till he became the most famous and useful of all the apostles.

If we turn from the Bible, and look out into the world around us, we may compare proud people to the tops of the mountains; these are bare and barren, and of little use to the world. We may compare humble people to the plains and valleys. These are fertile and beautiful, and are the greatest blessing to the world, in the abundance of grain, and fruit, and other good things which they yield.

And then, if we take notice of what is occurring in the scenes of daily life, we shall meet with incidents continually which furnish us with illustrations of the part of our subject now before us, that God crowns the humble with his blessing. Let us look at one or two of these illustrations.

"The Little Loaf." In a certain part of Germany, some years ago, a famine was prevailing, and many of the people were suffering from hunger. A kind-hearted rich man sent for twenty of the poorest children in the village where he lived, to come to his house. As they stood on the porch of his house, he came out to them bringing a large basket in his hand. He set it down before him and said: "Children, in this basket there is bread for you all. Take a loaf, each of you, and come back every day at this hour, till it shall please God to send us better times."

Then he left the children to themselves and went into the house, but watched them through the window. The hungry children seized the basket, quarreled and struggled for the bread, because each of them wished to get the best and largest loaf. Then they went away without ever thanking the good gentleman for his kindness.

But one little girl, named Gretchen, poorly but neatly dressed, remained, humbly standing by, till the rest were gone. Then she took the last loaf left in the basket, the smallest of the lot. She looked up to the window where the gentleman stood; smiled at him; threw him a kiss, and made a low curtsey in token of her gratitude, and then went quickly home.

The next day the other children were just as ill-behaved as they had been before, and the timid humble Gretchen received a loaf this time not more than half the size of the one she had on the previous day. But when she came home, and her poor sick mother cut the loaf open, a number of new silver pieces of money, fell rattling and shining out of it.

Her mother was frightened, and said, "Take the money back at once to the good gentleman; for it must certainly have dropped into the dough by accident. Be quick Gretchen! be quick!"

But when the little girl came to the good man and gave him her mother's message, he kindly said, "No, no, my child, it was no mistake. I had the silver pieces put into the smallest loaf as a reward for you. Continue to be as humble, peaceable, self-denying, and grateful as you have now shown yourself to be. A little girl who is humble enough to take the smallest loaf rather than quarrel for the larger ones, will be sure to receive greater blessings from God than if she had silver pieces of money baked in every loaf of bread she ate. Go home now, and greet your good mother very kindly for me." Here we see how God's blessing attends the humble.

"Humility Proving a Blessing." Some time ago a young man went into the office of one of the largest dry-goods houses in New York and asked for a situation. He was told to call again another day.

Going down Broadway that same afternoon, when opposite the Astor House, he saw an old apple woman, in trying to cross the street, struck by an omnibus, knocked down, and her basket of apples sent scattering into the gutter.

The young man stepped out of the crowd, helped the old woman to her feet, put her apples into her basket, and went on his way, without thinking of it.

Now a proud man would never have thought of doing such a thing as that. But this young man had learned the lesson of humility, and did not hesitate a moment to do this kind act.

When he called again to see about the situation, he was asked what wages he expected.

He stated what he thought would be right. His proposal was accepted. The situation was given him, and he went to work.

About a year afterwards, his employer took him aside one day, reminded him of the incident about the old apple woman; told him he was passing at the time, and saw it; and that it was this circumstance which induced him to offer the vacant situation to him, in preference to a hundred others who were applying for it.

Here we see what a blessing this young man's humility proved to him!

And thus we see that there are five good reasons why we should learn the lesson of humility. These are the *command* of Christ; the *example* of Christ; the *comfort* that humility gives; the *usefulness* to which it leads; and the *blessing* that attends it.

The first verse of the hymn we often sing contains a very suitable prayer to offer when we think of the lesson of humility we have now been considering:

> "Lord forever at thy side
> Let my place and portion be;
> Strip me of the robe of pride
> Clothe me with humility."

CHRIST AND THE LITTLE CHILDREN

IF, when Jesus was here on earth, he had shown a great interest in kings, and princes, in rich, and wise, and great men, it would not have been surprising; because he was a king and a prince, himself; he was richer than the richest, and wiser than the wisest, and greater than the greatest. But he did not do this. He took no particular notice of them; but he showed the greatest possible interest in children. When mothers brought their little ones to him, the disciples wanted to keep them away. They thought, no doubt, that he was too busy to take any notice of them. But they were mistaken. He was very busy indeed. He had many lessons to teach. He had sermons to preach; and sick people to heal; and blind eyes to open; and deaf ears to unstop; and lame men to make whole; and dead men to raise to life again. He had all his Father's will to make known to men; and all his Father's commandments to keep. He had to suffer, and to die for the sins of the world; that he might "open the kingdom of heaven to all believers." He was the busiest man that ever lived. Nobody ever had so much to do as he had. And yet, he was not too busy to attend to the little children. He had time to give to them. So he rebuked his disciples for trying to keep the children away from him. He told the mothers to bring them near. They did so. And then, one by one, "he took them up in his arms, put his hands upon them and blessed them." And when he had done this, as though that were not enough, he spoke those precious, glorious, golden words:—"*Suffer the little children to come unto me, and forbid them not, for of such is the kingdom of heaven,*" "verily I say unto you, whosoever shall not receive the kingdom of God as a little child, he shall not enter therein."

These things are told us by three of the evangelists. St. Matthew mentions them in chapter xix: 13-15. St. Mark x: 13-16, and St. Luke xviii: 15-17.

On another occasion, when he was in the temple, the children sang hosannas to him as the son of David. The chief priests and scribes were greatly displeased, when they heard it, and "said unto him, hearest thou what these say? and Jesus said unto them, yea: have ye never read, out of the mouths of babes and sucklings thou hast perfected praise?" Matt. xxi: 15, 16. Here he quoted from the Old Testament (Ps. viii: 2) to prove to them from their own scriptures, that God loves little children, and delights to have them engage in his service, and sing his praises.

And there was one other occasion on which Jesus spoke about the children, and showed his interest in them. This was after his resurrection. We read about it in St. John xxi: 15-18. He met his disciples, one day, on the shore of the sea of Galilee. Peter, who had shamefully denied his Master on the night in which he was betrayed was present with them. Jesus said to him, as if to remind him of his great sin, "Simon, son of Jonas, lovest thou me?" "Yea, Lord, thou knowest that I love thee," said the penitent disciple. "Feed my lambs," was his Master's reply. Here again, how beautifully Jesus showed his great love for the little ones of his flock!

From these different passages, we see clearly how dear little children are to the heart of our blessed Saviour! He is the only great Teacher who ever showed such an interest in children. And the religion of Jesus is the only religion which teaches its followers to love and care for the little ones. The worshipers of the idol Moloch, mentioned in the Bible, used to offer their children as burnt-sacrifices to their cruel god. Mahometans look upon their women and children as inferior beings. The Hindoos neglect their infants, and leave them exposed on the banks of the Ganges, or throw them into the river to be devoured by the hungry crocodiles. In the city of Pekin many infants are thrown out into the streets every night. Sometimes they are killed by the fall. Sometimes they are only half killed, and linger, moaning in their agony, till the morning. Then the police go around, and pick them up, and throw them all together into a hole and bury them.

In Africa, the children are sometimes buried alive; and sometimes left out in the fields or forests for the wild beasts to devour them. In the South Sea Islands three-fourths of all the children born used to be killed. Sometimes they would strangle their babies. Sometimes they would leave them, where oxen and cattle would tread on them, and trample them to death; while, at other times, they would break all their joints, beginning with their fingers and toes, and then go on to their wrists, and elbows, and shoulders. How dreadful it is to think of such practices! And when we turn from these scenes of heart-rending cruelty and think of the gracious Saviour,—the "gentle Jesus, meek and mild," stretching forth his arms in loving tenderness, and uttering the sweet words,—"Suffer the little children to come unto me, and forbid them not; for of such is the kingdom of God,"—what a wonderful contrast it makes!

And when we think of all that Jesus did and said to show his interest in children, we may well ask ourselves such questions as these,—Why was it so? What did he do it for? And when we come to look carefully into this part of the life of Christ, we can see four great things in it; and these are the reasons why Jesus did and said so much about children.

In the first place we see—GREAT LOVE—*in the interest Christ manifested towards the young.*

It was the same love which brought him down from heaven, and made him willing to become a little child himself; the same love which made him willing to live in poverty—and suffer the dreadful death upon the cross that led him to show such interest in the little ones. But if he had not told us himself how he feels on this subject, we could not have been sure of it. Children might well have said, when they heard about the love of Christ, "Yes, we have no doubt that Jesus does love grown up people, men and women in general. We believe this because the Bible tells us so; but how do we know that he loves us children?" If he had not told us so himself, we could not have been sure of it. But we know it now. And when we hear, or read of the love of Christ, we may be sure that it takes the children in.

During a famine in Germany, a family became so poor that they were in danger of starving. The father proposed that one of the children should be sold, and food provided for those that remained. At last the mother consented; but then the question arose which one of the four should be selected. The eldest, their first-born, could not be spared; the second looked like the mother, the third was like his father, and they could not give either of them up; and then the youngest—why, he was their pet, their darling, how could they give *him* up? So they concluded that they would all perish together, rather than part with one of their little ones. When those children knew of this, they might very well feel sure that their parents loved them. But Jesus did more than this for us, he was willing to die upon the cross, and he did so die, that "not one of his little ones should perish."

"Being Loved Back Again." Little Alice Lee sat in her rocking chair. She was clasping a beautiful wax doll to her bosom, and singing sweet lullabies to it. But every little while she looked wistfully at her mother. She was busy writing, and had told Alice to keep as quiet as possible till she got through.

It seemed a long time to Alice; but after awhile her mother laid down her pen, and pushed aside her papers, and said:—"Now I am through for to-day, Alice, and you can make as much noise as you please."

In a moment Alice laid down her doll, and running to her mother, threw her arms round her neck, and nestled sweetly in her loving bosom.

"I'm so glad," said Alice, "I wanted to love you so much, mamma."

"Did you, darling?" and the mother clasped the little one tenderly in her arms. "I am very glad that my little girl loves me;" replied her mother, "but I thought you were not very lonely while I was writing; you and dollie seemed to be having a good time together."

"Yes, we had, mamma; but I always get tired of loving dollie after awhile."

"Do you, dear? Tell me why?"

"O, because she never loves me back again."

"And is *that* why you love me?"

"That is *one why*, mamma; but not the first one, or the best one."

"And what is the first, and best?"

"Why, mamma, can't you guess?" and the little girl's blue eyes grew very bright, as they gazed earnestly into her mother's face. "It's because you loved me when I was too little to love you back; *that's* why I love you so."

And what a reason this is why we should love Jesus! He loved us when we were too little to love him back. The Bible says—"We love him because *he first* loved us." He loved us before we knew him, or had ever heard of him. He loved us before we were born. Before the world was made Jesus thought of you and me, and loved us. This is what he means when he says:—"*I have loved thee with an everlasting love.*" Jer. xxxi: 3. This means a love that never had a beginning, and that will never have an end. This is very wonderful. And when we think of it, we may well sing out our thankfulness in the words of the hymn:

> "I am glad that our Father in heaven
> Tells of his love in the Book he has given;
> Wonderful things in the Bible I see;
> This is the sweetest, that Jesus loves me.
> I am so glad that Jesus loves me,
> Jesus loves—*even me.*"

And when we think of all the kind words and actions of Jesus, by which he showed his interest in little children, the first thing that we see in them is—great love.

Now, let us take another look at this part of our Saviour's life, and the second thing that we see in it is—GREAT WISDOM.

It is wise to take care of the children and try to bring them to Jesus when young, *because then they are easily controlled.*

Suppose we plant an acorn in a corner of our garden. After awhile a green shoot springs out from it. We go to look at it when it is about a foot high. We find it getting crooked; but with the gentlest touch of thumb and finger, we can straighten it out. We wish it to lean in a particular direction. We give it a slight touch, and it leans just that way. Afterwards we conclude to have it lean in the opposite direction. Another slight touch, and it takes that direction. It is true, as the poet says, "Just as the twig is bent, the tree's inclined." But, suppose we let it grow for twenty or thirty years, and then come back to it. It is now a great oak tree. There is an ugly twist in its trunk. We try to straighten it out; but in vain. No power on earth can do that now. You can cut it down; or saw it up; or break it into splinters; but you cannot straighten it.

Suppose, that you and I should go to one of the highest summits of the Rocky Mountains. In a certain place there, we should find two little fountains springing up near each other. With the end of a finger we might trace the course in which either of those little springs should flow. We could lead one down the eastern side of the mountains, and the other down the western side. It would be very easy to control them then. But suppose now we travel down the side of the mountain till we reach the plain, at its base. Now see, yonder is a great river, rolling on its mighty flood of waters. That is what the little spring has grown to. It is too late to control it now. The time for controlling it was up yonder near the spring.

It is easy to control the spring; it is very hard to control the river. Jesus wished to control the spring when he directed us to bring the children to him. And in this he showed his wisdom.

It is wise to take an interest in children, and bring them early to Jesus—*because they have great influence in the world.*

Who can tell the influence that children are exerting in the world? We have an illustration of this in the words that were once spoken by Themistocles, the celebrated Grecian governor and general. He had a little boy, of whom his mother was very fond and over whom the child had very great influence. His father pointed to him, one day, and said to a friend, "Look at that child; he has more power than all Greece. For the city of Athens rules Greece; I rule Athens; that child's mother rules me, and he rules his mother."

I feel sure our Saviour must have felt very much as some one has done, who writes in this way about

THE GOOD THAT CHILDREN DO.

"A dreary place would be this earth
  Were there no little people in it;
The song of life would lose its mirth
  Were there no children to begin it;

"No little forms, like buds to grow,
    And make the admiring heart surrender;
No little hands, on breast and brow,
    To keep the thrilling love-chords tender.

"No babe within our arms to leap,
    No little feet towards slumber tending;
No little knee in prayer to bend,
    Our loving lips the sweet words lending.

"Life's song indeed would lose its charm,
    Were there no babies to begin it;
A doleful place this world would be,
    Were there no little people in it."

And if children have so great an influence in the world it was wise in Jesus to desire to have them brought early to him that they might learn to use that influence in the best possible way.

And then it was wise in Jesus to desire this, again, *because bringing children to him prevents great trouble, and secures great blessing.*

We are all familiar with Dr. Watts' sweet hymn, which says:

" 'Twill save us from a thousand snares
    To mind religion young."

Here is a striking illustration of this truth in the history of:

"One Neglected Child." A good many years ago, in one of the upper counties of New York, there was a little girl named Margaret. She was not brought to Christ, but was turned out on the world to do as she pleased. She grew up to be perhaps the wickedest woman in that part of the country. She had a large family of children, who became about as wicked as herself; her descendants have been a plague and a curse to that county ever since. The records of that county show that two hundred of her descendants have been criminals. In a single generation of her descendants there were twenty children. Three of these died in infancy. Of the remaining seventeen, who lived to grow up, nine were sent to the state prison for great crimes; while all the others were found, from time to time, in the jails, the penitentiaries, or the almshouses. Nearly all the descendants of this woman were idiots, or drunkards, or paupers, or bad people, of the very worst character. That one neglected child thus cost the county in which she lived hundreds of thousands of dollars, besides the untold evil that followed from the bad examples of her descendants. How different the result would have been if this poor child had been brought to Jesus and made a Christian when she was young!

"The Result of Early Choice." Here is a short story of two boys, of the choice they made when young, and the different results that followed from that choice.

A minister of the gospel was preaching on one occasion to the convicts in the state prison of Connecticut. As he rose in the desk and looked around on the congregation, he saw a man there whose face seemed familiar to him. When the service was over he went to this man's cell, to have some conversation with him.

"I remember you very well, sir," said the prisoner. "We were boys in the same neighborhood; we went to the same school; sat beside each other on the same bench, and then my prospects were as bright as yours. But, at the age of fourteen, you made choice of the service of God, and became a Christian. I refused to come to Christ, but made choice of the world and sin. And now, you are a happy and honored minister of the gospel, while I am a wretched outcast. I have served ten years in this penitentiary and am to be a prisoner here for life."

Jesus knew what blessings would follow to those who were early brought to him, and we see that there was great wisdom in the words that he spake when he said—"Suffer the little children to come unto me."

Christ and the Little Children 201

In the next place there was—GREAT ENCOURAGE-MENT—*in what Jesus did and said about children.*

If a company of boys or girls should try to get into the presence of a monarch, some great king, or emperor, they would find it a pretty hard thing to do. At the door of the palace they would meet with soldiers or servants, the guards of the queen or king. They would say to the children—"what do you want here?" And if the children should say, "Please sir, we wish to go into the palace and see the queen," the answer would be: "Go away; go away. The queen is too busy. She has no time to attend to little folks like you." And the children would have to go away without getting to see the queen.

But, Jesus is a greater king than any who ever sat upon an earthly throne. He has more to do than all the kings and queens in the world put together. And yet he never gave orders to the angels, or to any of his servants to keep the children away from him. On his great throne in yonder heavens he says still, what he said when he was on earth—"Suffer the little children to come unto me, and forbid them not." And he says this on purpose to encourage the children to come to him. And the thought that Jesus loves them and feels an interest in them has encouraged multitudes of little ones to seek him and serve him. Here are some illustrations of this:

"Learning to Love Jesus." "A little girl came to me one day," said a minister of the gospel, and said, "'Please sir, may I speak to you a minute?' I saw that she was in some trouble; so I took her kindly by the hand, and said, 'Certainly, my child. What do you wish to say?'

"'Please, sir,' said she, as her lip quivered and tears filled her eyes, 'it's a dreadful thing; but I don't love Jesus.'

"'And are you not going to love him?' I asked.

"'I don't know; but please sir, I want you to tell me how.' She spoke sadly, as if it was something she never could do.

"'Well,' I said, 'St. John, who loved our Lord almost more than any one else ever did, says that "we love him because he first loved us." Now if you go home to-night, saying in your heart, "*Jesus loves me,*" I think that to-morrow you will be able to say—"I love Jesus."'

"She looked up through her tears, and repeated the words very softly, 'Jesus loves me.'

She began to think about it on her way home, as well as to say it. She thought about his life, about his death on the cross, and about his sweet words to the little ones, and she began to feel it too.

"The next evening she came to see me again; and, putting both her hands in mine, with a bright happy face, she said:

"'Oh! please sir, I love Jesus now; for I know he does love me so!'"

Here was a little one encouraged to come to Jesus by thinking of the interest he feels in children.

"Doesn't He Love to Save?" A mother had just tucked her little boy in bed, and had received his good-night kisses. She lingered awhile, at his bedside, to speak to him about Jesus, and to see if he was feeling right toward him. He was a good, obedient boy, but that day he had done something that grieved his mother. He had expressed his sorrow for it, and asked his mother's forgiveness. As she stooped down for the last kiss, he said—"Is it all settled, mother?"

"Yes, my child," she said, "it's all settled with me; but have you settled it all with Jesus?"

"Yes, mother: I've asked him to forgive me: and I believe him when he says he will; for *doesn't he love to help and save children?*" "He does, my child, he does," said his mother, as she gazed on his happy little face, lighted up with the joy of that gospel, so often hidden from the wise and prudent, but revealed to babes.

Here we see how this little fellow was encouraged to seek Jesus from the assurance that he feels an interest in children, and loves to help and bless them.

"Love Leads to Love." A little boy named Charley stood at the window with his mother one morning, watching the robins as they enjoyed their morning meal of cherries from the tree near their house. "Mother," said Charley, "How the birdies all love father."

"They do," said his mother, "but what do you suppose is the reason that the birdies love your father?"

This question seemed to set Charley to thinking. He did not answer at first, but presently he said, "Why mother all the creatures seem to love father. My dog is almost as glad to see him as to see me. Pussy, you know, always comes to him, and seems to know exactly what he is saying. Even the old cow follows him around the meadow, and the other day I saw her licking his hand, just as a dog would. I think it must be because father loves them. You know he will often get up and give pussy something to eat; and he pulls carrots for the cow, and pats her; and somehow I think his voice never sounds so sweet as when he is talking to these dumb creatures."

"I think his voice is very pleasant when he is talking to his little boy," said his mother.

Charley smiled, and said, "That's so, mother. Father loves me, and I love him dearly. But he loves the birdies too I am sure. He whistles to them every morning when they are eating their cherries, and they don't seem a bit afraid of him, although he is near enough to catch them. Mother I wish everything loved me as they do father."

"Do as father does, Charley, and they will. Love all things and be kind to them. Don't kick the dog, or speak roughly to him. Don't pull pussy's tail, nor chase the hens, nor try to frighten the cow. Never throw stones at the birds. Never hurt nor tease anything. Speak gently and lovingly to them and they will love you, and everybody that knows you will love you too."

Now Charley's father, in acting as he did, was trying to make all the dumb creatures about him know that he was their friend; that he loved them, and had nothing but kindness in his heart towards them. In this way he encouraged them to come to him, and not be afraid of him.

And this is just the way in which Jesus was acting when he did and said so much to show his interest in children. He wants them all to understand that he is their friend; that he loves them, and wants them to come to him and love and serve him. And so every child who hears or reads about Jesus may feel encouraged to say:

> "Once in his arms the Saviour took
>   Young children just like me,
> And blessed them with his voice and look
>   As kind as kind could be.
>
> "And though to heaven the Lord hath gone,
>   And seems so far away,
> He hath a smile for every one
>   That doth his voice obey.
>
> "I'd rather be the least of them
>   That he will bless and own,
> Than wear a royal diadem,
>   And sit upon a throne."

And so we may well say that in what Jesus did and said about the children there is great encouragement.

And then there are—GREAT LESSONS—*too, in this part of the life of Christ.*

There are two lessons taught us here. One is about *the work we are to do for Jesus here on earth.* When Jesus said to Peter, "Lovest thou me? Feed my lambs," he meant to teach him, and you, and me, and all his people everywhere, the best way in which we can show our love to him. The lambs of Christ here spoken of mean little children, wherever they are found. And to feed these lambs is to teach them about Jesus. When we are trying to bring the young to Jesus and teaching them to love and serve him, then we are doing the work that is most pleasing to him:—the work that he most loves to have his people do. It was thinking about this that first led me to begin the work of preaching regularly to the young. And this is the lesson that Jesus would have all his people learn when he says to each of them:—"Lovest thou me? Feed my lambs."

"The Angel in the Stone." Many years ago there was a celebrated artist who lived in Italy, whose name was Michael Angelo. He was a great painter, and a great sculptor, or a worker in marble. He loved to see beautiful figures chiseled out of marble, and he had great power and skill in chiseling out such figures. One day, as he was walking with some friends through the city of Florence, he saw a block of marble lying neglected in a yard, half covered with dust and rubbish. He stopped to examine that block of marble. That day happened to be a great holiday in Florence and the artist had his best suit of clothes on; but not caring for this he threw off his coat, and went to work to clear away the rubbish from that marble. His friends were surprised. They said to him:—"Come on, let's go; what's the use of wasting your time on that good-for-nothing lump of stone?"

"O, there's an angel in this stone," said he, "and I must get it out."

He bought that block; had it removed to his studio, and then went to work with his mallet and his chisel, and never rested till out of that rough, unshapen mass of stone he made a beautiful marble angel.

Now, every child born into our world is like such a block of marble. The only difference is that children are living stones—marble that will last forever. And when we bring our children to Jesus, and by his help teach them to love and serve him, we are doing for them just what Michael Angelo was doing for his block of marble—we are getting the angels out of the stones. And this is what Jesus loves to have us do.

"How to Get the Angels Out." A Christian mother, whose children had all been early taught to love and serve Jesus, was asked the secret of her success in bringing up her children. This was her answer:—"While my children were infants on my lap, as I washed them day by day, I raised my heart to God that he would wash them in that blood which cleanseth from all sin; as I clothed them in the morning, I asked my heavenly Father to clothe them with the robe of Christ's righteousness; as I provided them food I prayed that God would feed their souls with the bread of heaven, and give them to drink of the water of life. When I prepared them for the house of God I pleaded that their bodies might be made fit temples for the Holy Ghost to dwell in. When they left me daily for the week-day school, I followed their youthful footsteps with the prayer that their path through life might be like that of the just, which shineth more and more unto the perfect day. And night after night, as I committed them to rest, the silent breathing of my soul has been, that their heavenly Father would take them under his tender care and fold them in his loving, everlasting arms."

Let Christian mothers follow this example and they will not fail to bring the angel out from every block of living marble that God has given them.

"The Best Time for Doing This." A faithful minister of Christ had a dear only daughter. She had been a thoughtful praying child. When only twelve years old she had joined her father's church. She now lay on her dying bed. "As I sat by her bedside," says her father, "among the things she said which I shall never forget were these:—'Father you know I joined the church when I was young—very young. Some of our friends thought that I was too young. But, oh! how I wish I could tell everybody what a comfort it is to me now to think of it.' Then reaching out her hand—the fingers were already cold—and grasping mine, she said with great earnestness:—'Father, you are at wórk for the young. Do all you can for them while they are young. It's the best time—the best time. Oh! I see it now as I never did before. It is the best time—while they are young—the younger the better. Do all you can for them while they are very young.' And then she fell asleep in Jesus."

This is the lesson about the work we are to do for him on earth, that Jesus taught in what he said concerning the children.

But when we think of those sweet words of Jesus—"Of such is the kingdom of heaven," we are *taught a lesson about the company we shall meet there.* We learn from what our blessed Lord says on this subject that he saves all the little ones who die before they are accountable for their actions. And we know that of all the persons born into our world more than half of them die before they reach this age. And this makes it very certain that more than half the company of heaven will be made up of little children. This is a very sweet thought to those who have lost little ones; and to those who love them.

And some people think that when young children die and go to heaven, they will not grow up to be men and women, but will always remain children. The Rev. Mr. Bickersteth, of England, in speaking of a father meeting his little ones in heaven, who died years before he did, represents him as meeting them there, just of the same age and size as they were when they died. And then he expresses his own thought on this subject in a single line:

"A babe in glory, is a babe forever."

But God has not said anything on this subject in the Bible. And when he himself has not spoken on such a point as this, it is impossible for us to say certainly which way it will be. But when we get to heaven and find just how it is, we shall all agree that God's way is the best way.

And then Jesus shows us plainly *what our character must be if we hope to go to heaven and join the happy company there.*

These are the words he spake on this subject; "Verily I say unto you, whosoever shall not receive the kingdom of God as a little child, he shall not enter therein." Mark x: 15. Jesus refers here to some of the best things that we find marking the character of a good child. Such a child is gentle, and loving, and kind; and this must be our character, if we hope to enter heaven. Such a child is willing to be taught:—believes all that his parent or teacher tells him; and does everything that he is told to do; and such must our character be if we hope to enter heaven.

And so when we come to study out this part of our Saviour's life, and think of all that he did and said to show his interest in children, we see these four great things in it: viz., great love; great wisdom; great encouragement; and great lessons.

I know not how to express in a better way the feelings which should be in the heart of everyone, young or old, on thinking of this great subject, than in the words of one who has thus sweetly written:

> "Lamb of God! I look to Thee,
> Thou shalt my example be;
> Thou art gentle, meek and mild;
> Thou wast once a little child.
>
> "Fain I would be as Thou art,
> Give me thy obedient heart:
> Thou art pitiful, and kind;
> Let me have thy loving mind.
>
> "Let me above all fulfill
> God my heavenly Father's will;
> Never his good Spirit grieve,
> Only to his glory live.
>
> "Loving Jesus, gentle Lamb!
> In thy gracious hands I am;
> Make me, Saviour, what Thou art;
> Live thyself within my heart.
>
> "I shall then show forth thy praise;
> Serve thee all my happy days;
> Then the world shall always see
> Christ, the Holy Child in me."

THE TRANSFIGURATION

THIS was one of the most surprising scenes in the life of our blessed Lord. It forms a great contrast to the other events mentioned in his history. He "came to visit us in great humility." When we read how he was born in a stable, and cradled in a manger; how he had "not where to lay his head;" when we read of the lowliness, and poverty, and suffering that marked his course, day by day, we come naturally to think of him as "the man of sorrows and acquainted with grief." And though, when we remember how he healed the sick, and cast out devils, and raised the dead to life again; how he walked upon the waters, and controlled the stormy winds and waves with his simple word, he seems wonderful in his power and majesty; yet there is nothing, in all his earthly life, that leads us to think so highly of him, as this scene of the Transfiguration, of which we are now to speak.

The account of this event is given us by three of the evangelists. We find it described by St. Matt. xvii: 1-13. St. Mark ix: 2-13. St. Luke ix: 28-29.

A short time before this took place, Jesus had told his disciples how he was to go up to Jerusalem, to suffer many things, to be put to death, be buried, and be raised again on the third day. St. Matt. xvi: 21. He also told them of the self-denial, which all who became his disciples would be required to exercise. This was very different from what they were expecting and must have been very discouraging to them. They did not yet understand that their Master had come into the world to suffer and to die. Instead of this, their minds were filled with the idea that the object of his coming was to establish an earthly kingdom and to reign in glory. And, for themselves, they were expecting that they would share his glory and reign as princes with him. And so they must have been greatly troubled by his words. To encourage and comfort them, therefore, he told them that, before they died, some of them should "see the Son of Man coming in his kingdom."

And then, some days after this, he took three of his disciples, the favored John and James and Peter, and went up with them "into a mountain, apart by themselves, and was transfigured before them." We are not told what mountain it was that was thus honored. Mount Tabor, near Nazareth, on the borders of the Plain of Esdraelon, has long been regarded as the favored spot. But, in our day, many persons think that it was not on the top of Tabor, but on one of the summits of Mount Hermon, where this wonderful event took place. One of the principal objections to supposing that Tabor was the place is, that in those days there was a large fortress on the top of this mountain, and this, they think, would interfere with the privacy that would be desired on such an occasion. But, for myself, I still incline to think that Tabor was the mountain chosen. I went to the top of this mountain, when in Palestine. And though there is a large convent there now, yet the summit of Tabor covers a wide space of ground. And outside of the walls of the convent, and even out of sight of its walls, I saw a number of retired, shady places that would be particularly suitable for such a scene as this.

But, it is impossible to decide positively which was the Mount of Transfiguration. And it is not a matter of much consequence. Those who think it was Hermon are at liberty to think so; and those who think it was Tabor, have a right to their opinion, for none can prove that they are mistaken in thinking so.

And when we come to consider this great event in the life of our Saviour, there are *two* things to speak of in connection with it; these are the *wonders* we see in it; and the *lessons* we may learn from it. Or, to express it more briefly —The Transfiguration—its wonders, and its lessons.

There are three wonders to be spoken of, and three lessons to be learned from this subject.

The first wonder is—THE WONDERFUL CHANGE— that took place in the appearance of our Lord on this occasion.

Jesus went up the mountain with his disciples. It was probably at the close of one of his busy days that he did this. It would seem from St. Luke's account,—chap. ix: 32—that Peter and his companions were weary with the day's work, and soon fell asleep. But, while they were sleeping, Jesus was praying. And it was while he was engaged in prayer that the

Transfiguration took place. St. Luke tells us it was—"*as he prayed.*"

Let us notice now, what the different evangelists tell us about this change. St. Matthew says—"He was transfigured before them: and his face did shine as the sun, and his raiment was white as the light." St. Mark says, "His raiment became exceeding white as snow, so as no fuller"—one who cleans, or whitens cloth—"on earth can white them." St. Luke says—"As he prayed, the fashion of his countenance was altered, and his raiment was white and glistening."

These are the different accounts we have of this surprising scene. If the disciples had been awake when this marvellous change began to take place, we cannot for a moment suppose that they would have gone to sleep while the heavens must have seemed to be opening above them and this blaze of glory was shining around them. They were, no doubt, asleep when the transfiguration began. And, as we know that the taking of an ordinary light into the room where persons are asleep will often awaken them, it is not surprising that the disciples should have been aroused from their slumber by the flood of light and glory that was beaming round their Master then. How surprised they must have been when they opened their eyes on that scene! They would never forget it as long as they lived. It was more than half a century after this when St. John wrote his gospel; and it was, no doubt, to this scene that he referred when he said, in speaking of Jesus;—"*we beheld his glory, the glory as of the only begotten of the Father.*" St. John i: 14. And, not long before his death, St. Peter thus refers to it:—"We were eye-witnesses of his majesty. For he received from God the Father, honor and glory, when there came such a voice from the excellent glory, saying, This is my beloved Son in whom I am well pleased." II. Pet. i: 16, 17.

One object for which this wonderful transfiguration of our Lord took place was, no doubt, to give to the disciples then, and to the followers of Jesus in all coming time, an idea of what his glory now is in heaven, and of what it will be when he shall come again in his kingdom. He had told his disciples about his sufferings and death, and the shame and dishonor connected with them; and here, as if to counterbalance that, he wished to give them a glimpse of the glory that is to shine around him forever.

How wonderful it must have seemed to the astonished disciples! When they had last looked on their Master, before going to sleep, they had seen him as "the man of sorrows," in his plain everyday dress, such as they themselves wore: but, when they looked on him again, as they awoke from their sleep, they saw his face shining as the sun, and his raiment dazzling in its snowy whiteness.

To what may we compare this wonderful change? Suppose you have before you the bulbous root of the lily plant. You look at it carefully, but there is nothing attractive about it. How rough and unsightly it appears! You close your eyes upon it for a brief space. You open them again. But what a change has taken place! That plain-homely looking bulb has disappeared, and in its place there stands before you the lily plant. It has reached its mature growth. Its flower is fully developed and blooming in all its matchless beauty! What a marvellous change that would be! And yet it would be but a feeble illustration of the more wonderful change that took place in our Saviour at his transfiguration.

Here is another illustration. Suppose we are looking at the western sky, towards the close of day. Great masses of dark clouds are covering all that part of the heavens. They are but common clouds. There is nothing attractive or interesting about them. We do not care to take a second look at them. We turn from them for a little while, and then look at them again. In the meantime, the setting sun has thrown his glorious beams upon them. How changed they now appear! All that was commonplace and unattractive about them is gone. How they glow and sparkle! Gold, and purple, and all the colors of the rainbow are blending, how beautifully there! Are these the same dull clouds that we looked upon a few moments before? Yes; but they have been transfigured. A wonderful change has come over them. And here we have an illustration of our Lord's transfiguration. The first wonder about this incident in his life is the wonderful change which took place in his appearance then.

The second wonder about the transfiguration is—THE WONDERFUL COMPANY—*that appeared with our Saviour then.*

At the close of his temptation in the wilderness, Jesus had some wonderful company too, but it was different from what he had now. *Then,* we are told that *"angels came, and ministered unto him."* And in the garden of Gethsemane, when he was sinking to the earth, overcome by the terrible agony through which he was passing, he had more company of the same kind; for we read that—*"there appeared unto him an angel from heaven strengthening him."* St. Luke xxii: 43. But it was not the company of angels that waited on him at the time of his Transfiguration. No: but we read that, "there appeared unto him Moses, and Elias," or Elijah. And if we ask why did not the angels come to him now, as they did on other occasions? Why did these distinguished persons, of the Old Testament history, come from heaven to visit him in place of the angels? It is easy enough to answer these questions. This transfiguration of Christ took place, as he himself tells us, in order to give his disciples a view of the glory that will attend him when he shall come in his kingdom. When he shall appear, on that occasion, all his people will come with him. Those who shall have died before he comes will be raised from the dead and come with him, in their glorious resurrection bodies. And those who shall be living when he comes will, as St. Paul tells us,—*"be changed in a moment, in the twinkling of an eye"*—I. Cor. xv: 52, 53—and have beautiful, glorified bodies, like the bodies of those who have been raised from the dead. And both these classes of Christ's people were represented by the distinguished persons who formed the company that appeared with Jesus at the Transfiguration. Moses had been in heaven nearly fifteen hundred years when this scene took place. He had died, as other men do, and had been buried. It is supposed by many wise and good men that his body had been raised from the dead, that he might appear in it on this occasion. And thus Moses represented all the dead in Christ, who will be raised to life again at his coming. Elijah had been in heaven for almost a thousand years. He had never died, and never lain in the grave. He was translated. This means that he was taken up to heaven without dying. But St. Paul tells us that bodies of flesh and blood, like ours, cannot enter heaven. I. Cor. xv: 50. They must be changed, and made fit for that blessed place. And so, we know, that as Elijah went up to heaven, in his chariot of fire, the same wonderful change must have passed over his body which we have seen will take place with those of Christ's people who shall be living on the earth when he comes again.

Jesus was transfigured that we might know how he himself will appear when he comes in his kingdom. And Moses and Elias "appeared with him in glory," to show us how the people of Christ will appear when they enter with him into his kingdom. And this was a good reason why these very persons, and not the angels, should have formed the company that came to visit our Saviour on the Mount of Transfiguration. It was wonderful company indeed that waited on Jesus then. But, it was a wonderful occasion. None like it had ever occurred before; none like it has ever occurred since; and none like it will ever occur again till Jesus shall come in the glory of his heavenly kingdom. The second wonder of the Transfiguration was the wonderful company.

The third wonder connected with this great event was—THE WONDERFUL CONVERSATION—*that took place between Jesus and his visitors.*

All the three evangelists, who tell of the Transfiguration, speak of this conversation. St. Matthew and St. Mark merely state the fact that Moses and Elias "were talking with Jesus;" but they do not tell us the subject of the conversation, or what it was about which they talked. But St. Luke supplies what they leave out. He says, "*they spake of his decease, which he should accomplish at Jerusalem.*" This means that they talked about the death upon the cross which he was to suffer. And when we remember that these great and good men had just come down from heaven, where God, the loving Father of Jesus dwells, and where all the holy angels are; and that this was the only time when they were to be present with Jesus, and have an opportunity of talking with him, during all his life on earth, we may wonder why they did not choose some more pleasant subject of conversation. And yet they did not make a mistake. God the Father had sent them from heaven to meet his beloved Son on this occasion. And, no doubt, he had told them what subject they were to talk about, and what they were to say to Jesus, on that subject. And then they knew very well how Jesus felt about this matter. And painful as the death upon the cross would be, they knew it was the nearest of all things to the heart of Jesus. It was the will of his Father that he should die on the cross, and it was the delight of his heart—the very joy of his soul to do his Father's will. And here we learn the unspeakable importance of the death of Christ. The apostle Paul was showing his sense of its importance when he said, "God forbid that I should glory, save in the cross of our Lord Jesus." Gal. vi: 14. He puts the word *"cross"* of Christ, for the death of Christ, but it means the same thing.

Some one has compared the cross of Christ to a key of gold, that opens the gate of heaven to us, if we believe in Jesus; but if we refuse to hear and obey the words of Jesus, it becomes a key of iron, and opens the gate of destruction before us.

"The Power of the Cross." A heathen ruler had heard the story of the cross and desired to know its power. When he was sick and near his end, he told his servants to make him a large wooden cross, and lay it down in his chamber. When this was done, he said—"Take me now and lay me on the cross, and let me die there." As he lay there dying he looked in faith to the blood of Christ, that was shed upon the cross, and said—"*It lifts me up: it lifts me. Jesus saves me!*" and thus he died. It was not that wooden cross that saved him; but the death of Christ, on the cross to which he was nailed—the death of which Moses and Elias talked with him, that saved this heathen man. They knew what a blessing his death would be to the world, and *this* was why they talked about this death. Here is one of Bonar's beautiful hymns which speaks sweetly of the blessedness and comfort to be found in the cross of Christ.

> "Oppressed with noonday's scorching heat,
>   To this dear cross I flee;
> And in its shelter take my seat;
>   No *shade* like this to me!
>
> "Beneath this cross clear waters burst;
>   A fountain sparkling free;
> And here I quench my desert thirst,
>   No *spring* like this to me.
>
> "A stranger here, I pitch my tent
>   Beneath this spreading tree;
> Here shall my pilgrim life be spent,
>   No *home* like this to me!
>
> "For burdened ones a resting place
>   Beside this cross I see;
> Here, I cast off my weariness;
>   No *rest* like this for me!"

Moses and Elias understood how the blessing of the world was to flow out from that death upon the cross which Jesus was to suffer; and so, we need not wonder that during the short visit which they made to Jesus, amidst the glory of his Transfiguration, the subject, above all others, about which they desired to talk with him—was his death upon the cross,—

"his decease, which he should accomplish at Jerusalem."

These are the three great wonders of the Transfiguration—the wonderful change—the wonderful company—and the wonderful conversation.

And this brings us to the second part of our subject, which is—*the three lessons* taught by the Transfiguration.

The first of these is—THE LESSON OF HOPE.

One thing for which the Transfiguration took place was to show us what we may hope to be hereafter, if we are the servants of Christ. We are told how Jesus appeared on this occasion. His glory is described. The brightness and glory that shone around him exceeded that of the noonday sun. But there is no particular description given Moses and Elias. We are not told how they looked. It is only said of them that—"they appeared in *glory*." St Luke ix: 31. I suppose the meaning of this is that they shared in the glory which Jesus himself had when he was transfigured. Their raiment was as white as his; and the same brightness and beauty beamed forth from their faces which made his so glorious. They shared their Master's glory. And, if we are loving, and serving Jesus, this is what we may hope to share with him hereafter. This is what we are taught to pray for in the beautiful Collect for the sixth Sunday after the Epiphany. These are the words of that prayer: "O God, whose blessed Son was manifested that he might make us the sons of God, and heirs of eternal life; Grant us, we beseech thee, that having this hope, we may purify ourselves, even as he is pure; that when he shall appear again, with power and great glory, *we may be made like unto him in his eternal and glorious kingdom;* where, with thee, O Father, and thee, O Holy Ghost, he liveth and reigneth, ever One God, world without end. Amen."

And it is right to offer such a prayer as this, because the Bible teaches us to hope for this great glory. How well a hope like this may be called *"a hope that maketh not ashamed,"* Rom. v: 5; *"a good hope through grace,"* II. Thess. ii: 16; "that *blessed hope*," Tit. ii: 13; *"a lively hope,"* I. Peter i: 3. And how well it may be spoken of as *"a helmet"*—to cover the head in the day of battle; and as "an anchor" to keep the soul calm and steadfast when the storms of life are bursting upon it! Moses and Elias appeared with Jesus at his Transfiguration, and shared his glory on purpose to teach us this lesson of hope, and to show us what we shall be hereafter. We shall be as glorious as Jesus was on the Mount of Transfiguration! This seems something too great and too good to be true. But no matter how great, or how good it is—*it is true.* Jesus taught this lesson of hope when he said—speaking of the time when he shall come in his kingdom, "*Then shall the righteous shine forth as the sun in the kingdom of their Father,*" St. Matt. xiii: 43. He taught us the same lesson, in his prayer to his Father, when he said, speaking of all his people, "*And the glory which thou gavest me, I have given them,*" St. John xvii: 21. And the apostle John taught us the same lesson, when he said,—"We know that when he shall appear *we shall be like him,*" I. John iii: 2. These sweet passages make this lesson of hope very sure. And this is just the way in which we are made sure about other things we have not seen.

"How we Know There is a Heaven." A Sunday-school teacher was talking to one of her scholars about heaven and the glory we shall have when we reach that blessed place. He was a bright boy, about nine or ten years old, named Charlie. After listening to her for awhile, he said: "But you have never been there,

Miss D., and how do you know there really is any such place?"

"Charlie," said the teacher, "you have never been to London; how do you know there is such a city?"

"O, I know that very well," said Charlie, "because my father is there; and he has sent me a letter, telling me all about it."

"And God, my Father, is in the heavenly city," said Miss D., "and he has sent me a letter, telling me about the glory of heaven, and about the way to get there. The Bible is God's letter."

"Yes, I see," said Charlie, after thinking awhile, "there must be a heaven, if you have got such a nice long letter from there."

The lesson of hope is the first lesson taught us by the Transfiguration.

The next lesson taught us here is—THE LESSON OF INSTRUCTION.

The great event of the Transfiguration took place in our Saviour's life for *this* reason, among others, that we might learn from it *how we are to think of Christ.* While the disciples were gazing on the glory of that scene, and on the distinguished visitors who were there, there came a cloud and overshadowed them. This cloud, we may suppose, was like a curtain round Moses and Elias, hiding them from the view of the disciples. And, as Jesus in his glory was left alone for them to gaze upon, there came a voice from the overshadowing cloud, saying—*"This is my beloved Son; in whom I am well pleased."* This was the voice of God, the Father. It spoke out on this occasion to teach the disciples then, and you and me now, and all God's people in every age, what to think about Christ. God, the Father, tells us here what he thinks about him; and we must learn to think of him in the same way. His will, his command is that *"all men should honor the Son, even as they honor the Father,"* St. John v: 3. Moses and Elias were great men in their day. They appeared on this occasion to add to the honor of Christ. And then they disappeared, as if to show that they were nothing in comparison with him. He is the greatest and the best of all beings. He must be first. Prophets and priests, and kings, and angels even, are as nothing to him. We must love him—and honor him above all others. The words of the hymn we so often sing, show us how God would have us think and feel towards him:

> "All hail the power of Jesus' name,
>   Let angels prostrate fall;
> Bring forth the royal diadem,
> And crown him Lord of all.
>
> "Let every kindred, every tribe,
>   On this terrestrial ball,
> To him all majesty ascribe,
> And crown him Lord of all."

"**How Christ Should be Honored.**" There is a story told of the Emperor Theodosius the Great which illustrates very well how we should honor Christ. There were at that time two great parties in the church. One of these believed and taught the divinity of Christ—or that he is equal to God the Father. The other party, called Arians, believed and taught that Christ was not divine; and that he was not to be honored and worshiped as God. The Emperor Theodosius favored this latter party. When his son, Arcadius, was about sixteen years old, his father determined to make him a sharer of his throne, and passed a law that his son should receive the same respect and honor that were due to himself. And, in connection with this event, an incident occurred which led the emperor to see how wrong the view was which he held respecting the character of Christ, and to give it up. When Arcadius was proclaimed the partner of his father in the empire, the officers of the government, and other prominent persons, called on the emperor in his palace, to congratulate him on the occasion, and to pay their respects to his son.

Among those who thus came, was a celebrated bishop of the church. He was very decided in the views he held about the real divinity of Christ, and very much opposed to all who denied this divinity.

Coming into the presence of the emperor, the bishop paid his respects to him, in the most polite and proper manner. Then he was about to retire from the palace, without taking any special notice of the emperor's son. This made the father angry. He said to the bishop, "Do you take no notice of my son? Have you not heard that I have made him a partner with myself in the government of the empire?"

The good old bishop made no reply to this, but going to Arcadius, he laid his hand on his head, saying, as he did so—"The Lord bless thee, my son!" and was again turning to retire.

Even this did not satisfy the emperor, who asked, in a tone of surprise and displeasure, "Is *this* all the respect you pay to a prince whom I have made equal in dignity with myself?"

With great warmth the bishop answered—"Does your majesty resent so highly my apparent neglect of your son, because I do not treat him with equal honor to yourself? What, then, must the *Eternal God*—the King of heaven—think of you, who refuse to render to his only begotten Son, the honor and the worship that he claims for him?"

This had such an effect upon the emperor that he changed his views on this subject, and ever afterwards took part with those who acknowledged the divinity of Christ, and honored the Son, even as they honored the Father.

And so we see that the second lesson taught by the Transfiguration was the *lesson of instruction.* We must learn to think of Christ as the Father in heaven thinks of him.

And then there is—A LESSON OF DUTY—*that comes to us from this Transfiguration scene.*

We are taught this lesson by the last two words that were spoken, by the voice which the apostles heard from the cloud that overshadowed them. These are the words:—"*Hear Him.*" "This is my beloved Son, in whom I am well pleased: *Hear Him.*" This is God's command to every one of us. To hear Jesus, means to listen attentively to what he has to say, and to do it. And what does Jesus say to us? He says many things. But the most important thing he has to say to the young, is what we find in St. Matt. vi: 33: *"Seek ye* FIRST *the kingdom of God."* This means that we must give our hearts to Jesus, and serve him while we are young. We must do this *first,*—before we do anything else. We cannot hear or obey Jesus in anything, till we hear and obey him in this. And there are three good reasons why we should do this.

We should "hear him" because there is *safety* in it. We are exposed to dangers every day, and nothing will so help to keep us safe in the midst of these dangers as hearing Jesus, and doing what he tells us to do. Here is an illustration of what I mean.

"Life in the Midst of Danger." There was an alarm of fire one day, near one of our large public schools. The children in the school were greatly frightened. They screamed, and left their places, and began to rush to the windows and stairs. The stairway leading to the door was soon choked up; and although the fire never reached the school-house, many of the children had their limbs broken and were bruised and wounded in other ways.

But there was one little girl who remained quietly in her seat during all this excitement. When the alarm was over, and the wounded children had been taken home, and order was restored in the school, the teacher asked this little girl why she sat still in her seat, and did not rush towards the door, as the other girls had done.

"My father is a fireman," she said, "and he has always told me that if ever there was a cry of fire when I was in school, I must remain quiet in my seat, for that was the safest way. I was dreadfully frightened; but I knew that what father had told me was best; and so I sat still, while the others were running to the door." This little girl *heard* her father. She minded him. She did what he told her to do, and she found safety in doing so. And if we "*hear him*" of whom the voice from the Mount of Transfiguration speaks to us—we shall find safety from many a danger.

We ought to learn this lesson of duty, and "hear him," because there is *success* in it.

In old times, when the racers were running in the public games, if a man wished to be successful in the race, it was necessary for him to fix his eye on the prize, at the end of the race-course, and keep it fixed there till he reached the end. No one could have any success in racing who did not do this.

Here is an incident about some boys at play that illustrates the point now before us.

"How to Walk Straight." A light snow had fallen in a certain village, and some of the village boys met to make the best use they could of the new fallen snow. It was too dry for snowballing, and was not deep enough for coasting; so they thought they would improve the occasion by playing at making tracks in the snow.

There was a large meadow near by, with a grand old oak tree standing in the centre of it. The boys gathered round the tree, and stood, on opposite sides, each one with his back against the tree. At a given signal they were to start, and walk to the fence opposite to each of them; and then return to the tree, and see which had made the straightest track.

The signal was given. They started. They reached the fence, and returned to the tree. "Now, boys, who has made the straightest track?" said one of the boys, named James Allison.

"Henry Armstrong's is the only one that is straight at all," said Thomas Sanders.

"I don't see how we all contrived to go so crooked, when the meadow is so smooth, and there is nothing to turn us out of the way," said one of the boys.

And then, looking to their successful companion, they said—"Tell us, Harry, how you managed to make so straight a track?"

Now mark what Harry said:—"I fixed my eye on yonder tall pine tree on the other side of the fence towards which I was to walk, and never looked away from it till I reached the fence."

The other boys were walking without any particular aim in view. No wonder that their walk was crooked. After the apostle Paul became a Christian, he made one of the straightest tracks through this world to heaven that ever was made. And he made it in just the same way in which Harry Armstrong made his straight track through that meadow. We have seen what Harry said of his track through the snow; now see what St. Paul says of the way in which he made his straight track through this world to heaven. *This* is what he says:

"One thing I do; forgetting those things which are behind, and reaching forth unto those things which are before, I press toward the mark, for the prize of the high calling of God, in Christ Jesus," Phil. iii: 13, 14. This was just what the racer used to do in the ancient games, when he fixed his eye on the prize and pressed right forward till he reached it. And it was just what Harry Armstrong did in his play. He fixed his eye on the big pine tree and never turned to the right hand or to the left till he reached it. The apostle Paul fixed his eye on Jesus, and made a straight track through the world till he reached the glorious heaven where Jesus dwells. And, in doing this, the great apostle was only practising the lesson of duty taught by the voice that speaks from the Transfiguration scene. *"Hear him,"* said that voice. And if you and I listen to it, and obey it, as St. Paul did, it will lead us to follow him as he followed Christ; and then we shall make a straight path through this world to heaven, as he did in his Christian course. There is success in doing this.

And then there is—*profit*—in learning this lesson, as well as safety and success.

David says, when speaking of God's commands, "In keeping of them there is *great reward*," Ps. xix: 11. This is true of all God's commands; and it is especially true of the command we are now considering—"Hear him."

Samuel obeyed this command, and it made him a blessing and an honor to the nation of Israel. David obeyed it, and it made him one of the greatest and most successful kings. Daniel obeyed it, and it covered him with honor, and made him a blessing to his own nation, and to the church of Christ in every age.

"The Reward of Obedience." Here is an Eastern story which illustrates this point of our subject. The story says there was once an enchanted hill. On the top of this hill a great treasure was hidden. This treasure was put there to be the reward of any one who should reach the top of the hill without looking behind him. The command and the promise given to every young person who set out to climb that hill, were—do not look behind you, and that treasure shall be yours. But there was a threat added to the command and promise. The threat was, if you look behind, you will be turned into a stone. Many young persons started, to try and gain the prize. But the way to the top of the hill led them through beautiful groves, which covered the side of the hill. In these groves were birds singing sweetly, and sounds of music were heard, and melodious voices inviting those who passed by to stop and rest awhile. One after another of those who set out for the prize at the top of the hill would stop, and look round to see where the voices came from; and immediately they were turned into stones. "Hence," says the story, "in a little while the hillside was covered with stones, into which those had been turned who neglected the command given them when they started."

Of course there never was such a hill as this. But the story gives us a good illustration. Our life may well be compared to such a hill. The treasure, on the top of it, represents the reward that awaits us in heaven, if we serve God faithfully. The songs, and the voices, from the groves, on the hillside, represent the temptations that surround us in our daily paths. The lesson of duty that comes to us from the Transfiguration scene—"Hear him"—is the only thing that can preserve us from these temptations. If we hear Jesus when he says to us—"follow me;" if we give him our hearts and walk in his way, he will carry us through all temptations; he will bring us safely to the top of the hill; and the reward laid up there will be ours. Let us learn this lesson of duty, because there is safety in it; there is success in it; there is profit in it.

And so we have spoken of two things in connection with the Transfiguration; these are the wonders that attended it, and the lessons taught by it. The wonders are three—the wonderful change—the wonderful company—and the wonderful conversation; and the lessons are three—the lesson of hope—the lesson of instruction—and the lesson of duty.

In leaving this subject, let us lift up our hearts to Jesus, and say, in the beautiful language of the Te Deum:

> "Thou art the King of Glory, O Christ!
> Thou art the everlasting Son of the Father.
> When Thou hadst overeome the sharpness of death
> Thou didst open the kingdom of heaven to all believers.
> Thou sittest at the right hand of God,
> In the glory of the Father.
> We believe that thou shalt come to be our Judge.
> We therefore pray thee, help thy servants
> Whom thou hast redeemed with thy precious blood.
> Make them to be numbered with thy saints,
> In glory everlasting.   Amen."

THE LESSONS FROM OLIVET

OUR last chapter was on the Transfiguration. The next will be on The Last Supper. Between these two events in our Saviour's life, how many interesting incidents took place! How many important sayings that fell from his gracious lips during this period are written for our instruction by the four evangelists! There is, for instance, the beautiful lesson about what it is on which the value of our gifts depend. He taught this lesson when he saw the rich casting their gifts into the treasury. Among them came "a certain poor widow, casting in two mites. And he said, Of a truth I say unto you, that this poor widow hath cast in more than they all;—for she of her penury hath cast in all the living she had," Luke xxi: 1-4. But, from among all these, we have only room for one chapter. A dozen, or twenty chapters would be needed on this part of the life of Christ. Where there are so many that might be taken, it has been very difficult to decide which is the best. In deciding this matter, I do not think we could do better than join the company of the three favored disciples, Peter, John, and James, and go, in thought with them, as they followed their Master from his last visit to the temple in Jerusalem, up to the top of the Mount of Olives. There Jesus took his seat, and his disciples sat around him, anxious to ask him some questions about what he had said to them in the temple. We read in St. Mark xiii: 1-2, that as he was going out of the temple the disciples called his attention to the beauty of that sacred building and the great size and splendor of some of the stones that were in it. Then Jesus pointed to that great building, and told them that the time was coming when it would be destroyed, and "there should not be left one stone upon another that should not be thrown down." This filled the minds of the disciples with surprise and wonder. They supposed that their temple would last as long as the world stood. They thought that it was the end of the world of which Jesus was speaking; and they were very anxious that he should tell them something more about it. And so, as soon as they were seated around him, on the Mount of Olives, they said, "Tell us, when shall these things be? and what shall be the sign, when all these things shall be fulfilled?" St. Mark xii: 4.

And now, we may imagine ourselves sitting with Jesus and his disciples on the Mount of Olives. As we look down we see the city of Jerusalem spread out beneath our feet. We see its walls, and its palaces. And there, just before us, outshining everything in its beauty, is that sacred temple, that was "forty and six years in building." Its white marble walls, its golden spires, and pinnacles, are sparkling in the beams of the sun, as they shine upon them. No wonder the Jews were so proud of it! It was a glorious building.

But now Jesus is beginning to speak. Let us listen to what he says. The lessons that he taught on the Mount of Olives run all through the twenty-fourth and twenty-fifth chapters of St. Matthew. In the first of these chapters, Jesus gave them a sign, by which those who learn to understand what he here says, might know when his second coming is to take place. These are some of the lessons from Olivet. I should like, very much, to stop and talk about them. But this cannot be now. We pass over to the twenty-fifth chapter of St. Matthew. In this chapter we have three of our Saviour's parables. These are very solemn and instructive. They all refer to the judgment that must take place when Jesus shall come into our world again. The second of these parables is the one we are now to consider. It is called—"The Parable of the Talents." We find it in St. Matt. xxv: 14-30. And *the lessons from Olivet,* which we are now to try and learn, are all drawn from the words of our Saviour, contained in the verses just mentioned.

This, then, is our present subject—*The Lessons from Olivet.* And there are *four* lessons, in this part of our Saviour's discourse, of which we are now to speak. *The first is—the lesson about the Master. The second—the lesson about the servants. The third is—the lesson about the talents; and the fourth, the lesson about the rewards.*

*The lesson about—*THE MASTER—*is the first thing of which we are to speak.*

In the 14th verse of this 25th chapter of St. Matthew, Jesus speaks of himself as—"a man travelling into a far country,"—and of his people as—"his own servants." In the 19th verse he speaks of himself as "the lord of those servants, coming back, after a long time, to reckon with them."

In St. Luke xix: 11-27 we have another of our Saviour's parables, very similar to the one now before us. There, he speaks of himself as "a *nobleman* who went into a far country to receive for himself a kingdom, and to return." This language was borrowed from a custom that prevailed in those days. The headquarters of the government of the world then was in the city of Rome. The kings and rulers of different countries received their appointments to the offices they held from the Roman Emperor. Archelaus, the son of Herod, succeeded his father as king of Judea. But, it was necessary for him to go to Rome and get permission from the emperor to hold and exercise that office. He had done this, not very long before our Saviour applied to himself the words we are now considering. This was a fact well known. And this is the illustration which Jesus here uses in reference to himself. He is the Head—the Prince—the Lord—the Master of all things in his church. He spoke of himself to his disciples as their "Lord and Master," St. John xiii: 14. He tells us that he has gone to heaven, as Archelaus went to Rome, "to receive for himself a kingdom and to return." He said he would be absent "a long time," verse 19. And this is true. He has been absent more than eighteen hundred years. He said he would "return," or come again. And so he will. It is just as certain that he will come again as it is that he went away. And he will come, not in figure, or in spirit, but in person, as he went. Remember what the angels said about this to his disciples, at the time of his departure. "Ye men of Galilee, why stand ye gazing up into heaven? this same Jesus, which is taken from you into heaven, shall *so come, in like manner* as ye have seen him go into heaven," Acts i: 11. He said he would return, and so he will.

But, in the meantime, he would have us remember that he is still our Lord and Master. No master ever had such a right to be Lord and Ruler as he has. God the Father has appointed him to be "Head over all things to his church," Ephes. i: 22. He is our Master, because he *made* us. This is what no other ever did for his servants. He is our Master because he *preserves* us. We cannot keep ourselves for a single moment, but he keeps us all the time,—by night, and by day. And he is our Master because, when we had sold ourselves into sin, and were appointed unto death, *he redeemed us*. He bought us with the price of his own precious blood. He made our hands to work for him; and our feet to walk in his ways. He made our hearts to love him;—our minds to think about him; our eyes to see the beauty of his wondrous works, our ears to listen to his gracious words, and our lips and tongues to be employed in speaking and singing his praises.

We cannot be our own masters. "I am my own master!"—said a young man, proudly, to a friend who was trying to persuade him from doing a wrong thing; "I am my own master!"

"That's impossible," said his friend. "You can not be master of yourself, unless you are master of everything within, and everything around you. Look within. There is your conscience to keep clear, and your heart to make pure, your temper to govern, your will to control, and your judgment to instruct. And then look without. There are storms, and seasons; accidents, and dangers; a world full of evil men and evil spirits. What can you do with these? And yet, if you don't master them, they'll master you."

"That's so," said the young man.

"Now, I don't undertake any such thing," said his friend. "I am sure I should fail, if I did. Saul, the first king of Israel, wanted to be his own master, and failed. So did Herod. So did Judas. No man can be his own master. 'One is your Master, even Christ,' says the apostle. I work under his direction. He is my regulator, and when he is Master all goes right. Think of these words,—'*He is your Master, even Christ.*' If we put ourselves under his leadership we shall surely win at last."

And as we cannot be our own master, if we refuse to take Christ as our Ruler, there is nothing left for us but to have Satan as our master. These are the only two masters we can have. We must make our choice between them. If Jesus is not our Master, Satan must be. If Jesus is our Master here, he will share his glory with us hereafter. If we serve Satan here, we must share his punishment hereafter. This is one of the solemn lessons that Jesus taught on Olivet. He is speaking of the day of judgment. He represents himself as on the judgment-seat. Two great companies are before him. On his right hand are those who took him for their Master. To them he says—"Come, ye blessed children of my Father, inherit the kingdom prepared for you, from the foundation of the world," St. Matt. xxv: 34.

On his left are those who took Satan for their master. The awful words he speaks to them are:—"Depart from, ye cursed, into everlasting fire, prepared for the devil and his angels." St. Matt. xxv: 41.

This is our first lesson from Olivet—the lesson about the Master.

The second lesson from Olivet is the lesson about—THE SERVANTS.

We are told that before this nobleman went away to the far country, he called to him "his own servants." The nobleman here spoken of means Jesus, our blessed Master. And now the question is—who are meant by "his own servants?" He has three kinds of servants. The first kind is made up of those who serve him *ignorantly*. This takes in all those things that have no knowledge or understanding. There, for instance are the sun,—the moon,—the stars, —the mountains,—the hills,—the plains,—the valleys,—the rivers,—the seas,—the wind that blows,—the rains that descend,—and the dews that distil; these all serve God, without knowing it. He made them to serve him, and they do it; but they do it ignorantly. "His kingdom *ruleth over all,*" and it makes all these things his servants. They do exactly what they were made for, but they do it ignorantly.

And there is another class of our Lord's creatures who serve him *unwillingly*. This is a very large class. It takes in all the wicked men, and the wicked spirits who are to be found anywhere. They do not wish to serve God, and yet, in spite of themselves, they are obliged to do it. We see this illustrated, when we think of the way in which the crucifixion of our blessed Saviour was brought about. Satan stirred up the Jews to take Jesus and put him to death. God allowed them to do it. They did it of their own choice—as freely, and as voluntarily, as they ever did anything in their lives. They did it because they hated him, and wished to get him out of their way. So they nailed him to the cross in their malice and their rage. This was the very thing God had determined should be done, that he might save and bless the world. He allowed Satan, and the Jews, to do just what their wicked hearts prompted them to do; and then he overruled it for good. And, in this way, as David says, he "makes the wrath of man to praise him, and the remainder of it he restrains." And thus we see how evil men, and evil spirits, are God's servants *unwillingly*.

But then, there is another class of persons who serve God *willingly*. This takes in all those who know and love him. He speaks of them, in this parable as "*his own* servants." When they find out what he has done for them, the thought of it fills their hearts with love; and then they desire to serve him, and do all he tells them to do, in order to show their love to him. And this is what Jesus means when he says—"Take my yoke upon you; for my yoke is easy, and my burden is light." When we really love a person, anything that we can do for that person is easy and pleasant to us. And so it is the great love for Jesus, that his people have, which makes his yoke easy, and his burden light to them.

"How to Become a Willing Servant to Jesus." A little boy came to his grandmother one day, and asked her how he could become a Christian. She answered very simply, "Ask Jesus to give you a new heart, *and believe he does it when you ask him.*"

"Is that all?" said the little fellow joyfully; "oh! that is easy enough." So he went to his room, and kneeling beside his bed, asked Jesus to give him a new heart. He believed that the dear Saviour, who loves little children, did hear and answer his prayer. And he left his room with a happy heart, for he felt sure that he was now one of Christ's own loving children, and willing servants. And this is the way in which we must take the yoke of Jesus upon us, and become his willing servants. And then in everything that we do we can be serving him. As St. Paul says—"whether we eat or drink, or whatsoever we do, we can do all to the glory of God."

A good man once said "that if God should send two angels down from heaven, and should tell one of them to sit on a throne and rule a kingdom, and the other to sweep the streets of a city, the latter would feel that he was serving God as acceptably in handling his broom as his brother angel was in holding his sceptre. And this is true. We see the same illustrated in the fable of:

"The Stream and the Mill." "I notice," said the stream to the mill, "that you grind beans as well and as cheerfully as you do the finest wheat." "Certainly," said the mill; "what am I here for but to grind? and so long as I work, what does it signify to me what the work is?

My business is to serve my master, and I am not a whit more useful when I turn out the finest flour than when I turn out the coarsest meal. My honor is, not in doing fine work, but in doing any thing that is given me to do in the best way that I can." That is true. And this is just the way in which Jesus wishes us to serve him when he says to "*his own* servants," "Occupy till I come." This means serve me, in everything, as you would do if you saw me standing by your side.

"How to Serve God." Willie's mother let him go with his little sister into the street to play. She told them not to go off the street on which their house stood. Willie was a little fellow, and lisped very much in talking; but he was brave, and he was obedient. Presently his sister asked him to go into another street; but he refused. "Mamma thaid no," was Willie's answer. "The thaid we muthn't do off thith threet," said Willie in his lisping way. "Only just a little way round the corner," said his teasing sister. "Mamma'll never know it."

"But I thall know it my own thelf; and I don't want to know any thuch a mean thing; and I won't!" And Willie straightened himself, and stood up like a man. That was brave and beautiful in Willie. And that is the way in which we should try to serve our heavenly Master.

"How a Boy May Serve God." A gentleman met a little boy wheeling his baby brother in a child's carriage. "My little man," said the gentleman, "what are you doing to serve God?" The little fellow stopped a moment, and then, looking up into the gentleman's face, he said:—"Why, you see, Sir, I'm trying to make baby happy, so that he won't worry mamma who is sick." That was a noble answer. In trying to amuse his baby brother, and to relieve his poor sick mother, that little boy was serving God as truly and as acceptably as the angel Gabriel does when he wings his way, on a mission of mercy, to some far off world.

And this is the lesson about the servants that comes to us from Olivet.

The lesson about—THE TALENTS—*is the third lesson that comes to us from Olivet.*

This parable tells us that before the Master went away, he "called his own servants, and delivered unto them his goods. Unto one he gave five talents, to another two, to another one; to every man according to his several ability." verses 14, 15. In St. Luke's account of the parable, what the master gave to his servants is spoken of as *pounds*, and each servant is said to have received one pound. These talents or pounds both mean the same thing. They denote something with which we can do good, and make ourselves useful. And it is plain, from both these parables, that the Master gave at least *one* talent, or one pound, to each of his servants. None of them were left without some portion of their Master's goods. And the lesson from Olivet which comes to us here is that every one of us has a talent, or a pound, that our Master Jesus, has given us, and which he expects us to use for him. And the most important thing for us is to find out what our talents are, and how we can best use them, so as to be ready to give a good account of them when our Master comes to reckon with us.

A TALENT FOR EACH.

"God entrusts to all
 Talents few or many;
None so young and small
 That they have not any.

"Little drops of rain
 Bring the springing flowers;
And I may attain
 Much by little powers.

"Every little mite,
  Every little measure,
Helps to spread the light,
  Helps to swell the treasure.

"God will surely ask,
  Ere I enter heaven,
Have I done the task
  Which to me was given?"

"One Talent Improved." One day, amidst the crowded streets of London, a poor little newsboy had both his legs broken by a dray passing over them. He was laid away, in one of the beds of a hospital, to die. On the next cot to him was another little fellow, of the same class, who had been picked up, sick with the fever which comes from hunger and want. The latter boy crept close up to his poor suffering companion and said:

"Bobby, did you ever hear about Jesus?"

"No, I never heard of him."

"Bobby, I went to the mission-school once; and they told us that Jesus would take us up to heaven when we die, if we axed him; and we'd never have any more hunger or pain."

"But I couldn't ax such a great gentleman as he is to do anything for me. He wouldn't stop to speak to a poor boy like me."

"But he'll do all that for you Bobby, if you ax him."

"But how can I ax him, if I don't know where he lives? and how could I get there when both my legs is broke?"

"Bobby, they told us, at the mission-school, as how Jesus passes by. The teacher said he goes around. How do you know but what he might come round to this hospital this very night? You'd know him if you was to see him."

"But I can't keep my eyes open. My legs feels awful bad. Doctor says I'll die."

"Bobby, hold up yer hand, and he'll know what you want, when he passes by." They got the hand up; but it dropped. They tried it again, and it slowly fell back. Three times they got up the little hand, only to let it fall. Bursting into tears he said, "I give it up."

"Bobby," said his tender-hearted companion, "lend me yer hand. Put your elbow on my piller: I can do without it." So the hand was propped up. And when they came in the morning, the boy lay dead; but his hand was still held up for Jesus. And don't you think that he heard and answered the silent but eloquent appeal which it made to him for his pardon and grace, and salvation, to that poor dying boy? I do, I do.

Bobby's friend had been once to the mission-school. He had but a single talent; but, he made good use of it when he employed it to lead that wounded, suffering, dying boy to Jesus.

"Good Friends." "I wish I had some good friends, to help me on in life!" cried lazy Dennis, with a yawn.

"Good friends," said his master, "why you've got ten; how many do you want?"

"I'm sure I've not half so many; and those I have are too poor to help me."

"Count your fingers, my boy," said the master.

Dennis looked down on his big, strong hands. "Count thumbs and all," added the master.

"I have; there are ten," said the lad.

"Then never say you have not ten good friends, able to help you on in life. Try what those true friends can do, before you go grumbling and fretting because you have none to help you."

Now, suppose that we put the word talents, for the word friends, in this little story. Then, we may each of us hold our two hands before us, and say "here are ten talents, which God has given me to use for him. Let me try and do all the good I can with these ten talents."

THE BEST THAT I CAN.

"'I cannot do much,' said a little star,
  'To make the dark world bright;
My silvery beams can not struggle far
  Through the folding gloom of night;
But I'm only a part of God's great plan,
And I'll cheerfully do the best I can.'

"A child went merrily forth to play,
  But a thought, like a silver thread,
Kept winding in and out, all day,
  Through the happy golden head.
Mother said,—'Darling, do all you can;
For you are a part of God's great plan.'

"So he helped a younger child along,
  When the road was rough to the feet,
And she sung from her heart a little song
  That we all thought passing sweet;
And her father, a weary, toil-worn man,
Said, 'I, too, will do the best I can.'"

"A Noble Boy." "Not long ago," said a Christian lady, "I saw a boy do something that made me glad for a week. Indeed it fills my heart with tenderness and good feeling whenever I think about it. But let me tell you what it was.

"As I was walking along a crowded street I saw an old blind man walking on without any one to lead him. He went very slowly, feeling his way with his cane.

"'He's walking straight to the highest part of the curb-stone,' said I to myself. 'And it's very high too. I wonder if some one won't help him and start him in the right direction.'

"Just then, a boy, about fourteen years old, who was playing near by, ran up to the old man and gently putting his hand through the man's arm, said:—'Allow me, my friend, to lead you across the street.' By this time there were three or four others watching the boy. He not only helped the old man over one crossing, but led him over another to the lower side of the street. Then he ran back to his play.

"Now this boy thought he had only done an act of kindness to that old man. But just see how much farther than that the use of his one talent went. The three boys with whom he was playing, and who had watched his kind act, were happier and better for it, and felt that they must be more careful to do little kindnesses to those about them.

"The three or four persons who stopped to watch the boy turned away with a tender smile upon their faces, ready to follow the good example of that noble boy. I am sure that I felt more gentle and loving towards every one, from what I saw that boy do.

"And then, another one that was made happy was the boy himself. For, it is impossible for us to do a kind act, or to make any one else happy, without feeling better and happier ourselves. To *be* good and to *do* good, is the way to be happy. This is our mission here in this world. Whatever talents our Master has given us, he intends that we should use them in this way."

"Tiny's Work for God." Two little girls, Leila and Tiny, were sitting, one summer day, under the tree which grew beside their home.

Both children had been quiet for a little while, when suddenly Tiny raised her blue eyes and said, "I *am* so happy, Leila. I do love the flowers, and the birdies, and you, and everybody so much." Then she added, in a whisper, "And I love God, who made us all so happy. Sister, I wish I could do something for him."

"Mother says if we love him, that is what he likes best of all," said Leila.

"Yes, but I do want to *do* something for him —something that would give me trouble. Can't you think of anything?"

Leila thought a little, and said, "Perhaps you could print a text for the flowers mother sends every week to the sick people in the hospital. They are so glad to have the flowers, and then the text might help them think about our Father in heaven."

"Oh! thank you, sister, that will be so nice! I will write—'Suffer the little children to come unto me, and forbid them not.'"

But Tiny was only a little over four years old, and it was hard for her to hold a pen, but she managed to print two letters every day till the text was finished. Then she went alone to her room, and laying the text on a chair, she kneeled down beside it, and said—"Heavenly Father, I have done this for you: please take it from Tiny, for Jesus Christ's sake. Amen." And God heard the prayer, for he always listens when children truly pray.

So Tiny's text was sent up to London, and a lady put a very pretty flower into the card and took it to the hospital. She stopped beside a bed where a little boy was lying. His face was almost as white as the pillow on which he lay, and his dark eyes were filled with tears.

"Is the pain very bad to-day, Willie?"

"Yes, miss; its dreadful-like. But it's not so much the pain as I mind. I'm used to that, yer know. Father beat me every day a'most, when he was drunk. But the doctor says I'm too ill for 'im to 'ave any 'opes for me, and I'm mighty afeard to die."

"If you had a friend who loved you, and you were well, would you be afraid to go and stay with him, Willie?"

"Why no, I'd like to go, in course."

"I have brought you a message from a Friend, who has loved you all your life long. He wants you to trust him, and to go and live with him. He will love you always, and you will always be happy."

Then the lady read Tiny's text, "*Suffer the little children to come unto me, and forbid them not.*" She told him how Jesus had died, and then had risen again, and had gone to heaven, to prepare a place for *him*, and for many other children. She told him how Jesus is still saying "Come," and his hand is still held out to bless.

So Willie turned to the Good Shepherd, and was no longer afraid. A few days afterwards he whispered—"Lord Jesus, I am coming;" and he died with Tiny's text in his hand.

That little girl used the talent that was given her, and it helped to bring a soul to Jesus.

EVERY TALENT USEFUL.

"Though little I bring,
  Said the tiny spring,
As it burst from the mighty hill,
  'Tis pleasant to know,
  Wherever I flow,
The pastures are greener still.

"And the drops of rain
  As they fall on the plain,
When parched by the summer heat,
  Refresh the sweet flowers
  Which droop in the bowers,
And hang down their heads at our feet.

"May we strive to fulfill
  All His righteous will,
Who formed the whole earth by His word!
  Creator Divine!
  We would ever be Thine,
And serve Thee—our God, and our Lord!"

Let us never forget this third lesson from Olivet, the lesson about,—the talents.

The fourth, and last lesson from Olivet is the lesson about—THE REWARDS.

The parable tells us that when the Master came back, and reckoned with his servants, he said to each of those who had made a right use of his talents:—"Well done, good and faithful servant, thou hast been faithful over a few things, I will make thee ruler over many things; enter thou into the joy of thy lord." In the parable in St. Luke we are told that the servant who had gained ten pounds was made ruler over ten cities; and he who had gained five pounds was made ruler over five cities. This shows us that God will reward his people, hereafter, according to the degree of faithfulness with which each one shall have used the talents given to him. And this is the lesson which the apostle Paul teaches us when he says that, "Every man shall receive *his own reward* according to *his own labor.*" I. Cor. iii: 8.

All the willing, loving servants of God will receive a crown of life when Jesus comes to reckon with them. But those crowns will not be all alike. They are spoken of as "crowns of gold:" Rev. iv: 4; as "crowns of glory:" I. Peter v: 4, and as "crowns of life:" Rev. iii: 11. But still there will be very great differences between these crowns. Some will be simply crowns of gold, or of glory, without any gems or jewels to ornament them. Some will have two or three small jewels shining in them. But, others again will be full of the most beautiful jewels, all glittering and sparkling with glory. And this will all depend upon the way in which those who wear these crowns used their talents while they were on earth, and the amount of work they did for Jesus. There is an incident mentioned in Roman history about a soldier, which illustrates this part of our subject very well.

"The Faithful Soldier and His Rewards." This man had served forty years in the cause of his country—of these, ten years had been spent as a private soldier, and thirty as an officer. He had been present in one hundred and twenty battles, and had been severely wounded forty-five times. He had received fourteen civic crowns, for having saved the lives of so many Roman citizens; three mural crowns, for having been the first to mount the breach when attacking a fortress; and eight golden crowns, for having, on so many occasions, rescued the standard of a Roman legion from the hands of the enemy. He had in his house eighty-three gold chains, sixty bracelets, eighteen golden spears, and twenty-three horse trappings,—the rewards for his many faithful services as a soldier. And when his friends looked at all those honors and treasures which he had received, from time to time, how well they might have said as they pointed to those numerous prizes—that he had "received *his own reward*, according to *his own labor*," and faithfulness! And so it will be with the soldiers of the cross, who are faithful in using the talents given them by their heavenly Master.

"A Great Harvest from a Little Seed." Some years ago there was a celebrated artist in Paris whose name was Ary Scheffer. On one accasion he wished to introduce a beggar into a certain picture he was painting. Baron Rothschild, the famous banker, and one of the richest men in the world, was a particular friend of this artist. He happened to come into his studio at the very time he was trying to get a beggar to be the model of one which he desired to put into his painting.

"Wait till to-morrow," said Mr. Rothschild, "and I will dress myself up as a beggar, and make you an excellent model."

"Very well," said the artist, who was pleased with the strangeness of the proposal. The next day the rich banker appeared, dressed up as a beggar, and a very sorry looking beggar he was. While the artist was engaged in painting him, another friend of his came into the studio. He was a kind-hearted, generous man. As he looked on the model beggar, he was touched by his wretched appearance, and as he passed him, he slipped a louis d'or—a French gold coin, worth about five dollars of our money—into his hand. The pretended beggar took the coin, and put it in his pocket.

Ten years after this, the gentleman who gave this piece of money received an order on the bank of the Rothschilds for ten thousand francs. This was enclosed in a letter which read as follows:

"Sir: You one day gave a louis d'or to Baron Rothschild, in the studio of Ary Scheffer. He has invested it, and made good use of it, and to-day he sends you the capital you entrusted to him, together with the interest it has gained. A good action is always followed by a good reward.
"James De Rothschild."

In those few years that one gold coin, of twenty francs, had increased to ten thousand francs. And this illustrates the way in which Jesus the heavenly Master rewards those who use their talents for him. See how he teaches this lesson, when he says—"Whosoever shall give to drink unto one of these little ones a cup of cold water only in the name of a disciple, verily I say unto you, he shall in *no wise lose his reward.*" St. Matt. x: 42. And in another place we are told that the reward shall be "an hundred fold," and shall run on into "everlasting life." St. Matt. xix: 29. How sweetly some one has thus written about

THE REWARD OF HEAVEN.

"Light after darkness, gain after loss,
Strength after weariness, crown after cross;
Sweet after bitter, song after sigh,
Home after wandering, praise after cry;
Sheaves after sowing, sun after rain,
Light after mystery, peace after pain;
Joy after sorrow, calm after blast,
Rest after weariness, sweet rest at last;
Near after distant, gleam after gloom,
Love after loneliness, life after tomb.
After long agony, rapture of bliss,
Christ is the pathway leading to this!"

The last lesson from Olivet is the lesson about the rewards. And taking these lessons together, let us remember that they are—the lesson *about the Master:* the lesson *about the servants:* the lesson *about the talents:* and the lesson *about the rewards.*

The Collect for the thirteenth Sunday after Trinity is a very suitable prayer to offer after meditating on the lessons from Olivet:

"Almighty and merciful God, of whose only gift it cometh that thy faithful people do unto thee true and laudable service: Grant, we beseech thee, that we may so faithfully serve thee in this life, that we fail not finally to attain thy heavenly promises; which exceed all that we can desire; through the merits of Jesus Christ our Lord. AMEN!

THE LORD'S SUPPER

WE are approaching now the end of our Saviour's life. The last week has come, and we are in the midst of it. This is called Passion week. We commonly use this word *passion* to denote anger. But the first and true meaning of the word, and of the Latin word from which it comes, is—suffering. And this is the sense in which we find the word used in Acts i: 3. There, St. Luke, who wrote the Acts, is speaking of Christ's appearing to the apostles, after his resurrection, and he uses this language: "To whom he showed himself alive, after his *passion;*" or after his suffering and death.

In the midst of this last week—this passion week—one of the interesting things that Jesus did was to keep the Jewish Passover for the last time with his disciples. This Passover feast had been kept by the Jews every year for nearly fifteen hundred years. It was the most solemn religious service they had. It was first observed by them in the night on which their nation was delivered from the bondage of Egypt and began their march towards the promised land of Canaan. We read about the establishment of this solemn service in Exodus, twelfth chapter.

The first Passover took place on the fourteenth day of the month Nisan. This had been the seventh month of the year with the Jews. But God directed them to take it for their first month ever afterwards. They were to begin their year with that month. Every family was to choose out a lamb for themselves, on the tenth day of the month. They were to keep it to the fourteenth day of the month. On the evening of that day, they were to kill the lamb. The blood of the lamb was to be sprinkled on the two side-posts and upper lintels of every door. They were to roast the lamb and eat it, with solemn religious services. And, while they were doing this, the angel of the Lord was to pass over all the land of Egypt, and, with his unseen sword, to smite and kill the first-born, or eldest child, in every family, from Pharaoh on his throne to the poorest beggar in the land. But the blood, sprinkled on the door-posts of the houses in which the Israelites dwelt, was to save them from the stroke of the angel of death as he passed over the land. And so it came to pass. The solemn hour of midnight arrived. The angel went on his way. He gave one stroke with his dreadful sword—and there was a death in every Egyptian family. But in the blood-sprinkled dwellings of the Israelites, there was no one dead. What a wonderful night that was! Nothing like it was ever known in the history of our world. It is not surprising that the children of Israel, through all their generations, should have kept that Passover feast with great interest—an interest that never died out, from age to age. Nor do we wonder that our blessed Saviour looked forward longingly to the occasion when, for the last time, he was to celebrate this Passover with his disciples. As they began the feast he said to them, "With desire I have desired" that is, I have earnestly, or heartily desired "to eat this passover with you before I suffer," St. Luke xxii: 15. It is easy to think of many reasons why Jesus should have felt this strong desire. Without attempting to tell what all those reasons were, we can readily think of some things which would lead him, very naturally, to have this feeling. It was the last time he was to eat this Passover with them on earth. This showed that his public work, for which he came into the world, was done. He had only now to suffer and die; to rise from the dead, and then go home to his Father in heaven.

This Passover had been one of the services established and kept for the purpose of pointing the attention of men to himself as the Lamb of God who was to take away the sins of the world. And now, the time had come when all that had thus been pointed out concerning him, for so many hundred years, was about to be fulfilled. He, the one true Lamb of God, had come. He was about to die for the sins of the world. Then the Jewish church would pass away, and the Christian church would take its place. And then the blessings of true religion, instead of being confined to one single nation, would be freely offered to all nations; and Jews and Gentiles alike, would be at liberty to come to Christ, and to receive from him pardon, and grace, and salvation, and every blessing.

There was enough in thoughts like these to make Jesus long to eat this last Passover with his disciples. In each of the four gospels we have an account of what took place when the time came for keeping this Passover. What is said concerning it we find in the following places: St. Matt. xxi: 17-30, St. Mark xiv: 12-26, St. Luke xxii: 7-39. St. John begins with the thirteenth chapter, and ends his account at the close of the seventeenth chapter. He is the only one of the four evangelists who gives a full and particular account of the wonderful sayings of our Lord in connection with this last passover, and of the great prayer that he offered for all his people.

Here is a brief outline of these different accounts. When the time came to keep the Passover, Jesus sent two of his disciples from Bethany, where he was then staying, to Jerusalem. He told them, that, when they entered the city, they would meet a man bearing a pitcher of water. They were to ask him to show them the guest-chamber, where he and his disciples might eat the Passover together. There were always great crowds of strangers in Jerusalem at the time of this festival; and many furnished chambers were kept ready to be hired to those who wished them, for celebrating the Passover. This man, of whom our Saviour spoke, was probably a friend of his, and according to our Lord's word, he showed the disciples such a room as they needed. Then they made the necessary preparations; and, when the evening came, Jesus and his disciples met there to keep this solemn feast.

Many of the pictures that we see of this last Supper, represent the company as seated round a table, very much in the way in which we are accustomed to sit ourselves. But this is not correct. The people in those Eastern countries were not accustomed to sit as we do. On this occasion the roasted lamb, with the bread and wine to be used at the feast, was placed on a table, and the guests reclined on couches round the table, each man leaning on his left arm, and helping himself to what he needed with his right hand.

Various incidents took place in connection with this last Supper. The disciples had a contest among themselves about which of them should be greatest. This led Jesus, in the course of the evening, to give them the lesson of humility, by washing his disciples' feet, of which we have already spoken. Then he told them how sorrowfully he was feeling. He said they would all forsake him, and one of them would betray him that very night. This made them feel very sad. Each of them suspected himself—and asked sorrowfully—"Lord, is it I?" They did not suspect each other; and none of them seems to have suspected Judas Iscariot at all. Then Peter whispered to John, who was leaning on the bosom of Jesus, to ask who it was that was to do this? In answer to John's question, Jesus said it was the one to whom he should give a piece of bread when he had dipped it in the dish. Then he dipped the sop and gave it to Judas.

After this, we are told that Satan entered into him, and he went out and made preparation for doing the most dreadful thing that ever was done from the beginning of the world—and that was the betrayal of his great, and good, and holy Master, into the hands of his enemies. When Judas was gone, and before the Passover feast was finished, making use of some of the materials before him, Jesus established one of the two great sacraments to be observed in his church to the end of the world—the sacrament of the Lord's Supper—or the holy Communion.

This is St. Luke's account of the way in which it was done, chapter xxii: 19, 20—"And he took the bread, and gave thanks, and brake it, and gave unto them, saying, This is my body which is given for you: this do in remembrance of me. Likewise also the cup after supper, saying,

This cup is the New Testament in my blood, which is shed for you." St. Matthew adds, and—"for many."

Such is the account we have of the first establishment of the Lord's Supper. It was to take the place of the Jewish Passover, and to be observed by the followers of Christ all over the earth, until the time when he shall come again into our world.

And this solemn sacrament—this holy communion—this Supper of our Lord, ought to be observed, or kept, by all who love him, for three reasons: these are its connection with *the word of his command—the memory of his sufferings—and the hope of his glory.*

Jesus connected this sacrament with *the word of his command* when he said—"*This do*, in remembrance of me." St. Luke xxii: 19. This is the *command* of Christ. It is a plain, positive command. Jesus did not give this command to the apostles only, or to his ministers, or to any particular class of his followers, but to all of them. It was given first to his apostles, but it was not intended to be confined to them. Jesus does not say—"This do," ye who are my apostles; or, ye who are my ministers. He does not say—"This do," ye old men, or ye rich men, or ye great men; but simply, "This do." And the meaning of what he here says, is—"This do," all ye who profess to be my followers, all over the world, and through all ages. And the words that he spake on another occasion come in very well here: "If ye love me, keep my commandments." And *this* is one of the commandments that he expects all his people to keep. He points to his holy sacrament, which he has ordained in his church, and then to each one of his people he says—"This do." No matter whether we wish to do it or not; here are our master's words—"This do." No matter whether we see the use of it, or not; Jesus says—"This do." It is enough for each follower of Jesus to say, "here is my Lord's command; I *must* obey it."

In an army, if the general issues an order, it is expected that every soldier will obey it. And no matter how important, or useful, in itself considered, any work may be, that is done by one of those soldiers, yet, if it be done while he is neglecting the general's order, instead of gaining for that soldier the praise of the general, or of securing a reward from him, it will only excite his displeasure:—he will order that soldier to be punished.

But the church of Christ is compared in the Bible to an army. He is the Captain or Leader of this army. And one of the most important orders he has issued for his soldiers is—"This do in remembrance of me." If we profess to be the soldiers of Christ, and are enlisted in his army, and yet are neglecting this order, he never can be pleased with anything we may do while this order is neglected. We seem to see him pointing to this neglected order, and saying to each of us, as he said to Saul, the first king of Israel, by the prophet Samuel:—"Behold, to obey is better than sacrifice: and to hearken, than the fat of rams." I. Sam. xv: 22.

No age is fixed in the New Testament at which young people may be allowed to come to the sacrament of the Lord's Supper. But, as soon as they have learned to know and love Christ and are really trying to serve him, they ought to be allowed to come. And yet ministers and parents sometimes keep them back, and tell them they must wait, and be tried a little longer, before they receive the help and comfort of this ordinance of Christ, even when their conduct shows they are sincerely trying to love and serve the blessed Saviour.

If a farmer should send his servant out into the field, when winter was approaching, telling him to put the sheep into the fold, that they might be protected from the wolves, and from the cold, it would be thought a strange thing if he should allow him to bring the sheep into the shelter of the fold, and leave the little lambs outside. This is a good illustration to show the importance of taking care of the lambs. But it fails at one point. The shelter of the fold is absolutely necessary for the protection of the farmer's lambs. They could not live without it. If left outside of the fold they would certainly perish. But there is not the same necessity for admitting young people to the Lord's Supper. They are not left out in the cold, like the lambs in the field, even when not admitted to this holy ordinance. They are already under the care and protection of the good Shepherd. He can guard them, and keep them, and cause them to grow in grace, even though, for awhile, they do not have the help and comfort of this sacrament. And, if they are kept back through the fault or mistake of others, he will do so. This sacrament, like that of baptism, is, as the catechism says, "*generally necessary to salvation.*" This means that it is important "where it may be had." But, if circumstances beyond our control should prevent us from partaking of it, we may be saved without it. Still, I think that young people who give satisfactory evidence that they know and love the Saviour, and are trying to serve him, ought to be allowed to come forward to this holy sacrament.

Some people when urged to come to the Lord's Supper excuse themselves, by saying that—"they are not prepared to come."

But this will not release any one from the command of Christ—"This do."

What the preparation is that we need in order that we may come, in a proper way, to this holy sacrament, is clearly pointed out in the exhortation that occurs in the communion service of our church. Here the minister says—"Ye who do truly and earnestly repent of your sins, and are in love and charity with your neighbors, and intend to lead a new life, following the commandments of God, and walking from henceforth in his holy ways: draw near with faith, and take this holy sacrament to your comfort." And there is no excuse for persons not being in the state these words describe: for this is just what God's word, and our own duty and interest require of us. If we have not yet done what these words require, we ought to do it at once; and then there will be nothing in the way of our obeying the command of Christ, when he says—"This do, in remembrance of me." By all the authority which belongs to him our Saviour *commands* us to keep this holy feast. And the first reason why we ought to "do this," is because of its connection with the word of his command.

The second reason why we ought to "do this" —is because of its connection with the memory of his sufferings.

We are taught this by the word *remembrance*, which our Saviour here uses. He says, "This do in remembrance of me." This means in remembrance of my sufferings for you. And *this* is the most important word used by him when he established this sacrament. It is the governing word in the whole service. It is the word by which we must be guided in trying to understand what our Lord meant to teach us by all he did and said on this occasion.

You know how it is when we are trying to understand the music to which a particular tune has been set. There is always one special note in a tune, which is called the *key-note*. The leader of a choir, when they are going to sing, will strike one of the keys of the organ, or the melodeon they are using, so as to give to each member of the choir the proper key-note of the piece of music they are to sing. It is very important for them to have this key-note, because they cannot have a proper understanding of what they are to do without it. This holy sacrament of the Lord's Supper is like a solemn song. And the key-note of the music to which the song is set is this word—*remembrance*. It teaches us that the sacrament of the Lord's Supper is a *memorial* service. And, in going through the music to which the song of this service has been set, every note that we use must be a memorial note. And the language used by our blessed Lord when he established this Supper, or sacrament, must be explained in this way. When he broke the bread and gave it to his disciples, saying—"This is my body, which is given for you: this do in remembrance of me," he meant that we should understand him as saying—"This is the *memorial* of my body." And when he gave them the cup, and said—"This is my blood of the New Testament," he meant that we should understand him as saying—"This is the *memorial* of my blood." And we are sure that this was the meaning, for two reasons.

One reason for believing this is that *this was the way in which similar words had been used in the Jewish Passover, which Jesus and his disciples were then keeping.*

In the Passover service, when the head of the family distributed the bread, he always said—"This is the bread of affliction." When he distributed the flesh of the lamb, roasted for the occasion, he used to say—"This is the body of the Passover."

But every one knows, and every one admits, that the Jewish Passover was a *memorial* service. It was kept in memory of the wonderful deliverance of their forefathers from the bitter bondage of Egypt. And the words used at that service were memorial words. And so, when Jesus, a little while before, had given to his disciples the Passover bread, saying—"This is the bread of affliction:" he did not mean to say that *that* was the very same bread which their forefathers had eaten, in the time of their affliction in Egypt. What he meant to say was—this is the bread which you are to eat in *memory* of your forefathers' trial and deliverance. And when he gave to each of them a piece of the sacrificial lamb, saying, "This is the body of the Passover;" he did not mean that in any mysterious, or supernatural sense, *that* was the very lamb of which their forefathers had eaten on the solemn night of the Passover; he only meant that it was the body of which they were to eat in memory of the Passover. The Passover was a memorial service; and the words used at the Passover were memorial words.

And so, when Jesus went on, from the last Passover of the Jewish church, to the first sacramental feast of the Christian church, and began by saying, "This do in *remembrance* of me," what else could the apostles possibly have thought, but that he intended this new service of the Christian church to be a memorial service, just as the old festival of the Jewish church had been? When he gave them the broken bread, and said, "This is my body;" they could only have understood him as meaning this is the memorial of my body. And when he gave them the cup into which he had just poured the wine, and said: "This is my blood;" they could only understand him as meaning this is the memorial of my blood. And so, the sense in which he had just before used the words employed in the Jewish festival must have led the disciples to understand them in the same way when he used similar words in the Christian sacrament. This is a good, strong reason for thinking of this sacramental feast as a memorial service.

There is indeed, one point of difference between the Jewish Passover and the Christian sacrament, when we think of them as memorial services. The Jews kept their solemn festival in memory of a *dead* lamb—the Passover lamb that was put to death for them, but never came to life again. We keep our Christian sacrament in memory of the Lamb of God, who died for us indeed, but who rose from the dead, and is alive forevermore. As we keep this solemn festival, we may lift up our adoring hearts to him and say for ourselves personally,

> "O, the Lamb! the loving Lamb!
> The Lamb of Calvary!
> The Lamb that was slain, but liveth again,
> And intercedes for me!"

And though they are both memorial services, yet this one thought makes a world-wide difference between them. The bread and meat which the pious Jew ate, when he kept the Passover, and the wine which he drank on that occasion, would strengthen his body, but there was nothing connected with those material substances that would do any special good to his soul. It is different, however, with our Christian festival of the Lord's Supper. And this difference is clearly brought out in what we find in the catechism of our church on this subject. In speaking of this holy sacrament, the question is asked—"What are the benefits whereof we are partakers thereby?" And the answer to this question is—"The strengthening and refreshing of our souls, by the body and blood of Christ, as our bodies are by the bread and wine."

Here we see that while the Lord's Supper is a memorial service indeed, it is at the same time something more than that.

And then, the actual bodily presence of Christ with them must have compelled the apostles to understand the words he used on that occasion, in this memorial sense.

They could not possibly have considered him as meaning that the bread and wine which he gave them at that solemn service did, in any mysterious and supernatural way, become his actual flesh and blood; because, these were already before them in the form of his own body. And they could not be in his body and in the bread and wine, at the same time. The sense in which Jesus first used these words—"my body" and "my blood," was clearly the memorial sense. He meant his disciples to understand him as saying "Take this bread in remembrance of my body, which is to be crucified for you;" and "Take this wine in remembrance of my blood which is to be shed for you."

This was what he taught the apostles when he first used these words among them; and this was all he taught them; and we have no right to use these words in any other sense till our blessed Lord himself shall give us authority to do so.

Let us never forget the word—*remembrance*, as used by our Saviour here. It is the root out of which the whole tree of this solemn service grows. Let us hold on to this root word, and it will save us from the errors into which many have fallen in reference to this subject.

And, surely, there is nothing so precious for us to store away in our memories as the thought of Christ in the amazing sufferings he once bore for us, in the great work he is now doing for us, and in the saving truth he embodies in his own glorious character.

The story is told of Alexander the Great, that when he conquered King Darius he found among his treasures a very valuable box or cabinet. It was made of gold and silver, and inlaid with precious jewels. After thinking for awhile what to do with it, he finally concluded to use it as his choicest treasury, or cabinet, in which to keep the books of the poet Homer, which he was very fond of reading. Now, if we use our memory aright, it will be to us a treasury far more valuable than that jeweled box of the great conqueror. And the thought of Christ, not in his sufferings only, but in his work, and in his character, is the most precious thing to lay up in our memory. And if we keep this remembrance continually before us it will be the greatest help we can have in trying to love and serve him better.

Here is an illustration of what I mean, in a touching story. We may call it:

"Love Stronger than Death." Some years ago there was a great fire in one of our Western cities that stood in the midst of a prairie. A mother escaped from her burning dwelling. Her husband was away from home. She took her infant in her arms, and wrapped a heavy shawl round herself and the baby. Her little girl clung to the dress of her mother, and they went out into the prairie, to get away from the flames of the burning buildings. It was a wild and stormy winter's night and intensely cold. She tried to run; but burdened as she was that was impossible. Presently she found that the tall dry grass of the prairie had caught fire. It was spreading on every side. A great circle of flame was gathering round her.

A little way off she saw a clump of trees on a piece of rising ground. Towards that spot she directed her steps, and strained every nerve to reach it. At last she succeeded in doing so.

For a moment the poor mother and her child were comparatively safe. But, on looking around, she saw that the flames were approaching her from opposite directions. Escape was impossible. Death—a terrible death by fire, seemed to be the only thing before her. She might wrap herself in that great shawl, and perhaps live through it. But, there were the children. Of course a mother could not hesitate a moment what to do under such circumstances. Wrapping the baby round and round in the folds of the shawl, she laid it carefully down, at the foot of one of the trees. Then, taking off her outer clothing, she covered the other child with it. She laid her down beside the baby, and then stretched herself across them. In a few moments the helpless little ones were sound asleep. The long hours of the night passed. The raging flames licked up the withered foliage about that clump of trees, and then left their blackened trunks to the keenness of the wind and frost.

The next day the heart-broken husband and father returned to find his home burnt, and his family gone—he knew not whither. He set out to search for his lost treasures. He found them by that clump of trees. There lay his wife—her hair and eyebrows, her face and neck scorched and blackened by the fire—but her body frozen stiff. Whether she perished by the flames or the frost no one ever knew. But, on lifting her burnt form they found, warm and cozy beneath, her two sleeping children. The elder child as they roused her, opened her eyes exclaiming, "Mamma, is it morning?" Yes: it was morning with that faithful mother, in the bright world to which she had gone!

Now, suppose that those children, as they grew up, should have had preserved among their treasures a piece of the burnt dress, or a lock of the scorched hair, of their devoted mother. As they looked at it, every day, it would be in *remembrance* of her. How touchingly it would tell of her great love for them, in being willing to lay down her life to save theirs! And how that thought would thrill their hearts and make them anxious to do all they could to show their respect and love for such a mother!

And so the broken bread and the poured out wine of this solemn sacrament should melt our hearts in the remembrance of the wonderful love of Christ to us, and should lead us to show our love to him by keeping his commandments.

And as we keep this solemn memorial service, how well we may say, in the words of the hymn:

>"According to thy gracious word,
>   In meek humility,
> This will we do, our dying Lord,
>   We will remember thee.
> Thy body, broken for our sake,
>   Our bread from heaven shall be:
> Thy sacramental cup we take,
>   And thus remember thee.
>
> "Can we Gethsemane forget?
>   Or there thy conflict see,
> Thine agony and bloody sweat,
>   And not remember thee?
> When to the cross we turn our eyes,
>   And rest on Calvary,
> O Lamb of God, our sacrifice,
>   We must remember thee."

But Jesus has connected this blessed sacrament with the hope of his glory—as well as with the word of his command and the memory of his sufferings.

He made this connection very clear when he said at the institution of this solemn service—"I will not drink henceforth of this fruit of the vine until that day when I drink it new with you in my Father's kingdom." St. Matt. xxvi: 29. And the apostle Paul pointed out the same connection when he said, "As often as ye eat this bread, and drink this cup, ye do shew the Lord's death, *till he come.*" I. Cor. xi: 26. This sacrament of the Lord's Supper is the point of meeting between the sufferings of Christ and the glory that is to follow—between his cross, with all its shame and anguish, and his kingdom, with all its honor and blessedness.

We have sometimes heard or read of magicians who have pretended to have wonderful mirrors into which persons might look and see all that was before them in this life. If there were such a mirror, it would be a strange thing indeed to look into it and find out what was going to happen to-morrow, or next month, or next year, or twenty years hence. But, there never was any such mirror. As the apostle says,

"We know not what shall be on the morrow." No mortal man can tell what will happen to him as he takes the very next step in life.

Yet, this solemn sacrament is like such a magical mirror. We can look into it and see, clearly represented there, what will happen to us in the future, not of *this* life indeed, but of the life to come. It leads our minds on to the marriage supper of the Lamb. And a voice from heaven declares—"Blessed are they who are called to the marriage supper of the Lamb." Rev. xix: 9. That marriage supper represents the highest joys of heaven. It gathers into itself all the glory and happiness that await us in the heavenly kingdom. And this sacramental service is the type or shadow of all the bliss connected with that great event in the future. If we are true and faithful partakers of this solemn sacrament—this memorial feast, we shall certainly be among the number of those whose unspeakable privilege it will be to sit down at the marriage supper of the Lamb, in heaven. There we shall be in the personal presence of Jesus, our glorified Lord. Our eyes "shall see the King in his beauty." And we shall see all his people too in the perfection of glory that will mark them there. And in happy intercourse with that blessed company we shall find all "the exceeding great and precious promises" of God's word fulfilled in our own personal experience.

And then there is nothing that can sustain and comfort us under the many trials of this mortal life like the hope of sharing this joy with our blessed Lord, when he shall come in the glory of his heavenly kingdom.

"The Hope of Glory." A Christian gentleman was in the habit of visiting, from time to time, a poor afflicted widow woman who lived in his neighborhood. She had once been very well off, and was the wife of a well-known and apparently successful merchant. But finally he failed in business and died soon after, leaving her alone in the world, and without anything to live on but what she could earn by her own labor.

After awhile her health failed, and then she was entirely dependent for her support on the kindness of her Christian friends. But she was always cheerful and happy. "On going in to see her one day," says this gentleman, "I found, on talking with her, that she was feeling very comfortable in her mind.

"'Tell me, my friend,' I asked, 'have you always felt as bright and cheerful as you seem to feel now?'

"'O, no,' she replied, 'very far from it. When my husband died, and I was left alone in the world, I used to feel very sad and rebellious. Many a time I was so sorrowful and despairing as to be tempted to take away my own life. But, in the good providence of God, I was led to read the Bible, and to pray for help from above. I became a member of the church. But, for a while, I did not find much comfort in my religion. And the reason of it was that I did not have very clear views of Christ as my Saviour, and of the wonderful things he has promised to do for his people in the future.

"'But, on one communion occasion, my minister preached on the words—"*Christ in you the hope of glory.*" That was a blessed communion to me. I saw then, as I had never seen before, how that sacred and solemn service was intended by him to be to all his people, at one and the same time, the means of preserving in their minds the remembrance of the sufferings he has borne for them in the past, and also of keeping alive in their hearts the hope of sharing in the glory which he has prepared for them in the future. And I have never had any trouble in my mind since then. My communion seasons were always bright and blessed seasons to me as long as I was able to go to church. And though I can no longer go up to the sanctuary and partake of the bread and wine, "the outward and visible signs" made use of in the heavenly feast; yet, blessed be God's holy name, I can, and do partake in a spiritual manner of that which those signs represent. I feel and know what it is to have "Christ in me the hope of glory." And this "satisfies my longing, as nothing else can do." I find peace and comfort in simply "looking unto Jesus." I have had much outward trouble and affliction since then. I live alone. There is no one here to help me. Sometimes I have nothing to eat, and but little to keep me warm. You see me *sitting* here now. Thus I have to spend my nights. My complaint is the dropsy, and this prevents me from lying down. *But I would not exchange my place as a forgiven sinner, with "Christ in me the hope of glory," for all the wealth and the honor that Queen Victoria could bestow upon me!*'"

What a blessed Saviour Jesus is, who can thus spread the sunshine of his peace and hope through the hearts and homes of the poorest and most afflicted in the land!

And thus, we have spoken of three good reasons, why all who love our Lord Jesus Christ should keep this solemn sacrament which he has ordained; we should do it because we see in it—*the word of his command—the memorial of his sufferings—and the hope of his glory.*

And when we partake of this solemn ordinance ourselves, or see others partaking of it, how well we may say in the beautiful lines of Havergal, the English poetess:

> "Thou art coming! At thy table
> We are witnesses for this,
> While remembering hearts thou meetest,
> In communion closest, sweetest,
> Earnest of our coming bliss.
> Showing not thy death alone,
> And thy love exceeding great,
> But thy coming, and thy throne,
> All for which we long and wait.
>
> "O the joy to see thee reigning,
> Thee, our own beloved Lord;
> Every tongue thy name confessing,
> Worship, honor, glory, blessing,
> Brought to thee with glad accord,
> Thee our master and our Friend,
> Vindicated and enthroned;
> Unto earth's remotest end,
> Glorified, adored, and owned."

"THIS DO IN REMEMBRANCE OF ME."

THE
LIFE OF JESUS CHRIST
FOR THE YOUNG

CONTENTS

VOLUME IV

CHAPTER		PAGE
I	Jesus in Gethsemane	1
II	The Betrayal and Desertion	29
III	The Trial	59
IV	The Crucifixion	89
V	The Burial	121
VI	The Resurrection	151
VII	The Ascension	179
VIII	The Day of Pentecost	211
IX	The Apostle Peter	239
X	St. John and St. Paul	271
	Analytical Index	301
	Index of Poems	319

JESUS IN GETHSEMANE

IN sailing across the ocean, if we attempt to measure the depth of the water in different places, we shall find that it varies very much. There are hardly two places in which it is exactly the same. In some places it is easy enough to find the bottom. In others, it is necessary to lengthen the line greatly before it can be reached. And then there are other places where the water is so deep that the longest line ordinarily used cannot reach to the bottom. We know that there *is* a bottom, but it is very hard to get down to it.

And, in studying the history of our Saviour's life, we may compare ourselves to persons sailing over the ocean. The things that he did, and the words that he spoke, are like the water over which we are sailing. And when we try to understand the meaning of what Jesus said and did, we are like the sailor out at sea who is trying to fathom the water over which he is sailing, and to find out how deep it is. And in doing this we shall find the same difference that he finds. Some of the things that Jesus did and said are so plain and simple that a child can understand them. These are like those parts of the ocean where a very little line will reach the bottom. Other things that Jesus did and said require hard study, if we wish to understand them. But then, there are other parts of the sayings and doings of Jesus which the best and wisest men, with all their learning and study, cannot fully understand or explain. These are like those places in the sea where we cannot reach the bottom with our longest lines.

We find our illustration of this in the garden of Gethsemane. Some of the things that were done and said there we can easily understand. But other things are told us, of what Jesus did and said there which are very hard to explain.

In speaking about this part of our Saviour's life, there are two things for us to notice. These are what we are *told* about Gethsemane, and what we are *taught* by the things that took place there. Or, a shorter way of stating it will be to say that our subject now is—*the facts—and the lessons of Gethsemane.*

Let us look now at the facts that are told us about Gethsemane. It is a fact that there was such a place as Gethsemane, near Jerusalem, when Jesus was on earth, and that there is such a place there now. It is a fact that Gethsemane was a garden or orchard of olive trees then, and so it is still. Everyone who goes to Jerusalem is sure to visit this spot, because it is so sacred to all Christian hearts on account of its connection with our Saviour's sufferings. The side of the Mount of Olives on which Gethsemane stands is dotted over with olive trees. A portion of the hill has been enclosed with stone walls. This is supposed to be the spot where our Lord's agony took place. Inside of these walls are eight large olive trees. They are gnarled and crooked, and very old. Some suppose they are the very trees which stood there when Jesus visited the spot, on the night in which he was betrayed. But this is not likely. For we know that when Titus, the Roman general, was besieging Jerusalem, he cut down all the trees that could be found near the city. But the trees now there have probably sprung from the roots of those that were growing in Gethsemane on this very night.

It is a fact that after keeping the last Passover, and observing, for the first time the Lord's Supper with his disciples, Jesus left Jerusalem near midnight with the little band of his followers. He went down the side of the hill on which the city stood and crossed the brook Kedron on the way to Gethsemane. It is a fact that on going into the garden he left eight of his disciples at the entrance. It is a fact that he took with him the chosen, favored three, Peter, James, and John, and went further into the garden. It is a fact that then he "began to be sorrowful and very heavy. Then saith he —my soul is exceeding sorrowful, even unto death." It is a fact that he withdrew from the three disciples, and, alone with God, he bowed himself to the earth, and prayed, saying, "O, my Father, if it be possible, let this cup pass from me." It is a fact that after offering this earnest prayer he returned to his disciples and found them asleep, and said to Peter, "What! could ye not watch with me one hour? Watch and pray, that ye enter not into temptation." It is a fact that he went away again, "and being in an agony he prayed more earnestly, and his sweat was, as it were, great drops of blood falling down to the ground." It is a fact that in the depths of his agony, "there appeared unto him an angel from heaven strengthening him." We are not told what the angel said to him. No doubt he brought to him some tender, loving words from his Father in heaven, to comfort and encourage him. It is a fact that he returned to his disciples again and found them sleeping, for their eyes were heavy. It is a fact that he went away again, and prayed, saying, "O, my Father, if this cup may not pass from me except I drink it, thy will be done." It is a fact that he returned the third time to his disciples, and said—"Sleep on now, and take your rest: behold the hour is at hand, and the Son of Man is betrayed into the hands of sinners. Rise, let us be going: behold he is at hand that doth betray me." And it is a fact that, immediately after he had spoken these words, the wretched Judas appeared with his band to take him. These are the facts told us by the evangelists respecting Jesus and his agony in Gethsemane. They are very wonderful facts, and the scene which they set before us in our Saviour's life is one of the most solemn and awful that ever was witnessed.

And now, let us go on to speak of *the lessons taught us by these facts.* These lessons are *four.*

The first lesson we learn from Gethsemane is a lesson—ABOUT PRAYER.

As soon as this great trouble came upon our blessed Lord in Gethsemane, we see him, at once separating himself from his disciples, and seeking the comfort and support of his Father's presence in prayer. And this was what he was in the habit of doing. We remember how he spent the night in prayer before engaging in the important work of choosing his disciples. And now, as soon as the burden of this great sorrow comes crushing down upon him, the first thing he does is to seek relief in prayer.

The apostle Paul is speaking of this, when he says, "he offered *up prayers and supplications, with strong crying and tears, unto him that was able to save him from death, and was heard in that he feared."* Heb. v: 7. This refers particularly to what took place here in Gethsemane. The earnestness which marked our Saviour's prayers on this occasion is especially mentioned. He mingled tears with his prayers. It appears from what the apostle here says, that there was something connected with his approaching death upon the cross that Jesus particularly feared. We are not told what it was. And it is not worth while for us to try and find it out, for we cannot do it. But the prayer of Jesus, was not in vain. "He was heard, in that he feared." No doubt this refers to what took place when the angel came to strengthen him. His prayer was not answered literally. He was not actually saved from death; but he was saved from what he feared in connection with death. Our Lord's experience, in this respect, was like that of St. Paul when he prayed to be delivered from the thorn in the flesh. The thorn was not taken away, but grace was given him to bear it, and that was better than having it taken away. The promise is—"Cast thy burden upon the Lord, and he shall sustain thee." Ps. lv: 22. And so, from the gloomy shades of Gethsemane, with our Saviour's agony and bloody sweat, there comes to us a precious lesson about prayer. We see Jesus praying under the sorrows that overwhelmed him there: his prayer was heard, and he was helped.

And thus, by the example of our blessed Lord, we are taught, when we have any heavy burden to bear, or any hard duty to do, to carry it to the Lord in prayer.

Let us look at some examples from every day life of the benefit that follows from prayer.

"Washington's Prayer." General Washington was one of the best and greatest men that this country, or any other, ever had. He was a man of piety and prayer.

While he was a young man, he was appointed by Governor Dinwiddie, of Virginia, to the command of a body of troops, and sent on some duty in the western part of that state. A part of these troops was composed of friendly Indians. There was no chaplain in that little army, and so Washington used to act as chaplain himself. He was in the habit of standing up, in the presence of his men, with his head uncovered, and reverently asking the God of heaven to protect and bless them in the work they were sent to do. And no doubt, the great secret of Washington's success in life, was his habit of prayer. He occupied many positions of honor and dignity during his useful life. But, never did he occupy any position in which he appeared so manly, so honorable, and so truly noble, as when he stood forth, a young man, in the presence of his little army, and tried to lift up their thoughts to God above, as the one "from whom all blessings flow."

"Praying Better Than Stealing." A poor family lived near a wood wharf. The father of this family got on very well while he kept sober; but when he went to the tavern to spend his evenings and his earnings, as he did sometimes, then his poor family had to suffer. One winter, during a cold spell of weather, he was taken sick from a drunken frolic. Their wood was nearly gone.

After dark one night, he called his oldest boy John to his bedside, and whispered to him to go to the wood wharf and bring an armful of wood.

"I can't do that," said John.

"Can't do it—why not?"

"Because that would be stealing, and since I have been going to Sabbath-school, I've learned that God's commandment is, 'Thou shalt not steal.'"

"Well, and didn't you learn that another of God's commandments is—'Children, obey your parents?'"

"Yes, father," answered the boy.

"Well, then, mind and do what I tell you."

Johnny was perplexed. He knew there must be some way of answering his father, but he did not know exactly how to do it. The right thing would have been for him to say that, when our parents tell us to do what is plainly contrary to the command of God, we must obey God rather than men. But Johnny had not learned this yet. So he said:

"Father, please excuse me from stealing. I'll ask God to send us some wood. Praying's better than stealing. I'm pretty sure God will send it. And if it don't come before I come home from school at noon to-morrow, I will go and work for some, or beg some. I can work, and I can beg, but I can't steal."

Then Johnny crept up into the loft where he slept, and prayed to God about this matter. He said the Lord's prayer, which his teacher had taught him. And after saying—"give us this day our daily bread;" he added—"and please Lord send us some wood too, and let father see that praying is better than stealing—for Jesus' sake. Amen."

And at noon next day when he came home from school, as he turned round the corner, and came in sight of their home, what do you think was the first thing he saw? Why, a load of wood before their door! Yes, there it was. His mother told him the overseers of the poor had sent it. He did not know them. He believed it was God who sent it. And he was right.

The first lesson from Gethsemane is about prayer.

The second lesson from this hallowed spot is— ABOUT SIN.

Here, in Gethsemane, we see Jesus engaged in paying the price of our redemption: this means, what he had to suffer for us before our sins could be pardoned. The pains and sorrows through which Jesus passed, in the agony of the garden, and the death on the cross: the sighs he heaved—the groans he uttered—the tears he shed—the fears, the griefs, the unknown sufferings that he bore—all these were part of the price he had to pay, that we might be saved from our sins.

When we read of all that Jesus endured in Gethsemane: when we hear him say—"my soul is exceeding sorrowful, even unto death:" when we see him fall to the earth, in such an agony that "his sweat was, as it were, great drops of blood falling down to the ground:" we may well ask the question—what was it which caused him all this fearful suffering? And there is only one way of answering this question; and this is by saying *that he was bearing the punishment of our sins.* There was nothing else that could have made him feel so sad and sorrowful. But *this* explains it all. Then, as the prophet says— "He was wounded for our transgressions, he was bruised for our iniquities;—and the Lord had laid on him the iniquity of us all." Is. liii: 5, 6. Our sins had provoked the wrath of God against us, and Jesus was bearing that wrath for us. In all the world, there is nothing that shows so clearly what a fearful thing sin is, as the awful sufferings of Jesus when he was paying the price of our sins, or making atonement for us. And it is by knowing what took place in Gethsemane, and on Calvary, and *only* in this way, that we can learn what a terrible evil sin is, and how we are to be saved from it.

Some years ago, there was a good Christian lady in England who had taken into her family a deaf and dumb boy. She was anxious to teach him the lesson of Gethsemane and Calvary; that Christ had suffered and died for our sins. Signs and pictures were the only means by which she could teach him. So she drew a picture of a great crowd of people, old and young, standing near a deep, wide pit, out of which smoke and flames were issuing, and into which they were in danger of being driven.

Then she drew the figure of one who came down from heaven, representing Jesus, the Son of God. She explained to the boy that when this person came, he asked God not to throw those people into the pit, because he was willing to suffer and to die for them, that the pit might be shut up and the people saved.

The deaf and dumb boy wondered much: and then made signs that the person who offered to die was only one, while the guilty ones who deserved to die were many. He did not understand how God could be willing to take one, in the place of so many. The lady saw the difficulty that was in the boy's mind. Then she took a gold ring off from her finger, and put it down by the side of a great heap of withered leaves, from some faded flowers, and then asked the boy, by signs, which was the more valuable, the one gold ring, or the many withered leaves? The boy took in the idea at once. He clapped his hands with delight, and then by signs exclaimed—"The one—the golden one." And then to show that he knew what this meant, and that the life of Jesus was worth more than the world of sinners for which he died, he ran and got his letters, and spelled the words—"Good! The golden one good!"

The deaf and dumb boy had learned two great lessons that day. For one thing he had learned this lesson about sin which we are trying to learn from Gethsemane. He saw what a dreadful thing sin is, when it was necessary for Jesus to die before it could be pardoned. And then, at the same time, he learned a lesson about Jesus. He saw what a golden, glorious character he is: that he is perfect man, and perfect God. This made his blood *so* precious that the shedding of that blood was a price sufficient to pay for the sins of the whole world.

And now, let us see, for a moment, how much good is done by telling to poor sinners this story of Gethsemane and Calvary, and of the sufferings of Jesus there. Here is an illustration of the power of this story, for which we are indebted to one of the Moravian Missionaries in Greenland.

Kazainak was a robber chief, who lived among "Greenland's icy mountains." He came, one day to a hut, where the missionary was engaged in translating into the language of that country the gospel of St. John. He saw the missionary writing and asked him what he was doing. Pointing to the letters he had just written, he said those marks were words, and that the book from which they were written could speak. Kazainak said he would like to hear what the book had to say. The missionary took up the book, and read from it the story of Christ's crucifixion. When he stopped reading the chief asked:

"What had this man done, that he was put to death? had he robbed any one? or murdered any one? had he done wrong to any one? Why did he die?"

"No," said the missionary. "He had robbed no one; he had murdered no one; he had done no wrong to any one."

"Then, why did he die?"

"Listen," said the missionary. "Jesus had done no wrong; but Kazainak has done wrong. Jesus had robbed no one; but Kazainak has robbed many. Jesus had murdered no one; but Kazainak has murdered his brother; Kazainak has murdered his child. Jesus suffered that Kazainak might not suffer; Jesus died that Kazainak might not die."

"Tell me that again," said the astonished chief. It was told him again, and the end of it was that the hard-hearted, blood-stained murderer became a gentle, loving Christian. He never knew what sin was till he heard of Christ's sufferings for it.

The second lesson we learn from Gethsemane is—the lesson about sin.

The third lesson from Gethsemane is the lesson ABOUT SUBMISSION.

Jesus taught us in the Lord's prayer to say, "Thy will be done on earth, as it is in heaven." And this is one of the most important lessons we ever have to learn. It is very easy to say these words—"Thy will be done;" but it is not so easy to feel them, and to be and do just what they teach. The will of God is always right, and good, and holy. Everything opposed to his will is sinful. St. Paul tells us that—"sin is the transgression of the law." To *transgress* a law, means to walk over it, or to break it. But the law of God is only his will made known. And so, everything that we think, or feel, or say, or do, contrary to the will of God—is sin. And when we remember this it should make us very anxious to learn the lesson of submission to the will of God. If we could all learn to do the will of God as the angels do, it would make our earth like heaven. And this is one reason why Jesus was so earnest in teaching us this lesson. He not only *preached* submission to the will of God, but *practised* it. When he entered Gethsemane, he compared the dreadful sufferings before him to a cup, filled with something very bitter, which he was asked to drink. Now, no person, however good or holy he may be, likes to endure dreadful sufferings. It is natural for us to shrink back from suffering, and to try to get away from it. And this was just the way that Jesus felt. He did not love suffering any more than you or I do. And so, when he prayed the first time in Gethsemane, with those terrible sufferings immediately before him, his prayer was—"Father, if it be possible, let this cup pass from me." But the cup did not pass away. It was held before him still. He saw it was his Father's will for him to drink it. So, when he prayed the second time, his words were—"O, my Father, if this cup may not pass from me, except I drink it: *thy will be done!*" This was the most beautiful example of submission to the will of God the world has ever seen.

When Adam was in the garden of Eden he refused to submit to the will of God. He said, by his conduct, "Not *thy* will, but *mine* be done:" and that brought the curse upon the earth, and filled it with sorrow and death. When Jesus was in the garden of Gethsemane, he submitted to the will of God. He said, "Not *my* will, but *thine* be done." This took away the curse which Adam brought upon the earth, and left a blessing in the place of it—even life, and peace, and salvation.

We ought to learn submission to the will of God, because he knows what is best for us.

"The Curse of the Granted Prayer." A widowed mother had an only child—a darling boy. Her heart was wrapped up in him. At one time he was taken very ill. The doctor thought he would die. She prayed earnestly that his life might be spared. But she did not pray in submission to the will of God. She said she did not want to live unless her child was spared to her. He was spared. But, he grew up to be a selfish, disobedient boy. One day, in a fit of passion, he struck his mother. That almost broke her heart. He became worse and worse; and, at last, in a drunken quarrel, he killed one of his companions. He was taken to prison; was tried—condemned to be hanged—and ended his life on the gallows. That quite broke his mother's heart.

Now God, in his goodness, was going to save that mother from all this bitter sorrow. And would have done so if she had only learned to say—"Thy will be done." She would not say that. The consequence was that she brought on herself all that heart-breaking sorrow.

And then we ought to learn submission to the will of God—*because, whatever he takes away from us—he leaves us so many blessings still!*

Here is a good illustration of this part of our subject. Some years ago, in a town in New England, there was a minister of the gospel who was greatly interested in his work. But he was attacked with bleeding of the lungs and was obliged to stop preaching and resign the charge of his church. About the same time his only child was laid in the grave; his wife, for a time, lost the use of her eyes; his home was broken up, and his prospects were very dark. They had been obliged to sell their furniture and take boarding at a tavern in the town where they lived. But, under all these trials, he was resigned and cheerful. He felt the supporting power of that precious gospel which he had so loved to preach. His wife had not felt as contented and cheerful under their trials as he was.

One day, as he came in from a walk, she said to him: "Husband dear, I have been thinking of our situation here, and have made up my mind to try and be patient and submissive to the will of God."

"Ah," said he, "that's a good resolution. I'm very glad to hear it. Now, let us see what we have to submit to. I will make a list of our trials. Well, in the first place, we have a comfortable home; we'll submit to that. Secondly, we have many of the blessings of life left to us; we'll submit to that. Thirdly, we are spared to each other; we'll submit to that. Fourthly, we have a multitude of kind friends; we'll submit to that. Fifthly, we have a loving God, and Saviour, who has promised to take care of us, and 'make all things work together for our good;' we'll submit to that.

This was a view of their case which his wife had not taken. And so by the time her husband had got through with his fifthly, her heart was filled with gratitude, her eyes with tears, and she exclaimed: "Stop, stop; please stop, my dear husband; and I'll never say another word about submission."

The lesson of submission is the third lesson that we are taught in Gethsemane.

The last lesson for us to learn from this solemn scene in our Saviour's life is a lesson—ABOUT TENDERNESS.

Jesus taught us this when he came back, again and again, from his lonely struggles with the sufferings he was passing through, and found his disciples asleep. It seemed very selfish and unfeeling in them to show no more sympathy with their Master in the time of his greatest need. He had told them how full of sorrow he was, and had asked them to watch with him. Now, we should have supposed that, under such circumstances, they would have found it impossible to sleep. They ought to have been weeping with him in his sorrow, and uniting in prayer to God to help and comfort him. But, instead of this, while he was bearing all the agony and bloody sweat which was caused him by their sins, *they were fast asleep!* If Jesus had rebuked them sharply for their want of feeling, it would not have been surprising. But, he did nothing of the kind. He only asked, in his own quiet, gentle way—"could ye not watch with me one hour?" And then he kindly excused them for their fault, saying—"The spirit indeed is willing, but the flesh is weak!" How tender and loving this was! Here we have the lesson of tenderness that comes to us from Gethsemane. We see here, beautifully illustrated, the gentle, loving spirit of our blessed Saviour. And the exhortation of the apostle, is—"Let *this mind be in you, which was also in Christ Jesus."* Phil. ii: 5.

Someone has well said, that "the rule for us to walk by, if we are true Christians, is, when any one injures us, *to forget one half of it, and forgive the rest."* This is the very spirit of our Master. This was the way in which he acted towards his erring disciples in Gethsemane. And, if all who bear the name of Christ were only trying to follow his example, in this respect, who can tell how much good would be done?

Here are some beautiful illustrations of this lesson of tenderness and forbearance which Jesus taught us in Gethsemane.

"The Influence of This Spirit in a Christian Woman." A parish visitor had a district to attend to which contained some of the worst families in town. There was a sick child in one of those families. The visitor called on her every day. The grandfather of this child was a wicked, hardened man, who hated religion and everything connected with it. He had a big dog that was about as savage as he was himself. Every day, when he saw this Christian woman coming to visit the sick child, he would let loose the dog on her. The dog flew at her, and caught hold of her dress. But she was a brave woman, and stood her ground nobly. A few kind words spoken to the dog took away all his fierceness. She continued her visits, day after day, bringing to the poor child such nice things as she needed. At first the dog was set upon her every day; but as she went on in her kind and gentle way, the old man began to feel ashamed of himself; and before a week was over, when he saw this faithful Christian woman coming to the suffering little one, instead of letting loose the dog upon her, he would take his pipe out of his mouth with one hand and lift the cap from his head with the other, and make a polite bow to her, saying, "Good morning, ma'am: werry glad to see you."

And so the spirit of Christ, as practised by that good woman, won the way for the gospel into that home of sin and misery, and it brought a blessing with it, as it always does.

"The Spirit of Christ in a Little Girl." "Sitting in school one day," says a teacher, "I overheard a conversation between a little girl and her brother. He was complaining of various wrongs that had been done to him by another little boy belonging to the school. His face grew red with anger, and he became very much excited in telling of all that this boy had done to him. He was going on to say how he intended to pay him back, when his sister interrupted him by saying, 'Brother, please don't talk any more in that way. Remember that *Charley has no mother.*'

"Her brother's lips were closed at once. This gentle rebuke from his sister went straight to his heart. He walked quietly away, saying to himself—'I never thought of that.' He remembered his own sweet home and the teaching of his loving mother; and the question came up to him—'What should I be if I had no mother?' He thought how lonely Charley must feel, and how hard it must be for him to do right *without a mother.* This took away all his anger. And he made up his mind to be kind and forbearing to poor Charley, and to try to do him all the good he could. This little girl was following the example of Christ, and we see what a good effect it had upon her brother."

"A Boy with the Spirit of Christ." Two boys —Bob Jones and Ben Christie—were left alone in a country school-house between the morning and afternoon sessions. Contrary to the master's express orders Bob Jones set off some fireworks. When afternoon school began, the master called up the two boys, to find out who had done the mischief.

"Bob, did you set off those fireworks?"

"No, sir," said Bob.

"Did you do it, Ben?" was the next question.

But Ben refused to answer; and so the master flogged him severely for his obstinacy.

At the afternoon recess the boys were alone together. "Ben, why didn't you deny it?" asked his companion.

"Because there were only us two there, and one of us must have lied," said Ben.

"Then why didn't you say I did it?"

"Because you had said you didn't, and I would rather take the flogging than fasten the lie on you."

Bob's heart melted under this. Ben's noble spirit quite overcame him. He felt that he never could allow his companion to lie under the charge of the wrong that he had done.

As soon as the school began again, Bob marched up to the master's desk, and said:

"Please, sir, I can't bear to be a liar. Ben Christie didn't set off these fire-crackers. I did it, and he took the flogging rather than charge me with the lie." And then Bob burst into tears.

The master looked at him in surprise. He thought of the unjust punishment Ben had received, his conscience smote him, and his eyes filled with tears. Taking hold of Bob's hand, they walked to Ben Christie's seat; then the master said aloud:

"Ben, Ben, my lad, Bob and I have done you wrong; we both ask your pardon!"

The school was hushed and still as the grave. You might almost have heard Ben's big-boy tears dropping on his book. But, in a moment, dashing the tears away, he cried out—"Three cheers for the master." They gave three cheers. And then Bob Jones added—"And now three cheers for Ben Christie"—and they made the school-house ring again with three rousing cheers for Ben.

Ben Christie was acting in the spirit of Christ in what he did that day. And in doing so he did good to his companion, Bob Jones. He did good to the master, and to every scholar in the school.

And there is no way in which we can do so much real good to all about us as by trying to catch the spirit and follow the example of our blessed Saviour.

And so, when we think of Jesus in Gethsemane, let us never forget *the facts and the lessons* connected with that sacred place. The facts are too many to be repeated. The lessons are four. There is the lesson about prayer; the lesson about sin; the lesson about submission; and the lesson about tenderness.

And, as we leave this solemn subject, we may each of us say, in the words of the hymn:

> "Can I Gethsemane forget?
> Or there thy conflict see,
> Thine agony and bloody sweat,
> And not remember thee?
>
> "Remember thee, and all thy pains,
> And all thy love to me;
> Yes, while a breath, a pulse remains,
> Will I remember thee.
>
> "And when these failing lips grow dumb,
> And mind, and memory flee,
> When thou shalt in thy kingdom come,
> Jesus, remember me."

THE BETRAYAL AND DESERTION

ONE of the darkest chapters in the history of our Saviour's life is this now before us. Here we see him betrayed into the hands of his enemies by one of his disciples and deserted by all the rest.

In studying this subject, we may look at the history of the betrayal and desertion, and then consider some of the lessons that it teaches.

The man who committed this awful crime was *Judas Iscariot*. He was one of the twelve whom Jesus chose, in the early part of his ministry, to be with him, all the time, to see all the mighty works that he did, and to hear all that he said in private as well as in public. He is called Judas *Iscariot,* to distinguish him from another of the disciples of the same name, viz., Judas, the brother of James. Different explanations have been given of the meaning of this name Iscariot. The most likely is, that it was used to denote the place of his birth. If this be so, then it was written at first, Judas-Ish-Kerioth —which means a man of Kerioth. And then this would show us that he belonged to a town in the southern part of Judah, called Kerioth.

We know nothing about Judas before we hear him spoken of as one of the twelve apostles. In the different lists of the names of the apostles, he is always mentioned last, because of the dreadful sin which he finally committed. When his name is mentioned he is generally spoken of as "the traitor"—or as the man "which also betrayed him." Jesus knew, of course, from the beginning, what kind of a man Judas was, and what he would do in the end. But, we have no reason to suppose that Judas himself had any idea of committing this horrible crime when he first became an apostle; or that the other apostles ever had the least suspicion of him. There can be no doubt that he took part with the other apostles when Jesus sent them before his face to "preach the gospel of the kingdom," and to perform "many mighty works." Yes, Judas, who afterwards betrayed his Master, preached the gospel and performed miracles in the name of Jesus. His fellow-disciples, so far from suspecting any harm of him, made him the treasurer of their little company, and let him "have the bag" and manage their money affairs. And *this*, may have been the very thing that ruined him.

The first time that we see anything wrong in Judas is at the supper given to our Lord at Bethany. We read about this in St. John 12: 1-9. On this occasion, Mary, the sister of Lazarus, brought a very precious box of ointment, and anointed the feet of Jesus with it. Judas thought this ointment was wasted, and asked why it had not been sold for three hundred pence, and given to the poor. This would be about forty-five or fifty dollars of our money. It is added—"This he said, not because he cared for the poor; but because he was a thief, and had the bag, and bore what was put therein." None of his disciples suspected Judas of being a thief at this time. These words were added, long after the death of Judas, when his true character was well known.

But, when Jesus rebuked Judas for finding fault with Mary, and praised her highly for what she had done, he was greatly offended. And then, it seems, he first made up his mind to do that terrible deed which has left so deep and dreadful a stain upon his memory. For we read—St. Matt. xxvi: 14-16—"Then one of the twelve, called Judas Iscariot, went unto the chief priests and said unto them, What will ye give me, and I will deliver him unto you? And they covenanted with him for thirty pieces of silver. And from that time he sought opportunity to betray him." The paltry sum for which Judas agreed to betray his Master was about fifteen dollars of our money—the price of a common slave.

Very soon after this Jesus met his disciples in that upper chamber of Jerusalem, to eat the Passover together for the last time. And Judas came with them. How could the wretched man venture into the presence of Jesus, when he had already agreed to betray him?

But Jesus knew all about it. How startled Judas must have been when he heard Jesus say before them all—"One of you shall betray me." It is probable that Jesus said this to drive Judas out from his presence, for it must have been very painful to him to have him there. And, after Jesus had given the sop to Judas, to show by this that he knew who the traitor was, we read that—"Satan entered into him. Then Jesus said unto him, That thou doest do quickly." Then he "went immediately

The Betrayal and Desertion

out;" and hastened to the chief priests to make arrangements for delivering Jesus unto them.

It is clear, I think, from this that Judas was not present while Jesus was instituting the Lord's Supper. It must have been a wonderful relief to Jesus when Judas left their little company. And we are not surprised to find it written—"When he was gone out Jesus said, Now is the Son of man glorified, and God is glorified in him," St. John xiii: 31. Then followed the Lord's Supper; and the glorious things spoken of in the 14th, 15th, and 16th chapters of St. John, and the great prayer in the 17th chapter. After this came the agony in the garden of Gethsemane.

Just as this was over, Judas appeared with the band of soldiers and servants of the chief priests "with lanterns, and torches, and weapons." Jesus went forth to meet them, and asked whom they were seeking. They answered, "Jesus of Nazareth. Jesus saith unto them, I am he. As soon as he had said unto them I am he, they went backward and fell to the ground." Then Judas came to Jesus according to the signal he had given them, and said, Hail, Master, and kissed him. But Jesus said unto him, Judas, betrayest thou the Son of man with a kiss? Then Peter drew his sword to defend his Master, and struck a servant of the high-priest, and cut off his right ear. Jesus touched the ear, and healed it; and told Peter to put up his sword. Then they came to Jesus and bound him, and led him away to the high-priest; and it is added: *"Then all the disciples forsook him and fled."* He was betrayed by one of his own disciples and forsaken by all the rest.

Nothing is said about Judas during the time of the trial of Jesus. Some suppose that he expected our Lord would deliver himself out of the hands of his enemies. We have no authority for thinking so. But, when he found, at last, that Jesus was condemned and was really to be put to death, his conscience smote him for what he had done. He brought back the thirty pieces of silver—the beggarly price he had received for betraying his Master—and threw them down at the feet of the chief priests, saying—"I have sinned, in that I have betrayed the innocent blood. And they said—What is that to us? See thou to that. And he went and hanged himself."

This was the end of the wretched man, so far as this world is concerned. And such is the history of the betrayal and desertion of Jesus.

We might refer to many lessons taught us by this sad history, but we shall speak of only four. Two of these relate to Jesus, and two of them to Judas.

One of the lessons about Jesus, taught us here, refers to—THE LONELINESS OF HIS SUFFERINGS.

We all know how natural it is, when we are in trouble, to desire to have one near who loves us. The very first thing a child does when worried about anything is to run to its mother and throw itself into her loving arms. It would almost break the child's heart if it could not have its mother's presence and gentle sympathy at such a time.

And it is the same when we grow older. We naturally seek the company of our dearest friends in times of trouble. And it adds greatly to our suffering if we cannot have those we love near us when we are in sorrow. But, in the history of our Saviour's betrayal and desertion, we see how it was with him. In the midst of his great trouble, when the wrath of God, occasioned by our sins, was pressing heavily upon him, he was betrayed into the hands of his enemies by one of the little band of his own chosen followers. How much this must have added to his sorrow! And if the rest of his apostles had only stood by him faithfully, as they had promised to do, during that night of sorrow, it would have been some comfort to him. But they did not. As soon as they saw the traitor Judas deliver him into the hands of his enemies, we read these sad, and melancholy words, "*Then all the disciples forsook him, and fled!*" How hard this must have been for Jesus to bear! The cup of his sorrows was full before; *this* must have made it overflow. He knew it was coming. For, not long before, he had told them that "the hour was coming, when they would be scattered, and *leave him alone.*" This shows how deeply he felt, and feared this loneliness. Seven hundred years before he came into our world, the prophet Isaiah represented him as saying—"I have trodden the wine-press *alone*," chap. lxiii: 3. And this was what he was doing now. In the midst of the multitudes he came to save he was left—alone. There was not an earthly friend to stand by him—to speak a kind word to him—or to show him any sympathy in this time of his greatest sorrow. The only comfort left to him was the thought that his Father in heaven had not forgotten him.

The Betrayal and Desertion

When he spoke of his disciples leaving him alone, he said, "*And yet, I am not alone, because the Father is with me.*" St. John xvi: 32.

Jesus never forgets how lonely he felt at this time; and he loves to come near and comfort us when we are left alone. We should always remember at such times how well able he is to help and comfort us.

Here are some simple illustrations of the blessing which those find who look to Jesus in their loneliness.

An aged Christian was carried to a consumptives' hospital to die. He had no relation or friend to be near him except the nurse and the doctor. Yet he always seemed bright and happy. The doctor, in talking with him one day, asked him how it was that he could be so resigned and cheerful? His reply was—"When I am able to think, I think of Jesus; and when I am not able to think of him, *I know he is thinking of me.*"

And this was just the way King David felt when he said, "I am poor and needy; yet the Lord thinketh upon me."

"Not Alone." Little Bessie was sitting on the piazza. The nurse came in and found her there. "Ah! Bessie dear, all alone in the dark," said the nurse, "and yet not afraid?"

"No, indeed," said little Bessie, "for I am not all alone. God is here. I look up and see the stars, and God seems to be looking down at me with his bright eyes."

"To be sure," said the nurse, "but God is up in the sky, and that is a great way off."

"No," said Bessie; "God is here too; sometimes He seems to be clasping me in his arms, and then I feel so happy."

"The Help of Feeling Jesus Near." There was a poor man in a hospital. He was just about to undergo a painful and dangerous operation. They laid him out ready, and the doctors were about to begin, when he asked them to wait a moment. "What shall we wait for?" was the inquiry of one of the doctors.

"Oh, wait a moment," said he, "till I ask the Lord Jesus Christ to stand by my side. I know it will be dreadful hard to bear; but it will be such a comfort to think that Jesus is near me."

One thing we are taught by the betrayal and desertion of Christ, is the loneliness of his sufferings.

Another thing, taught us by this part of our Saviour's history is—HIS WILLINGNESS TO SUFFER.

We often make up our minds to suffer certain things, because we have no power to help it.

But it was not so with Jesus. He had power enough to have saved himself from suffering, if he had chosen to do so. Sometime before this, when he was speaking to his disciples about his death, or, as he called it, laying down his life, he said—"No man taketh it from me, but I lay it down of myself. *I have power to lay it down, and I have power to take it again.*" John x: 18. And he showed plainly what his power was at the very time of his betrayal. When his enemies came to take him, he "went forth, and said unto them, Whom seek ye? They answered him, Jesus of Nazareth. Jesus saith unto them, I am he." John xviii: 4. But he put such wonderful power into these simple words—"*I am he*"—that, the moment they heard them, the whole multitude, soldiers, servants, and all, fell to the ground before him. It was nothing but the power of Jesus which produced this strange effect. It seems as if Jesus did this, on purpose to show that the mighty power by which he had healed the sick, and raised the dead, and cast out devils, and walked on the water, and controlled the stormy winds and waves, was in him still. He was not taken by his enemies because he had no power to help himself. The same power which made his enemies fall to the ground with a word could have held them there while he walked away; or could have scattered them, as the chaff is scattered by the whirlwind; or could have made the earth open and swallow them up. But he did not choose to exercise it in any of these ways. He was *willing* to suffer for us; and so he allowed himself to be taken.

As the Jews were seizing him Peter drew his sword, and smote one of the servants of the high-priest, and cut off his right ear. Jesus touched the ear, and healed it, in a moment, thus showing again what power he had. Then he told Peter to put up his sword, and said— "Thinkest thou that I cannot now pray to my Father, and he shall presently give me more than twelve legions of angels?" St. Matt. xxvi: 53. A full Roman legion contained six thousand men. Jesus had power enough in his own arm to keep himself from being taken, if he had chosen to use it. And more than seventy thousand angels would have flown with lightning speed to his deliverance, if he had but lifted his finger; or said—"come." There was so much power in himself, and so much power in heaven, at his command, that all the soldiers Rome ever had could not have taken him, unless he had been willing to be taken. But he *was* willing. And when they came to crucify him, all the nails ever made could not have fastened him to the cross, unless he had been willing to be fastened there. But his wonderful love for you and for me and for a world of lost sinners, made him willing to be fastened there, to suffer and to die, that our sins might be pardoned and that we might enter heaven.

And it is the thought of this amazing love of Christ, making him willing to suffer for us, which gives to the story of the cross the marvellous power it has to melt the hardest hearts and win the worst of men to his service. There is a power in love to do what nothing else can do,—to make men good and holy. And this is what we are taught when told that—"Christ suffered for sins, the just for the unjust, that he might bring us to God." I. Peter iii: 18. And when we find people acting in this way towards each other in every-day life it has just the same effect. Here is an illustration of what I mean. We may call it:

"The Power of Love; or, The Just for the Unjust." In a town near Paris, is a school for teaching poor homeless boys who are found wandering about the streets of that city and are growing up in idleness and crime.

When one of the boys breaks the rules of the school and deserves punishment, the rest of the school are called together, like a jury, to decide what shall be done with the offender. One of the punishments is confinement for several days in a dungeon, called "the black-hole." The prisoner is put on a short allowance of food, and, of course, forfeits all the liberties of the other boys.

After the boys have, in this way, passed sentence on one of their companions and the master approves of it, this question is put to the rest of the school:—"Will any of you become this boy's substitute? *i. e.*, take his place, and bear his punishment, and let him go free?" And it generally happens that some little friend of the criminal comes forward and offers to bear the punishment instead of him. Then the only punishment the real offender has to bear is to carry the bread and water to his friend as long as he is confined in the dungeon. In this way, it generally happens that the most stubborn and hard-hearted boys are melted down, by seeing their companions willingly suffering for them what they know they deserved to suffer themselves.

Not long ago, a boy about nine or ten years old, named Pierre, was received into this school. He was a boy whose temper and conduct were so bad that he had been dismissed from several schools. He behaved pretty well at first; but soon his bad temper broke out, and one day he quarrelled with a boy about his own age, named Louis, and stabbed him in the breast with a knife.

Louis was carried bleeding to his bed. His wound was painful, but not dangerous. The boys were assembled, to consult about what was to be done with Pierre. Louis was a great favorite with the boys, and they all agreed at once that Pierre should be turned out of the school and never allowed to come back.

This was a very natural sentence under the circumstances, but the master thought it was not a wise one. He said that if Pierre was turned out of school, he would grow worse and worse, and probably end his life on the gallows. He asked them to think again. They then agreed upon a long imprisonment, without saying how long it was to be. They were asked as usual, if any one was willing to go to prison instead of Pierre. But no one offered and he was marched off to prison.

After some days, when the boys were all together, the master asked again if any one was willing to take Pierre's place. A feeble voice was heard, saying—"I will." To the surprise of every one this proved to be Louis—the wounded boy, who was just getting over the effect of his wound.

Louis went to the dungeon and took the place of the boy who had tried to kill him; while Pierre was set at liberty. For many days he went to the prison carrying the bread and water to Louis, but with a feeling of pride and anger in his heart.

But at last he could bear it no longer. The sight of his kind-hearted, generous friend, still pale and feeble from the effects of his wound, pining in prison—living on bread and water—and willingly suffering all this *for him*—who had tried to murder him—this was more than he could bear. His fierce temper and stubborn pride broke down under it. The generous love of Louis had fairly conquered him. He went to the master, fell down at his feet, and with bitter tears confessed his fault, begged to be forgiven, and promised to be a good boy.

He kept his promise, and became one of the best boys in the school.

And so it is the love of Christ in being willing to suffer for us that wins the hearts and lives of men to him, and gives to the story of the cross all its power.

The willingness of Christ to suffer is the second thing taught us by the history of the betrayal and desertion.

These are the two things taught us about Jesus by this history: his loneliness in suffering, and his willingness to suffer.

But, there are are two things taught us about Judas, also, by this history.

One of these is—THE POWER OF SIN.

The sin of Judas was covetousness, or "the love of money." The apostle Paul tells us that this—"is the root of all evil." I. Tim. vi: 10. The little company of the apostles made Judas their treasurer. He carried the purse for them. He received the money that was contributed for their expenses, and paid out what was needed from day to day. We may suppose that, soon after his appointment to this office, he found himself tempted to take some of this money for his own use. Perhaps he only took a penny or two, at first, but then he soon went on to take more. Now, if he had watched and striven against this temptation, at the very first, and had prayed for strength to resist it, what a different man he might have been! There is an old proverb which says—"*Resist the beginnings.*" Our only safety is in doing this. Judas neglected to resist the beginning of his temptation and the end of it was his ruin. We never can tell what may come out of one sin that is not resisted.

If you want to sink a ship at sea, it is not necessary to make half a dozen big holes in her side; one little hole, which you might stop with your finger, if left alone, will be enough to sink that ship. Judas gave himself up to the power of one sin, and *that* led him on to betray his Master.

Let us look at some illustrations of the power of one sin.

"Clara's Obstinacy." Little Clara Cole was saying her prayers one evening before going to bed. Part of her evening prayer was the simple hymn—"And now I lay me down to sleep." When she came to the last line she stopped short and would not say it. "Go on, my dear, and finish it," said her mother. "I can't," she said, although she knew it perfectly well, and had said it hundreds of times before. "Oh, yes! go right on, my child."

"No; I can't." "My dear child, what makes you talk so? Say the last line directly."

But, in spite of her mother's positive commands and loving entreaties, Clara was obstinate, and would not do it. "Very well," said Mrs. Cole at last: "you can get into bed; but you will not get up till you have said that line."

Next morning Mrs. Cole went into Clara's room as soon as she heard her stir. "Now, Clara," she said pleasantly, "say the line, and jump up."

"I can't say it," said Clara, obstinately, and she actually lay in bed all that day, and part of the next rather than give up. The second day was her birthday and a number of little girls had been invited, in the evening, to her birthday party. That little, strong, cruel will of hers held out till three o'clock; then she said, "I pray the Lord my soul to take," and bursting into tears asked her mother's forgiveness.

How much power there was in that one sin! No one can tell what trouble it might have caused that poor child if she had not been taught to conquer it. But after that it never gave her much trouble.

"One Drop of Evil." "I don't see why you won't let me play with Willie Hunt," said

Walter Kirk, with a frown and a pout. "I know he doesn't always mind his mother. He smokes segars, and once in a while he swears just a little; but I've been brought up better than that; he won't hurt me. I might do him some good."

"Walter," said his mother, "take this glass of pure water, and put just one drop of ink into it."

Walter did so, and then in a moment exclaimed, "Oh! mother, who would have thought that one drop would blacken a whole glass so!"

"Yes, it has changed the color of the whole. And now just put one drop of clear water in it, and see if you can undo what has been done."

"Why, mother, one drop, or a dozen, or fifty won't do that."

"That's so, my son; and that is the reason why I don't want you to play with Willie Hunt. For one drop of his evil ways, like the drop of ink in the glass, may do you harm that never can be undone."

Here we see the power of a single sin.

"One Worm Did It." One day a gentleman in England, went out with a friend who was visiting him, to take a walk in the park. As they were walking along, he drew his friend's attention to a large sycamore tree, withered and dead.

"That fine tree," said he, "was killed by a single worm."

In answer to his friend's inquiries, he said:

"About two years ago, that tree was as healthy as any in the park. One day I was walking out with a friend, as we are walking now, when I noticed a wood-worm about three inches long forcing its way under the bark of the tree. My friend, who knew a great deal about trees, said—'Let that worm alone, and it will kill this tree.' I did not think it possible, and said—'well, we'll let the black worm try, and see what it can do.'"

The worm tunnelled its way under the bark. The next summer the leaves of the tree dropped off, very early. This year the tree has not put out a single green leaf. It is a dead tree. That one worm killed it.

Here we see the power of one sin. The third lesson taught us by the history of the betrayal and desertion, is—the power of sin.

The fourth lesson taught us by this history is— THE GROWTH OF SIN.

Solomon says, "The beginning of strife"—and the same is true of all sin—"is as when one letteth out water." Prov. xvii: 14. There is a bank of earth that keeps the water of a mill-dam in its place. You notice one particular spot where the bank seems weak. The water is beginning to make its way through. At first, it only just trickles down, drop by drop. By and by, the drops come faster. Now, they run into each other, and make a little rill. Every moment the breach grows wider and deeper, till, at last, there is a roaring torrent rushing through that nothing can stop.

Every sin is like a seed. If it be planted in the heart and allowed to spring up, no one can tell what it will grow into. Suppose, that you and I knew nothing about the growth of trees. We are sitting under the wide-spreading branches of a vast oak tree. A friend picks up a tiny, little acorn, and holding it up before us, says—"This giant tree, under whose shade we are sitting, has all grown out of a little acorn, like this." It would seem impossible to us. We could hardly be made to believe it. But we need no argument to prove this. We know it is so.

But the growth of sin in the hearts and lives of men is quite as surprising as the growth of trees in the forest. We see this in the case of

The Betrayal and Desertion

Judas. Suppose that we could have seen him when he first let his love of money lead him to do wrong. Perhaps he only stole a penny or two, at first. That was not much. And then, suppose we had not seen Judas again till the night in which he had made up his mind to commit that greatest and most awful of all sins—the sin of betraying his Master! what a wonderful change we should have seen in him! The growth of a river from a rill—of a giant oak from a tiny acorn—would not be half so surprising as the monstrous growth in wickedness that we should have seen in Judas. When we saw him committing his first sin, he was like a little child. When we saw him committing his last awful sin—the child had sprung up into a huge, horrible giant. Jesus said he had become a devil. St. John vi: 70. How fearful it is to think of such growth in wickedness! And yet, if we allow the seed of sin to be sown in our hearts, and to spring up there, we cannot tell but what its growth may be as fearful in us as it was in Judas.

Let us look at some illustrations of the growth of sin.

"The Growth of Lying." Some time ago a little boy told his first falsehood. It was like a solitary little thistle seed, sown in the mellow soil of his heart. No eye but that of God saw him as he planted it. But, it sprung up—O, how quickly! and, in a little time, another seed dropped from it into the ground, and then another, and another, each in its turn bearing more and more of those troublesome thistles. And now, his heart is like a field of which the weeds have taken entire possession. It is as difficult for him to speak the truth as it is for the gardener to clear his land of the ugly thistles that have once gained a rooting in the soil.

"The Snake and the Spider." A black snake, about a foot long, lay sunning itself on a garden-bed one summer's day. A spider had hung out his web on the branches of a bush, above where the snake lay. He saw the huge monster lying there, for huge indeed he was compared to the little spider, and he concluded to take him prisoner. But, you ask, is not the snake a thousand times stronger than the spider? Certainly he is. Then how can he take him prisoner? Well, let us see how he did it. The spider spun out a fine, slender thread. He slipped down, and touched the snake with it. It stuck. He took another, and touched him with that, and that stuck too. He went on industriously. The snake lay quiet. Another, and another thread, was fastened to him, till there were hundreds and thousands of them. And, by and by, those feeble threads, not one of which was strong enough to hold the smallest fly, when greatly multiplied, were strong enough to make the snake a prisoner. The spider webbed him round and round, till, at last, when the snake tried to move, he found it was impossible. The web had grown strong out of its weakness. By putting one strand here, and another there, and drawing, first on one, and then on another, the spider had the snake bound fast, from head to tail, to be a supply of food for himself and family for a long while.

And so, if we give way even to little sins, they may make us their prisoner as the spider did the snake, and before we are aware of it, we may be bound hand and foot and unable to help ourselves.

"Sin Like a Whirlpool." The Columbia river, in Oregon, has a great bend in it at one place where it passes through a mountain range. When the water in the river is high there is a dangerous whirlpool in this part of the river. An officer connected with the United States Exploring Expedition was going down this river, some years ago, in a boat which was manned by ten Canadians. When they reached this bend in the river, they thought the water was so low that the whirlpool would not be dangerous. So they concluded to go down the river in the boat, as this would save them the labor of carrying the boat with its baggage across the portage to the place where they would take the river again below the rapids. But, the officer was put on shore, to walk across the portage. He had to climb up some high rocks. From the top of these rocks he had a full view of the river beneath and of the boat in her passage. At first, she seemed to skim over the waters like a bird. But, soon he saw they were in trouble. The struggles of the oarsmen and the shouts of the man at the helm showed that there was danger from the whirlpool, when they thought there would be none. He saw the men bend on their oars with all their might. But, in spite of all, the boat lost its straightforward course, and was drawn into the whirl. It swept round and round, with increasing force and swiftness. No effort they could make had the least control of it. A few more turns, each more rapid than the rest, and at last, the centre was reached; and the boat,

THE BETRAYAL AND DESERTION 55

with all her crew, was drawn into the dreadful whirlpool, and disappeared. Only one of the ten bodies was found afterwards, in the river below; and that was all torn and mangled by the rocks, against which it had been dashed.

Just such a whirlpool is sin. Judas was drawn into it when he first gave way to his covetousness and began to steal money from the purse with which he was entrusted. Like the men in the boat, he soon lost all control of himself and was carried round and round, till at last he was "drowned in destruction and perdition."

And thus we have considered the history of the betrayal and the lessons that it teaches. Two of these lessons refer to Jesus. They show us the *loneliness* of his sufferings, and his *willingness* to suffer. Two of them refer to Judas. They show us the *power*, and the *growth* of sin.

There is a beautiful Collect in the Prayer Book which is very suitable to use in connection with such a subject as this. It is the Collect for the Fourth Sunday after Epiphany, and teaches us to pray thus:

"O God, who knowest us to be set in the midst of so many and great dangers, that by reason of the frailty of our nature, we cannot always stand upright; grant to us such strength and protection as may support us in all dangers, and carry us through all temptations, through Jesus Christ, our Lord. Amen."

The blessings asked for in this prayer are just what we need amidst the dangers and temptations that surround us in this evil world. If we only obtain for ourselves "the strength and protection" here prayed for, and which God has promised to give to those who truly seek it, we need not be afraid either of the power or the growth of sin. This strength will be a safeguard to us against the power of sin, and this protection will check the growth of sin in our hearts. It will indeed, "support us in all dangers, and carry us through all temptations." If Judas had used such a prayer as this, and had earnestly sought "the strength and protection" here spoken of, he would never have been known as "the traitor," and the end of his earthly life would never have been wound up with this shameful sentence—"he went and hanged himself." But, as wrecks along the shore show us where the danger lies, so, when we see the wrecks we should try to avoid the rocks on which they struck and go on our way in safety.

I know not how to finish this subject better than for each of us to say, in the words of the hymn:

> "My soul, be on thy guard;
> Ten thousand foes arise;
> And hosts of sins are pressing hard
> To draw thee from the skies.
>
> "O watch, and fight, and pray;
> The battle ne'er give o'er;
> Renew it boldly every day,
> And help divine implore."

THE TRIAL

WE come now to another of the dark and sad chapters in the history of our Saviour's life. We have seen how he was betrayed by one of his disciples, and forsaken by all the rest. Then his enemies seized him, and led him away to those who had sent them—the priests and rulers of the Jewish church. We speak of what then took place at the *trial* of our Saviour. But it was only the form or mockery of a trial. It was not conducted at all in the way in which regular trials were required to be conducted among the Jews. The simple truth is that the enemies of Jesus had made up their minds to put him to death, and they merely pretended to have a trial because they were afraid to do it without.

And in studying this part of the life of our Saviour, we may look, very briefly, at the history of his trial; and then at some of the lessons that it teaches us.

When the band of soldiers and servants had seized Jesus, and made him prisoner, they led him away to the house of Caiaphas the high-priest. He had gathered together the chief-priests and other members of the Jewish high council, called the Sanhedrim. This was the highest court among the Jews. It was composed of seventy, or seventy-two of the oldest, the most learned, and honorable men of the nation. The high-priest was generally the president of this council. Their usual place of meeting was in one of the courts of the temple. But, on special occasions, they met in the house of the high-priest, as they did now. Jesus was brought before this council. Here they tried to bring some charge against him of teaching false doctrines, or of doing something contrary to the laws of their church. But though they had hired many false witnesses against him, the witnesses did not agree in their testimony, and they found it impossible to prove anything wrong against him.

Then the high-priest made a solemn appeal to him, and asked him to say whether he was the Son of God. "Jesus saith unto them—I am.

Hereafter shall the Son of man sit on the right hand of the power of God." Then they said he was guilty of blasphemy, and deserved to be put to death. St. Matt. xxvi: 59-66; St. Mark xiv: 55-64; John xviii: 19-24.

After this, the servants of the priests blindfolded Jesus, and began to mock him, to smite him, to spit on him, and to say all manner of insulting and blasphemous things to him. St. Matt. xxvi: 67, 68; St. Mark xiv: 65; St. Luke xxii: 62-65.

Then the priests and other members of the council seem to have gone home, leaving Jesus to the mockery and insults of the servants. As soon as it was morning the priests and scribes met again. They asked him once more if he were the Christ, the Son of God. Again he declared that he was. Then they arose and led him to Pilate, the Roman governor, to get his consent for them to put him to death. This was necessary because Jerusalem was then under the power of the Romans, and no one but the governor, whom they appointed, had the power of putting a prisoner to death according to law.

But, when the priests brought Christ before Pilate, they changed their plan. They did not accuse him of blasphemy now, because they knew very well that Pilate would not care at all about that. So they pretended that he had been trying to stir up the people in opposition to the Roman government. This was a very serious charge, and one for which, if it could be proved, the punishment would be death.

But, they could not prove their charge. As soon as Pilate looked on Jesus, he seemed to be satisfied that he was an innocent man. Then he took him aside and had a long conversation with him, alone by himself. The result of this was that Pilate was perfectly satisfied of the innocence of Jesus, and was resolved to release him.

But, on returning to the judgment hall and telling the Jews what he wished to do, he found that they would not listen to this for a moment. Thus he was in trouble, and knew not what to do. Just then something was said about Galilee. This was in the northern part of Palestine, and out of the dominion of Pilate. Herod was the governor of Galilee. He happened to be in Jerusalem at that time. Pilate resolved to send his prisoner to him, and hoped in this way, to get rid of any further trouble in connection with him.

So Jesus was sent to Herod—the Herod under whose dominion John was beheaded. He asked him many questions; but Jesus declined to answer one of them. Then Herod, with his men of war, mocked him and sent him back to Pilate, only saying that he found no fault in him. St. Matt. xxvii: 1, 2, 11-14; Mark xv: 1-5; Luke xxiii: 1-12; John xviii: 28-38.

After this Pilate made several attempts to release Jesus; but the Jews were so fierce in their opposition that he was afraid to do it.

Then he thought he saw his way out of the difficulty by the help of a custom that had prevailed in connection with the feast of the Passover, which was then about to be kept. He had been in the habit of allowing the Jews to ask for the release of some prisoner who deserved to be put to death, and of setting him at liberty, when they requested it, while they were keeping the feast. There was a prisoner then in Jerusalem named Barabbas. He had been guilty of murder and other dreadful crimes. Pilate thought that when he should bring Jesus and Barabbas before the people, side by side, and offer to release to them whoever they should choose, they would be sure to ask for the gentle, loving Jesus, in preference to a wretched, blood-stained murderer. And no doubt they would, if they had been left to their own choice. But they were not so left. The priests and scribes had made up their minds that Jesus should be put to death. So they went about among the people, when this offer was made, and persuaded them to cry out—"Not this man, but Barabbas."

Thus Pilate was disappointed again.

While this was going on, his wife sent a message to him saying she had had a dream about this prisoner Jesus, which troubled her greatly. She said he was a just and good man, and begged her husband not to have anything to do with putting him to death. This made Pilate feel still more resolved than ever to let him ago.

Then he told the Jews that Jesus had done no wrong, and he would therefore chastise him and let him go. This made the Jews very furious. They told Pilate that if he let this man go, it would show that he was not a true friend of the emperor, Cæsar. They gave him to understand that they would complain of him to the emperor, and in this way he would be likely to lose his office. This alarmed him so that he could stand out no longer. He let the Jews have their way, and delivered Jesus up to them, to be crucified.

Then the soldiers took Jesus and stripped him of his own clothes, and put a purple robe upon him; and platted a crown of thorns and put it on his head, and bowed the knee before him in shameful mockery, and cried—"Hail! king of the Jews!" Then they smote him with the palms of their hands, and with the reed, and showed their utmost contempt by spitting on him. Then Pilate had him brought forth before the Jews, wearing the crown of thorns, and the purple robe, and pointing to him in scorn, said—"Behold the man! Behold your king!"

"And he delivered him to be crucified." St. Matt. xxvii: 11-30; St. Mark xv: 1-20; St. Luke xxiii: 1-25; St. John xviii: 13-24, 28-40; xix: 1-16.

Such is the history of our Saviour's trial.

And now, we may go on to speak of *five* lessons taught us by this history.

The first lesson is about—THE WEAK RULER.

We refer, of course, here to Pontius Pilate. We know very little about him beyond what we learn from the gospels. He belonged to a highly honorable Roman family. He had been the governor of Judea for several years. He was not a very cruel or oppressive ruler, although he sometimes did hasty and unjust things. Our

Saviour referred to one of these when he spoke of—"the Galileans whose blood Pilate had mingled with their sacrifices." We know none of the particulars of this event. But, from reading the history of our Lord's trial we can see, very well, what sort of a man Pilate was. He was a weak man. I do not mean weak in body, but weak in character. He could see what was right, and was willing to do it, if it could be done without injury to himself.

When Jesus was brought before him as a prisoner, he soon saw that he was an innocent man, and that it would be wrong to put him to death. But, at the same time, he saw that unless he did put him to death, he would give great offence to the Jews. And if he offended them, he was afraid they would complain of him to the emperor, and he would lose his office. And so his fear led him to condemn an innocent man to death, although he knew it was wrong to do so. He tried to get rid of the guilt connected with this act by washing his hands before the Jews, and saying "I am innocent of the blood of this just person: see ye to it." But this was very foolish. Why, all the waters in the ocean could not wash away the stain of the Saviour's blood from the hands of Pilate. He knew that the right thing for him to do was to let Jesus go: but he was afraid to do it. This shows what a weak man he was.

And the wrong that he did on this occasion did not save him from the dangers that he dreaded. The Jews did accuse him to the emperor for some other things. He lost his office in disgrace. And of what happened to him after losing his office, different accounts are given. One of the stories about him is that he retired into Switzerland and spent the rest of his days on a mountain, near the city of Lucerne. This mountain is named Pilatus after him. The story says that he lived a very unhappy life there, and that he finally drowned himself in a lake on the top of that mountain. But the things for us to remember about Pilate are that he was a weak man; that he committed a dreadful sin when he condemned Jesus to death; and that the punishment of his sin which followed him in this life was the loss of his office, and the deep disgrace which it has fastened on his name. Wherever the two great creeds of the church are repeated, all over the earth, we hear it publicly proclaimed that Jesus —"suffered under Pontius Pilate."

We see plainly illustrated in Pilate's case the punishment that followed from his weakness in not doing what he knew to be right. If we have the courage to refuse to do what is wrong, we shall always be rewarded for it.

"Brave Charlie." Two little boys were walking along a village street one day, when they stopped before the garden connected with a gentleman's house and gazed with admiration on the many beautiful flowers that were growing there. Presently the smaller of the two boys exclaimed, "Oh, how I wish I had one or two of those beautiful roses, to take home to my sick sister. Every day she says she wishes she could see some flowers again."

"Then, why don't you take some of them, you little goose," said the other boy. "Here, I am taller than you, and I can reach over the fence. I'll get some for both of us."

"No, no, Tim," said the little boy, seizing his arm; "I wouldn't steal even a flower, if I never had one in the world; but I'll go in and ask the lady for a rose for Ellen."

"Well, you'll only get sent away for your pains," said the older boy; "for my part I shall help myself."

But, just as Tim was reaching over the fence and had seized a branch of beautiful roses, the gardener spied him, and dropping a basket that was in his hand, he rushed after the boy and caught him. He gave him a sound flogging and told him that if he ever found him doing that again, he would have him put in jail as a thief.

In the meantime little Charlie had gone up the steps and rung the door-bell. The door was opened immediately by a kind-looking lady.

"Please, ma'am will you give me a rose or two for my sick sister?" asked Charlie.

"Yes, indeed, my little man," said the lady. "I have been sitting at the window and I heard your conversation with the boy who wished you to steal some of my roses; and I'm very glad to see that you would not steal 'even a flower.' Now come with me, and I will cut you a beautiful bunch of roses." Then she asked him about his mother and sister, and told him to come and get some flowers whenever his sister wanted them.

After this she went to see his sick sister and mother and helped them in many ways. She kept up her interest in Charlie, and when he had done going to school, she got him a nice situation and remained his friend for life.

And when we think of Pontius Pilate, the weak ruler, let us remember that if we do wrong, we must always suffer for it; and that if we do right God will surely reward and bless us.

"Dare to do right! dare to be true!
You have a work that no other can do;
Do it so bravely, so kindly, so well,
Angels will hasten the story to tell.

"Dare to do right! dare to be true!
The failings of others can never save you;
Stand by your conscience, your honor, your faith;
Stand like a hero, and battle till death.

"Dare to do right! dare to be true!
God, who created you, cares for you too—
Treasures the tears which his striving ones shed,
Counts, and protects every hair of your head."

The second lesson that we may learn from the history of Christ's trial is a lesson about—THE WICKED PRIESTS.

If our Saviour had been persecuted and put to death by infidels or by men who did not profess to be religious, it would not have been surprising. But, when we find that it was the priests—men occupying the highest places in the church, and whose business it was to study the Scriptures, and teach them to the people—when *these* were the men most forward in having Jesus put to death—it seems very strange. And yet, it was just so. When Jesus began his ministry, the priests were the first to oppose him. As he went on with the work of his ministry, they were always the most ready to persecute him, and give him trouble. And at the last, it was the priests who resolved he should be put to death and who took the lead in bringing about that awful result. It was the priests who hired Judas to betray him. It was the priests who brought false charges against him. And, when Pilate was willing to let him go, it was the priests who stirred up the people to insist on his being put to death. Jesus had come at the time and in the way that the prophets had said he should come; and yet the priests would not receive him. He had been loving, and gentle, and kind; and yet they hated him. He had spent his life in going about doing good; and yet the priests made up their minds that he must be put to death.

And the question that comes up here is—how was it possible that these men—these priests—should be so wicked? This is a very serious and important question. And the answer to it is this: that being ministers, or priests, or being engaged in the outward duties of religion will do us no good and make us no better than other people, unless we are careful to have our hearts made right in the sight of God; unless we are willing to believe what he tells us, and to think, and feel, and speak, and act, as he wishes us to do. The best things, when spoiled, always become the worst things. Women have many things that help to make them better than men. But a bad woman is always worse than a bad man. Satan was once an archangel. But he sinned. He fell. He is now an angel ruined, and this makes him the worst, the wickedest person to be found in all the universe.

There is one passage of Scripture which explains to us how it was possible for those priests to become so wicked. This passage is found in II. Thess. ii: 11, 12. Here the apostle Paul tells us that if we are not willing to let God be our teacher, and if we do not love the teachings that he gives us, God will let Satan come and deceive us, and lead us to believe what is not the truth. This will make us very wicked; and the end of it will be that our souls will be lost. This explains to us how it was that those Jewish priests became so wicked. They were not willing to let God be their Teacher. They would not receive the things that God had taught about Jesus in the Old Testament. Then Satan came and deceived them. He made them believe what was not true about Jesus. And it was *this* which led to their becoming such wicked men. They were the wickedest men in the world at the time they lived.

And this should make us very careful not to think too much of ourselves or of our own opinions. It should make us willing to believe all that God tells us about Jesus, or about ourselves, in the Bible, whether we understand it or not. This is the only way in which we can become wise, and good, and happy; and be kept from following the example of these wicked priests.

There is only room for one illustration here: "The Two Brothers." Some years ago there lived in the State of Rhode Island two boys who were brothers, twin-brothers. They grew up together. They both had the same home, the same education, and everything about them the same. They were very much alike in size and appearance. They were both bright, intelligent, sensible, good-natured boys. This continued till they were about sixteen years of age. Then one of them read an infidel book— called Paine's Age of Reason. He made up his mind to follow the teachings of that book. The other brother had read the Bible and resolved to take *that* as his guide and teacher through life. And from this time, the two brothers, who had been so much alike before, soon began to be very different from each other. One of them turned around and walked in a wrong way, the other went on in the right way. One of them fell into habits of intemperance, and so was led on to all kinds of wickedness. The other learned the lessons which the Bible teaches, and practised them in his daily life. One of them became an idle, worthless vagabond, while the other became a useful, prosperous, and happy citizen. One of them sank down to the low level of a wretched gambler, while the other rose to occupy a seat in the Legislature of the State in which he lived.

And the end of these two men was that one of them committed murder. He was put in prison; was tried, found guilty, condemned to be hanged, and died upon the gallows. The other lived a long and useful and happy life, and died at last loved and honored by all who knew him.

This is the lesson about the wicked priests.

The next lesson from this history of the trial is about—THE PATIENCE OF CHRIST.

There are many things told us of the life of Christ which are wonderful, but the most wonderful of all is his patience. There are other examples of patience in the Bible, but none that can be compared with the example of Jesus. The apostle James tells us of "the patience of Job." Ch. v: 11. He was indeed very patient. In one day he lost all his property and his children. The messengers that brought him the sad tidings of his losses followed each other, like the waves of the sea. It must have been very hard for him to bear. And if we had been told that he was very much excited and had said some very violent and bitter words on hearing of all that had happened to him, we should not have been at all surprised. But he did nothing of the kind. After hearing of all his terrible losses, he simply bowed himself to the earth, and said—"The Lord gave, and the Lord hath taken away; blessed be the name of the Lord." Job i: 21. Here is a noble example of patience.

Joseph was very patient. When he first saw his brethren, as they came down to Egypt to buy corn, he remembered all the bitter wrongs they had done to him. He was now the governor of all the land of Egypt. They were completely in his power. How easily he could have taken revenge upon them by throwing them all into prison or putting them to death! But there was no such feeling in his heart. He was forgiving and patient. He only thought of doing them good and showing them kindness.

But, all other examples of patience dwindle into nothing when compared to the example of Christ. What a beautiful picture of his patience the prophet Isaiah gives when he thus speaks of him: "He was oppressed and he was afflicted, yet he opened not his mouth; he is brought as a lamb to the slaughter, and as a sheep before her shearers is dumb, so he opened not his mouth." Is. liii: 7. He let his enemies say all manner of evil things against him falsely; he let them mock him,—and smite him on the face,—and spit upon him. Yes, he whom the angels of heaven had been accustomed to honor and worship, as they bowed in reverence before him, allowed himself to be so shamefully treated by sinful worms of the dust, by the very men he had come down from heaven to save; and yet, he never spoke one cross or angry word to them! How wonderful this was! How amazed the angels must have been when they saw it!

Oh! what an example of patience we have in Jesus! And if we call ourselves the friends and followers of Christ, let us try to have the same mind in us that was in him, by imitating the example of his patience. There is no way in which we can do so much good to others, and make them think well of the religion of Christ, as by trying to practise the same patience which he practised.

"How to Learn Patience." A good many years ago there was a celebrated physician in Germany, named Boerhave. He was famous for his learning and also for his piety. He had learned well this lesson of patience. One day he had been greatly provoked, but without getting angry in the least. A friend who had witnessed it, asked him if he knew what it was to be angry. "O, yes," said he, "my temper was naturally very violent and passionate."

"Then, pray tell me," said his friend, "how you ever learned to be so patient." Now mark what that great and good man said in answer to this inquiry.

"I learned to be patient," was his reply, "by doing two things; one was by thinking of Christ; the other was by asking him to help me."

We may all learn patience in this way.

"A Soldier's Example of Patience." Some years ago an English missionary in India baptized a soldier. This man had been a famous prize-fighter in England. He was a powerful, lion-looking, lion-hearted man. With a single blow he could level the strongest man to the ground. The men in his regiment were all afraid of him. He had not been in the habit of going to church, but, as he afterwards told the missionary, "he sauntered into the chapel one evening, hardly knowing where he was going." What he heard that night led him to repentance and he became a Christian. The change which took place in his temper and conduct was very surprising. The lion was changed into a lamb. A month or so after this, when they were dining in the mess-room one day, some of his comrades, who had always been afraid of him, began to ridicule him on account of his religion. One of them said, "I'll find out whether he is a real Christian or not;" and taking a bowl of hot soup, he threw it into his breast. The whole company were alarmed at this. They looked on in speechless silence, expecting to see the roused lion leap up, and spring in fury on his foe. But he quietly opened his waistcoat, and wiped his scalded breast.

Then turning calmly round he said, "This is what I must expect. If I become a Christian, I must suffer persecution. But my Saviour was patient, and I want to be like him." His comrades were filled with astonishment. But they were satisfied he was a true Christian and he had no more trouble from them. The patience of Christ is the third lesson for us to learn from his trial.

The fourth lesson taught us by this subject is— THE HUMILIATION OF CHRIST.

If we desired to put the whole history of the life of our blessed Saviour into a single sentence, I do not think we could find a better one than that which the apostle Paul uses when he says of him that—"*He humbled himself.*" Phil. ii: 8. Before he came into our world he was "in the form of God, and thought it not robbery to be equal with God." This means that he was God. Now if he had chosen to become an angel, holy, and pure, and good, he would have had to humble himself very much, even for that. But, instead of becoming an angel, he became a man. And, in becoming a man, he took our nature upon him in its fallen state. He was made like us in all points, except sin. How he humbled himself here! And, in coming into our world, if he had chosen to come as one of the richest men in it,—as a great king or emperor—that would have been an act of great humiliation. But he came as a poor man. He was one of the poorest men that ever lived on the earth. He had made the world, and was the owner of all its treasures, and yet he could say of himself with truth—"The foxes have holes, and the birds of the air have nests, but the Son of man hath not where to lay his head." What humiliation there was here! We see his humiliation in the poverty and suffering that he endured. His whole life was an act of humiliation. But how greatly this humiliation was increased during the time of his trial! Think how his back was torn by the cruel scourges! What humiliation was there! Think how he was mocked, and insulted! Think how the soldiers put an old purple robe upon him: how they platted a crown of thorns, and put it upon his head; how they put a reed in his hand in mockery for a sceptre: how they bowed the knee before him in scorn, and cried—"Hail! king of the Jews!" How wonderful this was O, never let us forget the humiliation of Christ! And when we think of all this—how can we, as Christians, ever feel proud? Our great duty is, as the apostle says, to be "clothed with humility." No wonder that Augustine, one of the old fathers of the early church, when asked—"What is the first thing for a Christian to learn?" should have said—"humility." "What is the second?"—"humility." "And what is the third?" should still have said—"humility."

"Examples of Humility." A converted South Sea Islander was helping to translate the New Testament into his native language. On coming to the passage, "Behold what manner of love the Father hath bestowed upon us, that we should be called the sons of God;" I. John iii: 1, he hastened to Mr. Williams, the missionary and said, "No, no, this is too much, too much! let us say—'Now are we allowed to kiss God's feet.'" That man was clothed with humility.

A pious nobleman in England was in the habit of attending a prayer meeting in the country village where he lived, and where a few of the poor people of the neighborhood were accustomed to assemble on a week-day evening. When he first came in they were surprised to see him, and they all rose up at once to offer him the best seat in the room. This troubled him greatly. He gently said to them, "Please take your seats my friends, and have the kindness not to do this again. When I go to the 'House of Lords,' I go as one of the lords of the realm. But when I come to this cottage prayer meeting, *I come simply as a disciple of Jesus among my fellow disciples,* and must be allowed to take any seat that may be empty." That nobleman was clothed with humility.

"The Humble King." A French monarch was found one day by some of his attendants engaged in instructing out of the Bible a boy belonging to his cook.

They said it was beneath his dignity as the King of France to be engaged in teaching the child of his cook. His answer was a noble one. "My friends," said he, "this boy has *a soul that is as precious as mine, and it was bought with the same precious blood.* If it was not beneath the dignity of my Saviour, the King of heaven, to die for him, it is not beneath my dignity as king of France to tell him what has been done for his salvation."

That king was clothed with humility. The humiliation of Christ is the fourth lesson taught us by this trial.

The last lesson we learn from the history of the trial is about—THE GLORY OF CHRIST.

Perhaps some may think it strange to speak of the glory of Christ in connection with this part of his history. Here we see him betrayed, and deserted by his own disciples. He is delivered into the hands of his enemies. They pretend to try him. But it is only the form of a trial through which he is made to pass. He is charged with great crimes. These cannot be proved against him. But still he is condemned to the most disgraceful of all deaths. He is handed to the soldiers to do what they please with him. And is it right to speak of the *glory* of Christ in connection with such scenes as these? Yes. For this was just what Jesus did himself. It was, as he was about to enter on all this humiliation and suffering, when Judas went out from his presence to betray him, that Jesus said:—"*Now* is the Son of man glorified." Thus he himself connected the thought of his glory with these very scenes. And surely he was not mistaken. He knew what he was saying.

Now just think what it is in which true glory consists. It is not in wearing fine clothes. It is not in occupying high positions. It is not in having people say fine and flattering things about us. No; but it is in thinking, and feeling, and saying, and doing, and suffering that which is right and according to the will of God. And *this* is just the position that Jesus was occupying during his trial. He was fulfilling the will of God in things that were the hardest of all for him to do and to suffer. And *that* was what made him glorious.

If we were asked to point to that part of our Saviour's life in which he appears to us in the greatest glory, there would probably be considerable difference of opinion among us. Some of us, no doubt, would point to his transfiguration; some to the times when he walked upon the water, or controlled the winds and the waves with his word; and others would point to the times when he healed the sick, or raised the dead, and cast out devils. But it was not so. No; but it was when he was betrayed and forsaken—when he was condemned to death, and mocked, and insulted by his enemies that Jesus appeared most glorious: for it was then that he was showing, in the strongest possible light, his desire to do his Father's will and the greatness of his love for the people he came to save. It is not clothing, but character that makes us great or glorious. And the more we try to be like Jesus, in doing the will of God as he did it, in this part of his life, the greater will be the glory belonging to us.

"The True Hero." A number of boys were playing after school one day. The playground was on the bank of a river. One of the biggest boys was named Tom Price. He was the strongest boy in the school. He loved to get up quarrels among the boys to show how easily he could whip any of them. But there was one boy in the school who never would fight. His name was Joe Wilson. He was not so big or so strong as Tom Price. But it was not this which made him unwilling to fight. He was trying to be a Christian. He knew it was wrong to fight, and so he always refused to do it.

One day Tom Price agreed with some of the other boys to try and force a fight on Joe Wilson. So while they were playing after school, Tom knocked Joe's cap off his head, and it fell into the river.

"Tom threw your cap over on purpose, Joe," said one of the boys; "fight him for it."

"Yes, give it to him, Wilson," said the other boys, "we'll see that you have fair play."

Price squared off and stood in a fighting position. "I won't fight," said Wilson. "I'm sorry you threw the cap over Price; for it was all but new, and I don't see any fun in such mischief. But, I'm not going to fight about it."

"Come on, if you dare," said Price, shaking his fist at him. All the boys gathered round and urged Wilson to "go on, and give it to him."

"No, I don't think it right to fight," said Wilson, "and I won't do it."

"Coward! coward! he's afraid," cried the boys. "I am not a coward," said Wilson; "I dare do anything that's right. But this is not right, and I wont do it."

"Go home, coward! go home, coward!" shouted the boys after him, as he turned to go home.

He had not gone far before there was a sound of a heavy splash. "He's in! He'll drown!—he can't swim! Price is drowning," cried the boys as they stood on the edge of the bank.

Joe Wilson heard these shouts and ran to the bank of the river. He saw Price struggling in the stream. The other boys were running about and shouting, but they were afraid to go in. In a moment Joe Wilson threw off his jacket, stepped back a few paces—ran—and jumped into the river. He swam out to Price —caught him by the hair of his head, and managed, though with great difficulty and at the risk of his own life, to bring him safely to the shore. Wilson walked quietly home, not only to change his wet clothes, but also to avoid the praise of those who but a moment ago were calling him a coward.

An old gentleman was standing there who had witnessed this whole scene. As soon as Wilson was gone, he called the boys to him and said: "Boys! learn a lesson from what has just taken place. Don't mistake a hero for a coward next time. The boy who is afraid to do what he knows to be wrong in God's sight, is the true hero. He is not afraid of anything else; not afraid of man—of danger—or of death."

The point of greatest glory in Joe Wilson's conduct that day was not when he bravely plunged into the river. No; but it was when he nobly stood his ground among his companions, and said "I think it wrong to fight; and I won't do it."

And so, even amidst the sorrowful scenes of our Saviour's trials, we see his glory shining out in the way in which he did and suffered what was according to the will of God.

And from this study of the trial of our Saviour, let us carry away with us the five lessons of which we have spoken.

These are the lesson about the weak ruler:—the wicked priests:—the patience—the humiliation—and the glory of Christ.

THE CRUCIFIXION

WE read in St. Matthew's gospel these three simple, but solemn words: *"They crucified him."* Chap. xxvii: 35. Here we have set before us the greatest event in the history of our Saviour while he was on earth. They tell us of the most important event that ever took place in our own world, or in any other world. We have no reason to suppose that Jesus ever took upon himself the nature of any other race of creatures, as he did take our nature. We have no reason to suppose that he ever died, in any other world, as he died in ours. How wonderful this makes the thought of his crucifixion! And how diligently we should study it, and try to understand what it was intended to teach! This is what we come now to do. And in doing this, the two great things for us chiefly to consider, are—*The history of the Crucifixion; and its Lessons.*

And in looking at this history the first thing for us to notice is—*the place of the crucifixion.*

In speaking of this place, St. Matt. xxvii: 33, says it was—"a place called Golgotha, that is to say a place of a skull." St. Luke xxiii: 33, says it was a place "called Calvary." Golgotha is a Hebrew word, and Calvary is a Latin word; but they both mean the same thing, namely a skull, or the place of a skull. Some have thought that this name was given to it because it was the spot where public execution took place and criminals were buried. But there is no proof of this. It is often spoken of as "the *hill* of Calvary": but it is never so called in the New Testament. It is supposed to have received its name from the fact of its being a smooth and rounded piece of ground, resembling somewhat the shape of a skull, and looking like what we call the brow of a hill. Exactly where this place was we cannot tell. In the Church of the Holy Sepulchre at Jerusalem they show a hole in a rock, which they pretend to say was the very hole in which the cross of Jesus was placed. But it is impossible to prove this. And the thought which shows how unlikely this is to be the Calvary where Jesus died is this, that Jesus died *outside* the walls of

Jerusalem, but this is *inside* the walls, and we know that the city at that time was much larger than the present city. The apostle Paul tells us that "Jesus suffered *without the gate.*" Heb. xiii: 13. We are sure then that Calvary, or Golgotha, the place of the crucifixion, was outside the walls of Jerusalem, but nigh unto the city. This is all that we can find about it with any certainty.

The *time of the crucifixion* is the next thing to consider. It was on Friday of the last week of his earthly life. What is called "Good Friday," in the week before Easter, known as Passion Week, is kept by a large part of the Christian Church in memory of this event.

As to the hour of the day when the crucifixion took place, there is some difference in the statements made by the different evangelists. St. Matthew says nothing about the hour when Jesus was crucified. He only says that during the time of the crucifixion, "from the sixth hour there was darkness over all the land unto the ninth hour." St. Matt. xxvii: 45. This means from twelve o'clock at noon, till three o'clock in the afternoon. St. Luke and St. John both say that it was—"*about* the sixth hour," when this great event took place. But it is clear from their way of speaking of it, that they did not wish to be understood as stating the time very exactly. St. Mark says—ch. xv: 25, "And it was the third hour, and they crucified him." There seems to be a disagreement between these statements. But it is easy enough to reconcile the difference. There are two ways of doing this. One is by supposing that when St. Mark says: "It was the third hour, and they crucified him," he was speaking of the time when they began to make preparations for the crucifixion, while St. Luke and St. John refer to the time when the preparations were all finished, and the crucifixion had actually taken place.

But there is another way of reconciling this apparent difference. The Jews were accustomed to divide their day into four parts, corresponding with the four watches into which the night was divided. Beginning at six o'clock in the morning, which was the time when their day commenced, they sometimes called the first three hours, from six to nine o'clock, the first hour. The next three hours, from nine to twelve o'clock, they called the second hour; and then, according to this way of reckoning, the three hours following, from twelve to three o'clock, would be the third hour. And if *this* was the way in which St. Mark was speaking, then his *third* hour would agree exactly with the sixth hour mentioned by St. Luke and St. John. And so, when we think of the time of the crucifixion, we may remember that Jesus hung upon the cross, in dreadful agonies, from "about" twelve o'clock at noonday until three in the afternoon. O, how long and painful those hours must have seemed to him!

The next thing to notice is—*the manner of the crucifixion*. Suppose that you and I had been standing on Calvary at the time of our Saviour's death: what should we have seen? Why, lying there on the ground, we should have seen the great wooden cross, on which Jesus was to suffer. It is made of two pieces. There is one long, upright piece of timber, and a shorter one fastened across this upright beam, at the upper end. There is Jesus standing by— bound, and bleeding, and crowned with thorns. The soldiers take him and lay his body on the cross, with his back towards it. They stretch out his arms to their full length, along the upper beam of the cross. They take heavy hammers and drive great rough nails through the palms of his hands, and through the tender part of his feet. How terrible the suffering caused by every blow of those hammers! And see, when this is done, the soldiers raise up the cross, and place the lower end of it in a hole they had prepared for it. It comes down with a jar. What terrible tortures that jar sends through every part of the suffering Saviour's frame! About the middle of the cross is a projecting piece of wood, to form a sort of seat, so as to prevent the whole weight of the body from hanging from the nails, and tearing the flesh of the hands and feet. And there the Son of God is left to suffer tortures that cannot be expressed, till death shall come and bring relief.

The witnesses of the crucifixion is the next thing of which to speak.

Near the cross was his mother and the good women who were her companions. John is the only one of the apostles found near the cross at the time when their Lord was crucified. The soldiers and the priests were there. The walls of Jerusalem were, no doubt, lined with people looking anxiously on; and crowds of strangers were standing by, beholding this sad event; for Jerusalem was always full of persons from a distance at that season who came to keep the feast of the Passover. And then, if our eyes had been opened, as the eyes of Elisha's servant were, (II. Kings vi: 17), so that we could have seen as spirits do, we should have beheld multitudes of angels among the spectators of the crucifixion. We should have seen them hovering over the cross and gazing with wonder on the sight that met their view there—the Son of God—hanging on the cross in agonies and blood!

The wonders attending the crucifixion is another thing to notice. There was the darkness over all the land from the sixth to the ninth hour, or from twelve to three o'clock. This was not a natural darkness caused by an eclipse of the sun, for the Jewish Passover was held at the time of the full moon, and it is impossible to have an eclipse then. No; it was a miraculous darkness. The sun hid his face, as if he was ashamed to look on and see

> "When God, the Mighty Maker died,
> For man, the creature's sin."

And then there was an earthquake. The great globe itself seemed to tremble at the thought of the dreadful deed that was taking place on its surface. The solid rocks were rent in pieces. The graves were opened, and many of the dead buried in them rose, and came back to life. And then, at the same time, the vail of the temple—that thick, strong vail—which hung between the holy place and the most holy place, without any one touching it, was rent in twain from the top to the bottom. This was done by miracle. If you and I had been there, with our eyes opened, as I said a little while ago, we should probably have seen two mighty angels, taking hold of that vail and rending it. These were the wonders that attended the crucifixion.

And then there are *the words spoken by Jesus on the cross*, to notice. Seven times the blessed Lord opened his mouth and spoke as he hung amidst the torturing agonies of the cross. The first time he spoke there, was to pray for his murderers. St. Luke xxiii: 34. Then he spoke to his disciple John, who was standing near the cross, and asked him to take care of his mother. St. John xix: 25-27. Then he answered the prayer of the dying thief, and told him he should be with him in paradise that day. St. Luke xxiii: 39-43. Then he said—"I thirst." St. John xix: 28. Then came the awful cry which he uttered when his Father in heaven forsook him and left him alone. St. Matt. xxvii: 46. Then he said—"It is finished!" St. John xix: 30. Then he "cried with a loud voice," and said—"Father, into thy hands I commend my spirit." St. Luke xxiii: 46. And then he meekly bowed his head and died.

Such is the history of the crucifixion—the most solemn, the most awful, the most important event that ever took place since the world was made.

A great many very valuable lessons are taught us by the history of the crucifixion. We can speak of only five.

The first lesson taught us by the crucifixion is—*the lesson of forgiveness.*

It was probably while the Roman soldiers were driving the rough nails through his tender hands and feet, or just after the cross was set up in its place, that Jesus taught us this lesson. He looked on his murderers with a pitying eye. If he had asked God to punish them, as they deserved for their cruelty, or if he had spoken to them ever so severely, it would not have been surprising. But though they were causing him so much suffering, when he had done them no harm, still there was not one angry feeling in his heart towards them, and not one unkind word fell from his lips. Instead of this, he lifted up his eyes to heaven, and offered the prayer—"*Father, forgive them; for they know not what they do.*" Here we have the most perfect pattern of forgiveness the world has ever known. If we wish to be true followers of Jesus, we must try to be like him in this respect. We must learn well this lesson of forgiveness.

"Examples of Forgiveness." Dr. Duff, the late excellent missionary to India, once read our Saviour's sermon on the mount to some Hindoo young men whom he was teaching. As he read on he came to the passage in which Jesus says, "I say unto you love your enemies, bless them that persecute you, and pray for them that despitefully use you, and persecute you." One of the young men was so impressed by our Saviour's words that he exclaimed, with great earnestness, "O how beautiful! how divine! this is the truth!" And for days and weeks afterwards he would exclaim, from time to time, "*Love your enemies!* who ever heard such teaching? How beautiful this is! This is heavenly teaching!"

"A Forgiving Boy." "Mamma," said little Charley, "now I've got a new sled, what shall I do with my old one?" Presently he added, "Mamma, there's a chance to do something real good."

"What is it, Charley?"

"Why, you see, mamma, if there's any boy I hate, it's Tim Tyson. He's always plaguing and teasing me and all the other little boys. It never does any good to get cross, for that is just what he likes: but then Tim likes sledding very much and he has no sled. I've a notion to give the old sled to him. It will show him that I forgive him. It might make him think, and do him good. Mightn't it?" "Yes, it might," said the mother.

So Tim got Charley's sled. The kind, forgiving spirit of the little boy he had teased so much touched him greatly. It made him think. It did him good. After that Tim never teased Charley again, or any of the other little boys.

"How a Bishop Taught Forgiveness." There was once a good bishop who lived at Alexandria in Egypt. One day a nobleman came to see him. He told the bishop about a person who had done him a great wrong. He got very angry about it. "I never will forgive him," said he, "as long as I live."

Just then the bell tinkled for prayers in the bishop's private chapel. He rose to go into the chapel and asked the nobleman to follow him. The bishop kneeled at the railing of the little chancel. He asked his friend to repeat the

Lord's prayer after him, sentence by sentence. This was done till they came to the sentence "Forgive us our trespasses, as we forgive those who trespass against us." When the bishop had offered this prayer he waited for the nobleman to say it after him, but he was silent. He said it again but there was no answer. Then the bishop was silent and gave his friend time to think. Presently the nobleman rose to his feet and said:

"I dare not offer that prayer, while I feel as I now do. It would be asking God never to forgive me. I must forgive if I expect to be forgiven."

Then he left the chapel, sought out the person who had injured him, and told him that he freely forgave him. After this he went back and finished his prayer with the good bishop.

The lesson of forgiveness, is one lesson taught us by the crucifixion of our Saviour.

The second lesson we are here taught is—*the lesson of duty to our parents.*

When we think of Jesus hanging on the cross and bearing all the dreadful pains of crucifixion, it seems to us that he must have been so fully occupied with his own terrible sufferings as to have had no thought or feeling for any one but himself. But it was not so. He did not forget his duty to his mother even then. He saw her standing by his cross weeping. Joseph, her husband, was no doubt dead. She would have no one now to take care of her. John, the disciple whom Jesus loved, was standing near his mother. Jesus looked at his mother, and told her to consider John as her own son. Then he looked at John, and turning his eye to the weeping Mary, he told John to treat her as his own mother. And from that time John took the mother of Jesus to his own home and took care of her, as if she had been his own mother. How thoughtful and tender this was in Jesus! How much it was like the loving Saviour! And how touchingly we may learn from this crucifixion scene the lesson of our duty to our parents, and especially to our mothers! No child can ever fully repay a faithful, loving mother for all that she has done. Let us try to follow the example which Jesus set us from the cross about our duty to our parents.

Let us look at some examples of those who have learned and practised this lesson.

"The Polish Prince." Here is a story of a Polish prince who had a very good father. This young man was in the habit of carrying the picture of his father in his bosom. And when he was tempted to do anything that was wrong, he would take out this picture and look at it, saying, "Let me do nothing that would grieve my good father."

"Ashamed to Tell Mother." Some boys were playing one day after school. Among them was a little fellow whom his companions were trying to tempt to do something wrong. "I can't do it," said he, "because I should be ashamed to tell mother of it."

"Well, but you needn't tell her; and she won't know anything about it."

"But I should know all about it myself, and I'd feel mighty mean if I wouldn't tell mother!"

The boys laughed at him and said: "The idea of a boy running and telling his mother every little thing! What a pity you weren't a girl!"

"You may laugh about it as much as you please," said the noble little fellow, "but I've made up my mind never, as long as I live, to do anything I would be ashamed to tell my mother." That boy was a hero. He was doing just what Jesus would have done in his place. Many a boy would have been saved from ruin if he had only acted in this way.

"Honoring His Mother." "Is there a vacant place in this bank, which I could fill?" asked a boy with a glowing face, as he stood, with cap in hand, before the president of the bank.

"There is none," was the reply. "Were you told that we wanted a boy? Who recommended you?"

"No one recommended me, sir," calmly said the boy. "I only thought I would see."

There was an honesty and manliness about the lad which pleased the president and led him to continue the conversation.

"You must have friends who could help you in getting a situation; have you told them?"

With a saddened feeling, the boy said: "My mother told me it would be useless to try without friends," then apologizing for the interruption, he turned to go away; but the gentleman detained him, saying: "Why don't you stay at school a year or two longer, my young friend, and then try to get a situation?"

"I have no time for school," was his reply. "I study at home, and keep up with the other boys as well as I can."

"Then you have had a place already," said the officer, "why did you leave it?"

"I have not left it, sir," quietly answered the boy.

"But you wish to leave it. What is the matter?"

The boy was confounded for a moment—but presently said—"I want to do more for mother, sir."

These brave words of the boy touched the gentleman's heart. And grasping the hand of the little fellow he said:—"My boy, what is your name? and where do you live? You shall have the first vacancy, for a boy, that occurs in the bank. And in the meantime if you need a friend, come to me. But now tell me frankly, why do you wish to do more for your mother? Have you no father?"

The boy's eyes filled with tears. He had to make an effort before he could speak. But recovering himself directly he said:

"My father is dead: my brothers and sisters are dead. My mother and I are left alone to help each other. But she is not strong, and I wish to do all I can for her. It will please her, sir, that you have been so kind to me, and I am very much obliged to you." And then leaving his name and residence with the gentleman, he made a bow and retired.

It was not long before the president of that bank called to see this boy and his mother. He cheered their hearts by telling them that he had a situation for the boy, who found a warm friend in him as long as he lived. God's blessing followed that boy, and he rose to occupy an important position in the bank. And God's blessing will always follow those who learn and practise the lesson Jesus taught us on the cross—of honoring our parents.

The third lesson we may learn from the crucifixion is about—*the power and willingness of Jesus to save.*

This lesson is taught us by what took place between Jesus and the dying thief, as they each hung upon the cross. Jesus was crucified between two thieves. One of them cast reproaches upon Jesus, as he hung by his side. The other rebuked his fellow thief; and then, turning his eyes towards Jesus, said—"Lord, remember me when thou comest into thy kingdom." Jesus at once heard and accepted his prayer, and told the thief that he should be with him in paradise that day. This was one of the most wonderful things that took place in connection with the crucifixion of our Saviour. There were many wonders in it. It was wonderful that this dying thief should have understood so clearly as he did the true character of Jesus. It was wonderful that he should have had faith to trust the salvation of his soul to one who was dying what seemed to be a criminal's death. It was wonderful that he should have repented truly of his sins, and have prayed earnestly, as he did, while hanging on the cross. It was wonderful that Jesus was able and willing to pardon him, to change his heart, and make him fit for heaven at the last hour of his life. And it was wonderful that Jesus was so ready to help and save another at the very time when he was suffering so much himself. The apostle Paul tells us that "he is able to save unto the *uttermost*, those who come unto God through him." Heb. vii: 25. There could not be a more striking illustration of the power and willingness of Jesus to save sinners than we have here in the case of the dying thief.

But illustrations of the same kind, though not so striking as this, do often occur.

"The Cleansing Fountain." There was once a man who had been a very great sinner. He had long been in the habit of committing all sorts of wickedness. But at last he grew weary of his evil ways, and wanted to become a Christian.

But he thought his sins were too great to be forgiven. A Christian man talked and prayed with him. To encourage him he repeated the first verse of the hymn, which says:

> "There is a fountain filled with blood
> Drawn from Immanuel's veins;
> And sinners plunged beneath that flood
> Lose all their guilty stains."

But the poor man shook his head, and said, "There's nothing in that for me. My sins are too great to be washed away." Then his friend repeated the second verse:

> "The dying thief rejoiced to see
> That fountain in his day;
> And there may I, though vile as he
> Wash all my sins away."

"That means *me*," said the penitent sinner. He was encouraged to pray to Jesus, and he found that he was able and willing to save him.

"Muckle Bess—A Hopeless Case." This was the name of a woman who lived in Scotland many years ago. Her history illustrates very well the point now before us, and shows the power and willingness of Christ to save. She was the daughter of a good, pious farmer. But she was led into evil company. She left her father's house, and became a most wicked and abandoned woman. She was a terror to every one, even to the wicked people among whom she had gone to live. At last she left them and spent her time in wandering among the highlands, living like a wild beast, stealing what she could get to eat, or to wear, and sleeping in barns or stables, in sheepfolds, or in the dens and caves of the mountains. She used to roam over the country begging, or stealing, cursing and swearing, and doing all sorts of wicked things. Everybody was afraid of her. No one thought of speaking to her, or even of praying for her; and every one looked upon her case as hopeless.

At one time, when Muckle Bess had passed middle life, there was a great religious interest among the churches in that part of the country.

On one Sabbath day they were holding services in the open air. A great crowd of people had gathered round the minister. To the surprise of every one, who should appear, at the outside of the crowd, but poor Bess. Ragged, and wild-looking, she seemed just like the witch of Endor. The women trembled at the sight of her, and the men thought she had only come for mischief. But she sat quietly down on the grass and listened to the preaching. It led her to think of her wicked life, and filled her heart with anguish. Presently she rose to her feet, stretched out her brawny arms, and cried in tones of agony that melted the hearts of all who heard her, "Oh, thou God o' my fathers; oh, thou God o' bonnie Scotland, that has been steeped in blood for thy name's sake; look on me a wretched sinner, who has scorned thee, and robbed thee, and defied thee! Hast thou na' promised cleansin' to them whose sins are scarlet and crimson? And whose sins are o' deeper dye than mine? God, be merciful to me a sinner!" And then she sank sobbing to the earth.

The stillness of death was over that congregation. The minister paused till poor Bess's sobs were no longer heard. Then he went on with the sermon. He spoke of the love of Christ in being willing to suffer and die for us. He told of his power and readiness to pardon and save all who truly turn to him, and referred to the case of the dying thief to prove the truth of what he said. This touched the heart of poor Bess, and led her to feel that there might be hope, even for her. Then she rose to her feet again, and cried, "Hear me, ye people o' God! Hear me, ye angels above! Hear me, ye powers o' evil, while I vow afore ye all, that I will e'en tak' him at his word, and leave it there!"

From that time Muckle Bess became a changed woman. She went back to her father's house to live. But she occupied her time in going from house to house, to tell the story of Jesus and his love. And the rest of her life she spent in speaking kind words and doing kind acts to all about her. She was never tired of telling, with tears of heartfelt gratitude, what Jesus had done for her soul.

How beautifully this story illustrates the power and willingness of Jesus to save!

The fourth lesson we learn from the crucifixion of Christ is about—*the depth of his sufferings*.

The sufferings of his body were very great. When the Roman soldiers beat him on the back with their rods, his flesh was torn, and made to quiver with pain. Then his brow was torn by the sharp points of the crown of thorns that were pressed upon his head. His hands and feet were torn by the rough, cruel nails that were driven through them. And when the cross was set upright in the earth, and his body was hanging by those nails, who can tell the agony that must have been wringing every nerve in it? Think of him as hanging thus for three or four dreadful hours! how long the moments must have seemed that made up those hours! And if he tried to change his position in the slightest degree, every movement must have increased the torture he was feeling a hundred fold.

But this was not all: this was not half the suffering that Jesus endured. If he had been feeling peaceful and comfortable in his mind while all this was going on, he would not have cared much for these bodily pains. But he had no such feeling. His mind or soul was enduring sufferings much worse than those which the scourges, and the crown of thorns, and the crucifixion, caused to his body. He said to his disciples as he entered Gethsemane—"My soul is exceeding sorrowful, even unto death." This was the sorrow he felt from thinking that his Father in heaven was angry with him, and was looking at him as if he were a sinner. He had taken our sins upon himself, and God was treating him as if he had really been a sinner. He was bearing the wrath of God that we had deserved for our sins. The apostle Paul tells us that—"He was made a curse for us." Gal. iii: 13. We cannot understand what Jesus had to feel when this curse came down upon him. But it was this which wrung from him that bitter cry when the darkness came around him, as he hung upon the cross,—"My God! My God! why hast thou forsaken me?"

This made the sufferings that Jesus bore for us greater than we can tell, and greater than we can understand.

This part of our subject we must leave without attempting any illustration. There never was any sorrow or suffering like that which he bore for us. I know of nothing that could be used as an illustration here. This thought of the sufferings of Christ is like one of those places in the ocean which is so deep that we cannot get a line long enough to reach the bottom.

And then the last lesson for us to learn from the crucifixion of Christ is about—THE WONDERS OF HIS LOVE.

The apostle Paul tells us that the love of Christ—"*passeth knowledge.*" Ephes. iii: 19. He says the riches of this love are "*unsearchable.*" The love of Christ is like a mountain, so high that we cannot climb to the top of it. It is like a valley, so deep that we cannot get down to the bottom of it. It is like a plain, so broad that we cannot get to the beginning of it, on the one hand, or to the end of it on the other. And when we are looking at Jesus as he hangs upon the cross, we are in the best position we ever can occupy for trying to understand the wonders of his love. It was the love of Jesus which made him willing to come down from heaven and "humble himself unto death, even the death of the cross." It was the love of Jesus which made him willing to be nailed to the cross, and to hang there in agony and blood, till as the Te Deum says, he had "overcome the sharpness of death, and had opened the kingdom of heaven to all believers." And as we stand before the cross of Christ, and think of the depth of his sufferings, and the wonders of his love, we may well ask in the language of the hymn:

>"O Lamb of God! was ever *pain*,
>Was ever *love* like Thine?"

And it is this wonderful love of Jesus, in dying for us, which gives to the story of the cross the strange power it has over the hearts of men.

"The Influence of the Love of Christ." We are so accustomed to hear of the blessed Saviour, and his amazing love, that it often gets to be a familiar story to us, and so it does not have its proper influence on our hearts. But it is different with the missionaries of the gospel. When they tell the heathen about Jesus, and his love, it is new to them, and sometimes it has a strange effect upon them. Here is an instance of this:

The Rev. Mr. Nott, an English missionary in the South Sea Islands, was reading the third chapter of the gospel of St. John to a number of the natives. Presently he came to that wonderful statement in the 16th verse, "God so loved the world that he gave his only begotten Son, that whosoever believeth on him should not perish but have everlasting life." When he heard this, one of the natives said, "What words were those you read? Let me hear those words again." The missionary read the verse again, slowly and deliberately. On hearing them again, the native rose and said, "Is that so? Can it be true that God loved the world, when the world did not love him?" "It *is* true," said the missionary. "And this is the message we bring you. If you believe in Jesus, and his love, it will save your soul, and make you happy forever." This wonderful love of Jesus won that heathen's heart, and he became a Christian.

This illustrates what the apostle Paul means when he says, "the love of Christ constraineth us." To constrain, means to draw. The power which the gospel has to draw men's hearts to God is in the love of Christ.

"The Power of Love." A teacher was giving a lesson to a class of children, on metals and minerals. They were told that gold could be melted, and that all metals could be melted. Then the teacher asked: "Can stones be melted?"

"Yes," said a little boy; "stones are melted in volcanoes."

"That is true; and now, can you tell me what can melt a heart as hard as stone?"

After thinking for a few minutes, the little boy said: "I think it is God only who can melt a hard heart."

"You are right, my child; and now can you tell me how does God melt hard hearts?"

"It is by his love."

"You are right again, my child; it is the love of God that melts stony hearts. And it is by giving his Son to die for us that God shows his love."

Here is a very striking story to show the power of the love of Christ in melting a hard heart. We may call it:

"Hope for the Lost." Charles Anderson was the son of a sailor. His father was drowned at sea. Charles was left an orphan, in a seaport town in England. Having no one to take care of him, he got in with bad boys, and grew up an idle, careless, swearing, drunken young man. In a drunken spree one night, he and his companions broke into a house and robbed it. He was taken to prison, tried, and sentenced to seven years' transportation to New South Wales. After his arrival there, thinking that he was unjustly punished, he became sulky, obstinate, and rebellious. He cared for no rules. He minded no orders, but did just as he pleased. For his bad conduct he was flogged again and again. But punishment did him no good. He grew worse and worse. He became so thoroughly bad and unmanageable that at last he was sentenced to receive three hundred lashes on his back, and to be chained for two years to a barren rock that stood by itself in the middle of the harbor of Sydney. The wretched man was fastened by his waist to this rock, with a chain twenty-six feet long.

He had irons on his legs and had hardly a rag to cover him. His only bed was a hollow place scooped out in the rock. He had no other shelter than a wooden lid, with holes bored in it. This was locked over him at night and removed in the morning. If he had been a wild beast, instead of a man, he could hardly have been treated worse. His food was pushed to him once a day, in a box, with a long pole. Sometimes people going by in boats, would throw him pieces of bread or biscuit. But no one was allowed to go near him or speak to him. Thus he spent two long years, a prisoner on that lonely rock. Of course, he grew no better, but worse, under such treatment. When his time was out, and he was released from the rock, he behaved so badly that very soon he was taken up again, and sent a prisoner to Norfolk Island, to work in chains for the rest of his life.

Now, what good could possibly be expected from such a man? None at all, if the same hard treatment had been continued towards him. But it was not continued. No, at Norfolk Island, he came under the care of a good Christian gentleman. This was Capt. Maconochie, an officer of the English army. He had great faith in the power of kindness and love. He found this man Anderson one of the very worst men he had ever met with; but he resolved to try the power of the gospel upon him. He treated him kindly, as one man ought to treat another. He got him to attend a night school which he had opened, and there had him taught to read. Then he persuaded him to join a Bible class which he taught. He showed an interest in him and sympathy for him. He often took him apart by himself and talked kindly to him. He told him of the wonderful love of Jesus, as shown in the story of the cross. This touched and melted the hard and stony heart of that desperate man. He wept like a child, at the thought of his life of sin. He prayed earnestly for pardon, and found it. Charles Anderson—the fierce, unmanageable man—the man who had been chained, like a wild beast to that lonely rock, became a Christian. And he was a thoroughly changed man in every respect. The change from midnight to mid-day, from mid-winter to mid-summer, is not greater than the change that appeared in him. From being an ill-tempered, gloomy, disobedient, idle man who was a plague to all about him, he became gentle, and kind, cheerful, obedient, and trustworthy; a man who gained the respect and the love of all who knew him. Capt. Moconochie got him released from being a prisoner, on account of his good behaviour. Then he took him into his own service, and a more useful and excellent servant he never had in all his life. Here we see the power of the love of Christ. And so when we think of the history of the crucifixion, let us remember these six things,—the place—the time—the manner—the witnesses—the wonders—and the words—which make up that history. And when we think of the lessons it teaches—let us remember the lesson of forgiveness—the lesson of duty to our parents—the lesson about the power and willingness of Christ to save—about the depths of his sufferings—and the wonders of his love.

We cannot better close this subject than with the words of the hymn we often sing:

> " When I survey the wondrous cross,
>   On which the Prince of glory died,
> My richest gain I count but loss,
>   And pour contempt on all my pride.
>
> " Forbid it, Lord, that I should boast,
>   Save in the cross of Christ my God,
> All the vain things that charm me most,
>   I sacrifice them to his blood.
>
> " See from his head, his hands, his feet,
>   Sorrow and love flow mingled down!
> Did e'er such love and sorrow meet,
>   Or thorns compose so rich a crown?
>
> " Were the whole realm of nature mine,
>   *That* were a tribute far too small;
> Love so amazing, so divine,
>   Demands my life—my soul—my all."

THE BURIAL

IN the last chapter, we left our blessed Lord hanging dead upon the cross. Deep darkness was spread over the land, as if to hide from view the awful wickedness which men were committing.

We have now to consider what became of the dead Saviour after this. When death enters our homes and lays his icy hand on some one whom we love, we know that the next thing to follow is the funeral. We have to make preparation, as Abraham said on the death of Sarah, his wife, to "bury our dead out of our sight." Gen. xxiii: 4. And so, after the crucifixion, or death of our Saviour, the next thing for us to consider is—his burial. We have an account of this burial in each of the four gospels. We can read all that is said about it in the following places: —St. Matt. xxvii: 56-66; St. Mark xv: 42-47; St. Luke xxiii: 50-56, and St. John xix: 38-42.

The history of the burial of Christ, given in these different places, briefly stated, is, that as soon as he was dead, and while he was yet hanging on the cross, two men came forward and took charge of his burial. One of these is called "Joseph of Arimathea." We know nothing about him before this. His name was never mentioned before, and after this it is never mentioned again in the Scriptures. What we are told about him is, that he was a rich man—an honorable counsellor, or a member of the Jewish Sanhedrim: he was a just and good man—a disciple of Jesus—but had kept his thoughts and feelings on this subject to himself, because he was afraid of the Jews. And with him came Nicodemus—of whom we read in the third chapter of St. John—who came to Jesus by night to have a talk with him on the subject of religion. He was also a member of the Jewish Sanhedrim, and "a ruler of the Jews." Joseph went boldly in before Pilate, and asked permission from him to take the body of Jesus down from the cross and have it buried. This was in the afternoon of the same day on which the crucifixion had taken place. Pilate was surprised to think that Jesus could have died so soon. Death by crucifixion, although very painful, was still a lingering death. It is said that cases have been known of persons who have hung upon the cross for two or three days before death put an end to their sufferings. We do not wonder, therefore, that Pilate should have felt surprised, when he heard that Jesus, who was crucified about twelve o'clock, should have been dead about three o'clock the same afternoon. He sent for the centurion, who had charge of the crucifixion, and asked if it was true that Jesus was already dead. The centurion had carefully examined the body, and told Pilate that he was really dead.

Then Pilate gave Joseph and Nicodemus permission to take down the body and bury it. Immediately they went back to Calvary and took the body of Jesus down from the cross. They could hardly do it by themselves, and they had, no doubt, engaged some other persons to help them. We are not told how the body was taken down. In the art gallery, at Antwerp in Belgium, there is a famous painting of this scene, by Rubens the celebrated Flemish artist. It is called—"The Descent from the Cross." Here, Joseph and Nicodemus are represented as having set up ladders against the cross. They have climbed up the ladder, and have drawn out the nails, and then we see them carefully handing down the dead body of our blessed Lord. This would be one way of taking the body down.

Another way would be to lift the cross up from the place in the earth, where it was fastened, and lay it carefully down on the ground, with the body of Jesus still nailed to it. It would be much easier to get the nails out, with the cross in this position, than while it was standing upright. But we are not told how it was done, and so we are at liberty to think of either of these ways as the one that was adopted. And now, the mangled body of the dead Saviour is removed from the cross. Then, it is reverently wrapped in the linen which Joseph had brought with him for this purpose. Nicodemus had brought a hundred pounds weight of spices, myrrh and aloes. These were probably in the form of powder. It was the custom of the Jews to use these spices in the burial of the dead, because they have the power of preventing decay from taking place immediately.

In a warm country like Palestine, decay begins very soon after death. And in a body that had been torn and mangled, as was the case with the body of Jesus, it would take place still sooner. And so the use of the spices was necessary.

The Burial

No doubt the wounds made by the nails in the hands and feet of our Saviour, and the gash of the spear in his blessed side, were gently filled with those powdered spices. And then the spices were put freely in between the folds of the linen that were wrapped about his dead cold limbs. The Jews did not use coffins. Their dead were only wrapped in grave-clothes, as was the case with Lazarus, and here with our Lord.

And now the preparations are made. The body is ready for the burial. And the grave is ready for the body. Near to Calvary, where Jesus was crucified, there was a garden. And in that garden was a new tomb, in which no dead body had ever lain. This tomb was dug out from the solid rock. The rocks around Jerusalem are filled with such tombs. They are not generally dug down below the surface of the ground, as we make our graves, but into the side of the rock, and on a level with the ground. This tomb belonged to Joseph of Arimathea. It had, no doubt, been made for himself and family. How little he thought when he had that new tomb made, that Jesus, the Son of God, and the Redeemer of the world, would be the first one to occupy it! What an honor and privilege Joseph had in being permitted to furnish the tomb in which the dead body of the Lord of life was to rest till the morning of the resurrection!

And now, the funeral procession is formed. Joseph and Nicodemus, and their helpers, take reverently hold of the body of Jesus, and bear it quietly and solemnly away to the open tomb in yonder garden. No doubt the good women, who lingered round the cross, joined in the procession, and followed the body of their Lord to the place where it was to lie. They reach the tomb. On the rocky floor of that tomb, the lifeless body of Jesus is gently laid. They linger in silence around it. They gaze at it with loving wonder and amazement. Then they go out. A great stone is rolled against the mouth of the tomb. And now, all that loving hearts can suggest, or willing hands can do for the buried one has been done. They pause awhile to meditate on that silent tomb, and then slowly retire to their homes, to prepare for the Jewish Sabbath, which began at six o'clock on Friday evening.

But there is one other thing to notice in connection with this burial. The priests had heard Jesus speak of rising from the dead on the third day. They went to Pilate and told him of this. They said they were afraid that his disciples might come by night and steal away his body, and then declare that he had risen from the dead. They asked him, therefore, to allow them to seal the stone over the mouth of the grave with his seal, and to have a guard of Roman soldiers appointed to keep watch over the tomb till the third day was passed. Pilate gave them leave to do this. And we read, "so they went and made the sepulchre sure, sealing the stone, and setting a watch." St. Matt. xxvii: 66.

Such is the history of the burial of our Saviour. And as we stand in thought before the silent tomb in which the body of Jesus is lying, we may well say, in the words of one of our hymns for Easter even:

> "All is o'er, the pain, the sorrow,
>   Human taunts, and Satan's spite;
> Death shall be despoiled to-morrow
>   Of the prey he grasps to-night,
> Yet once more, his own to save,
> Christ must sleep within the grave.
>
> "Fierce and deadly was the anguish
>   On the bitter cross he bore;
> How did soul and body languish,
>   Till the toil of death was o'er!
> But that toil, so fierce and dread,
> Bruised and crushed the serpent's head.

> "Close and still the tomb that holds him,
>   While in brief repose he lies;
> Deep the slumber that enfolds him,
>   Veiled awhile from mortal eyes;
> Slumber such as needs must be
> After hard won victory.
>
> "Near this tomb, with voice of sadness,
>   Chant the anthem sweet and low;
> Loftier strains of praise and gladness
>   From to-morrow's harps shall flow;
> Death and hell at length are slain,
> Christ hath triumphed, Christ doth reign."

This is the history of the burial of Christ. And now we may speak of four lessons taught us by this history.

The first lesson taught us is about—THE CERTAINTY OF HIS DEATH.

Sometimes the enemies of our religion have ventured to say that Jesus did not really die, but that he only fainted, or swooned, or appeared to die. But it is of the highest importance for us to know that Jesus did really die. When we are saying or singing that grand old anthem—the TE DEUM, we look up to Jesus and say, "When thou had'st *overcome the sharpness of death*, thou did'st open the kingdom of heaven to all believers." By Christ's overcoming the sharpness of death is meant his resurrection from the dead. But, if his resurrection was a real resurrection, then the death from which he rose, must have been a real death. We cannot come out of a state, or place, if we have never been in it. It is impossible that you, or I, for example, should go out of this church, unless we were first in it. And when we know that none of us could enter heaven, unless Jesus had really died for us, we see how important it is for us to be sure of the certainty of his death.

Now there was one thing connected with the burial of Christ which proves that he was really dead, and that was the drawing out of the nails from his hands and feet. When a great, rough nail or spike has been driven into a piece of solid wood, we know how hard it is to draw it out. There were two such spikes driven through the palms of the hands of Jesus, and two through his feet. In trying to draw these out, I suppose they must have made use of a large pair of pincers, or of a hammer with a claw on one side of it. As they came to those nails, one by one, they would have to get the nippers of the pincers or the claw of the hammer under the head of the nail. Then they would have to press down hard on the bruised and torn part of the hands and feet of our Saviour. Now this must have been so very painful that if he had only fainted on the cross this dreadful operation, as they went through with it four times, would certainly have brought him out from his fainting fit. But it did not. It had not the slightest effect upon him. There was no more feeling in his hands or feet than there was in the wood of the cross to which he was nailed. And this proves that he was really dead.

But then there was another thing that took place at the crucifixion of Jesus which also proves the certainty of his death. We read in St. John xix: 34—"But one of the soldiers with a spear pierced his side, and forthwith came there out blood and water." If Jesus had not been dead before this took place, that cruel spear, thrust into his heart, would certainly have killed him. If Jesus had been alive when the soldier did this, not blood and water, but only blood, would have flowed out from the wound which the spear made. And learned physicians who have examined this matter tell us that two things are clearly proved by this flowing out of blood and water from the wound which the soldier's spear had made in our Saviour's side. One of these is, that he was already dead. The soldier's spear did not kill him, but it proved that he was dead before the wound was made.

And then the other thing which it proved was that Jesus had died of a broken heart. In Dr. Hanna's "Life of Christ," Vol. III. pp. 369-379, may be found letters from several eminent Scottish physicians, showing that nothing but a broken heart could account for the flowing out of "blood and water" from the wound in our Saviour's side. It was not being nailed to the cross that killed our blessed Lord. Neither was it the wound made by the spear. No, but it was the great sorrow he had felt in being made to bear our sins, that had really broken his heart.

The sixty-ninth Psalm is one of the passages in the Old Testament that refers to Christ. It is he who is speaking there. And in the twentieth verse of that Psalm, we find him saying of himself, "*Reproach hath broken my heart.*" And so when we think of "the blood and water" that flowed out from his wounded side, and of the drawing out of those nails from his hands and feet, we may feel perfectly sure about the certainty of the death of Christ.

The next lesson that we learn from the burial of Christ is about—THE FULFILLMENT OF HIS WORD.

The prophet Isaiah had spoken about the death and burial of our Saviour seven hundred years before he was born into our world. In the ninth verse of the fifty-third chapter of his prophecy, where he is speaking of Jesus he says. "And he made his grave with the wicked, and with the rich in his death." This means that it was arranged, or intended, that he should be buried with the wicked, and yet it would so happen that he would be with the rich in his death. We can easily see how it was to be expected that Jesus would be buried with the wicked, because he died with them. He was crucified between two thieves. These thieves were buried "with the wicked," or in the place where common criminals were generally buried. And as Jesus had died with them, so it was to be expected that he would have been buried with them. And this is what would have happened if God had not ordered it otherwise. The disciples of Jesus had all forsaken him. And even if they had not done so, none of them were rich. Pilate would not have given them leave to take charge of the body of their dead Master. And if they had had it, they could not have procured a rich man's grave in which to bury it. It seemed impossible, therefore, that what Isaiah had spoken should come to pass. But that was the word of God. It was written in the scripture that Jesus was to be "with the rich in his death." And "the scriptures cannot be broken." God's word must be fulfilled. And so, just when Jesus was dying, Joseph of Arimathea, who had been a secret disciple of Jesus, made his appearance. He was a rich man. He had a sepulchre near at hand. He asked Pilate to let him have the body of Jesus, for the purpose of burying it. Pilate gave it to him. He buried it in his new tomb. And so the words of Isaiah were fulfilled to the very letter; although it seemed impossible before that such should have been the case. Jesus died with the wicked, and yet was buried with the rich. And here we see how wonderfully God's word was fulfilled.

And we meet with instances, continually, to show that God is still fulfilling his word in ways that are equally wonderful.

"Try It." A Christian woman, rich in faith, but poor in this world's goods, was greatly perplexed about the meaning of the words, "Give, and it shall be given unto you." She said to herself: "the best way to find out the meaning of such a promise, is to try it. I'll try it."

It was Saturday night. After buying what her children would need for Sunday, she had just two dollars left. Putting this money in her pocket, she went out. She had not gone far when a friend met her, who was in great distress, and asked the loan of two dollars. She gave the money to her friend, and resolved she would wait and see how God would fulfill his word.

Monday morning came. She had nothing with which to buy food for her family. While wondering what she should do, there came a knock at the door. On opening it a lady came in with a bundle in her hand. "Can you do some work for me?" she asked. "Certainly." "What will you charge?" The price was named. The lady put two dollars in her hand, saying, "This is more than you ask, but you may as well have it."

The good woman shouted for joy. She had tried God's promise, and had found out how wonderfully he fulfills his word.

"The Bullfinch." Andrew Austin lived in Scotland. He was a tailor by trade, a good, honest, Christian man, but very poor. At the time to which this story refers, he was in great trouble. Sickness in his family had used up all his money. The rent of his cottage was due, and he had nothing to pay it with. "What shall I do?" he said to himself, in great distress. He took down his Bible, and opened it at the book of Psalms. His eye rested on the fourth verse of the seventy-second Psalm—*"For he shall deliver the needy when he crieth."* He kneeled down and told God of his trouble, and asked him to fulfill that promise in his present distress. As he rose from his knees his heart was comforted, and he felt sure that God would fulfill his word and send, in some way, the help that was needed.

He resolved to go and see his landlord, and ask him to allow him a week's time in which to pay the rent.

Just as he opened the door to go out, a little bird flew past him, perched upon the mantle-shelf, and hopped about, chirping merrily. Andrew closed the door, and watched the movements of the little fellow with great interest. He saw that it was a bullfinch, a piping bullfinch. This is a bird something like a sparrow, with a round head and short thick bill. Bullfinches are great singers. They can learn tunes, and carry them all through nicely. While Andrew was watching the bird, it hopped on to the Bible which he had just been reading, and lifting up its little head began to sing the tune of "Old Hundred." Of course the bird only had the music without the words. But Andrew joined him, and put in the words:

> "Praise God, from whom all blessings flow;
> Praise him, all creatures here below;
> Praise him above, ye heavenly host;
> Praise Father, Son, and Holy Ghost."

When he got through singing this verse, the old man felt perfectly happy. Leaving the little stranger in his room, he went to see the landlord; and as he walked along he was repeating to himself the words of the twenty-third Psalm —"The Lord is my shepherd, I shall not want."

He found the landlord very pleasant. He readily gave him the additional time he wanted to make up his rent. As he was going home feeling very bright and cheerful, he was singing to a simple tune these words which just suited his circumstances:

> "The birds, without barn or storehouse, are fed;
> From them let us learn to trust for our bread;
> His saints, what is fitting, shall ne'er be denied,
> So long as 'tis written, 'The Lord will provide.'"

As he went on, he was spoken to by a servant in livery, whom he recognized at once as the footman of Lady Armistead, a rich and pious old lady, who lived at Basford Hall, about three miles from the village where he resided.

"You seem to be in good spirits, Andrew," said the servant, who was an old acquaintance. "You sing so well, one would think you had swallowed Lady Armistead's bullfinch. It's been missing these two days. I'm going home now, for it's no use seeking any more. Her ladyship takes on dreadfully about the bird, for it was a great favorite, and a regular tip-topper at singing."

Then Andrew asked him to go home with him, and said he should find his bird again. As they walked along towards the cottage, Andrew told his friend the story of his troubles; how he had prayed; what God had said to him out of his Book; and how the bullfinch came and cheered his heart; how he had been to the landlord's, and had got another week to turn round in; "and look you here John Morris, my rent'll be ready when it's wanted, as sure as my name's Andrew; for that bird was sent from my heavenly father, and brought me His message on its wings, 'for his mercy endureth for ever.'"

So John got the bullfinch and took it home to his mistress. When she heard about it, Lady

Armistead sent for the tailor. His simple story moved her to tears. She thought more of her bullfinch than ever, since God had made him a messenger of mercy to one of his suffering children. She gave the tailor money enough to pay his rent, and told him that he should have work from Basford Hall as long as he lived. "God bless your ladyship," said Andrew, with a grateful heart. Just then the bullfinch struck up its favorite tune, and Andrew joined in the song.

"Praise God from whom all blessings flow."

Lady Armistead smiled with sympathy, and Andrew added—"Yes, yes: Praise the Lord, for his mercy endureth forever."

Now, however long old Andrew might have lived after that, I think he would never read over that verse in the seventy-second Psalm —"He shall deliver the needy when he crieth," without remembering the lesson we are here taught by the burial of Christ—and that is, how wonderfully he fulfills his word.

The next lesson we learn from the burial of Christ is about—THE WORKING OF HIS PROVIDENCE.

Suppose we are looking at a great clock. Its wheels are moving slowly on. We listen, and hear it going—tick-tick-tick. The hands on the dial plate are getting near to twelve o'clock; and the very moment the minute hand comes over the figure 12, the hammer in the clock starts up, and begins to pound on the bell, and the clock strikes twelve. The maker of that clock arranged every part of its machinery in such a way that it would be sure to keep time and strike the hours as they came.

And the providence of God is just like such a clock. He is the maker of it. And he not only made the wheels of its machinery in the beginning, but he manages them all the time. He has his hand on every part of it. "God so loved the world that he gave his only begotten Son" to die for us. He was willing to have him crucified with wicked men. But he wished to have him buried with rich men. And seven hundred years before Jesus was born into our world he had said that it should be so. And when the time for Christ's burial came, the clock of his providence struck, just as he said it should do. Joseph of Arimathea was one of the wheels in this clock; and when the right time came, there he was—ready to bury the dead Saviour in his own new tomb. And thus, in the wonderful working of God's providence, it came to pass that Jesus was—"with the rich in his death." And as we think of ourselves, as standing by the tomb in which Jesus was buried, and seeing how strangely the prophecy about his burial was fulfilled, we cannot help wondering at the working of God's providence. It is true indeed, as the hymn says—that

> "God moves in a mysterious way,
>   His wonders to perform:
> He plants his footsteps in the sea,
>   And rides upon the storm."

And it is just the same now as it was then. Here are some examples of the working of this providence.

"The Raven of Winslade Quarry." Winslade is a small town in England, famous for its stone quarries. Some years ago an incident occurred there which strikingly illustrates this part of our subject. The men were at work in the lower part of the quarry. Directly above was a great mass of overhanging rocks. Dinner time came; but just as they were getting ready for it, a raven flew down, picked up the little parcel which contained one of the miners' dinner and flew away with it. The man of course did not want to lose his dinner, so he ran after the bird, thinking that she would soon have to stop, and lay down her heavy burden, and then he would get his dinner again.

His companions wished to see the fun and they joined in the chase. The bird was stronger than they thought and led them a long way off before she alighted. But, at last she flew down the side of a steep and dangerous precipice and laid her bundle on a projecting rock. She seemed to feel that she was safe there, and so she was, for no one was willing to risk his life by attempting to go down that perilous place. Then the men gave up the chase, and went back to the quarry. On reaching the spot they found to their surprise that a great mass of rock had fallen down just where they would have been eating their dinner. It would have crushed them to death if the raven had not come and taken them away in time to save them. Thus God made use of that bird to save the lives of those men. Here we see the wonderful working of God's providence.

"Delivered by a Dog." A minister of the gospel, who had a country parish in New England, tells this story:

"A farmer belonging to my parish, and who was quite well off, died suddenly. Shortly after his death his widow, who was a good Christian woman, concluded to give up the farm and take a small house in the neighboring village. The farm was sold and then an auction was held to sell the things on the farm and in the house, except the furniture that would be needed for the little house in the village.

"I went to see her," said the minister on the day of the sale. "I told her I thought she had done wisely in concluding to give up the farm, for it was half a mile away from any other house, and she would be lonely and unprotected there."

"'Oh! no,' she said, 'not unprotected; far from it! You forget that I am now under the special charge of that God "who careth for the widow and the fatherless," and who, I am sure, will protect us.'

"And now, let me tell you how God did protect them. There was a good deal of money in the house that night from the sale which had taken place. The only persons in the house were the mother with her three young children and their maid servant.

"Some time after going to bed she heard a strange and unusual noise at the back of the house. Then she was startled by the barking of a dog, apparently in the room under her chamber. This alarmed her still more as they had no dog of their own.

"She arose and dressed herself hastily. She awoke her maid and they went down stairs. They first looked into the room where they heard the dog. There they saw a huge black dog, scratching and barking furiously at the door leading into the kitchen. She told her servant to open the door where the dog was scratching. The girl was brave, and opened the door without a fear. In a moment the dog rushed out, and through the open door the widow saw two men at the kitchen window, which was also open. The men instantly turned to run, and the dog leaped through the window and ran after them. There was a fierce fight between them, but the men finally got away, though followed far off by the faithful dog.

"Mrs. M., and her maid fastened the window and doors, and concluded to sit up for the rest of the night, for, of course it would be impossible to sleep after what had taken place. They had hardly taken their seats before they heard their noble protector scratching at the outer door for admittance. They gladly let him in, and when he came up to them, wagging his great bushy tail, they patted and praised him for his goodness and courage. Then he stretched his huge form beside the warm stove, closed his eyes and went to sleep. The next morning they gave him a breakfast that any dog might have been glad to get. As soon as he had finished his breakfast, he went to the door, and stood impatiently whining till the door was opened, when off he ran in a great hurry, and they never saw him again.

"They had never seen the dog before, and knew not to whom it belonged. But the grateful widow felt sure that her Father in heaven had sent him for their protection that night. And her faith was stronger than ever at the mysterious working of his providence."

> "Say not, my soul, From whence
> Can God relieve my care?
> Remember that omnipotence
> Hath servants everywhere."

The last lesson taught us by the burial of Christ is—A LESSON OF COMFORT.

If Christ had not suffered, and died, and been buried for us, we should have no comfort when we come to die. The thought of having to lie down in the grave would have been terrible to us. But Jesus died and laid in the grave

The Burial

for us, on purpose that we might not be afraid to die.

It is true as the hymn says, that:

> "The graves of all his saints he blest
> When in the grave he lay."

David had learned this lesson, by faith in the promised Saviour, long before he came to earth, and it was this that enabled him to say, "Yea, though I walk through the valley of the shadow of death, I will fear no evil, for thou art with me; thy rod and thy staff they comfort me." Ps. 23:4.

And the apostle Paul had learned the same lesson, when he exclaimed so joyfully, "O death, where is thy sting? O grave, where is thy victory? Thanks be to God who giveth us the victory through our Lord Jesus Christ." I. Cor. xv: 55, 57.

Good Dr. Muhlenberg put this lesson very sweetly into a single verse of his beautiful hymn, when he said:

> "I would not live alway; no; welcome the tomb,
> Since Jesus hath lain there I dread not its gloom.
> There sweet be my rest, till he bid me arise,
> To hail him in triumph descending the skies."

The sweet Scottish poet Bonar had learned this lesson well, and was feeling the comfort which the thought of Christ's burial gives when he could think of dying and lying in the grave, and speak about it in these words:

> "I go to life and not to death;
> From darkness to life's native sky;
> I go from sickness and from pain
> To health and immortality.
>
> "Let our farewell, then, be tearless,
> Since I bid farewell to tears;
> Write this day of my departure
> Festive in your coming years.
>
> "I go from poverty to wealth,
> From rags to raiment angel-fair,
> From the pale leanness of this flesh
> To beauty such as saints shall wear.
>
> "I go from chains to liberty,
> These fetters will be broken soon;
> Forth over Eden's fragrant fields
> I'll walk beneath a glorious noon.
>
> "For toil there comes the crowned rest;
> Instead of burdens, eagles' wings;
> And I, even I, this life-long thirst
> Shall quench at everlasting springs."

We see the true effect of Christ's burial in the feeling of comfort which those who believe in him experience when they come to die. Here are some examples of what I mean.

When Dr. Watts was on his death-bed, he said, "I bless God that I can lie down at night without the slightest fear whether I wake in this world or another."

Another good minister, when asked how he felt at the approach of death, said,—"I am just going into eternity; but I bless God, I am neither ashamed to live, nor afraid to die."

During the reign of Henry VIII, of England, many good men were cruelly put to death for the sake of their religion. Among these was Dr. Fisher, Bishop of Rochester. When he came in sight of the scaffold on which he was to die, he took out of his pocket a Greek Testament, and looking up to heaven, said, "Now, O Lord, direct me to some passage which may comfort me in this trying hour." Then he opened the book, and his eye rested on this passage, "This is life eternal, to know thee, the only true God, and Jesus Christ whom thou hast sent." He closed the book and said, "Praised be God! this is all I need. This is enough for life, or for death; for time, or for eternity."

When the Rev. James Harvey came to his last sickness, his physician came in one day and told him he had but very little time to live.

"Then let me spend my last moments," said he, "in praising my blessed Saviour. Though my heart and my flesh fail, yet God is the strength of my heart, and my portion forever. St. Paul says: 'All things are yours, whether life or death; things present, or things to come; all are yours, and ye are Christ's, and Christ is God's.' Here is the treasure of a Christian, and a noble treasure it is. Death is ours. Jesus has made it our friend, by his death and burial. Praise God for this truth. And now welcome death! How well thou mayest be welcomed among the treasures of the Christian. 'For me to live is Christ, but to die is gain.'"

The Rev. William Janeway was another excellent and faithful minister of Christ. In his closing sickness, these were among the last words that he spoke: "I bless God I can die in peace. I know what that means, 'The peace of God which passeth all understanding shall keep your hearts.' It is keeping mine now. My joy is greater than I can express. Bless the Lord, O my soul, and all that is within me, bless his holy name. Now I can die. It is nothing. I long to die. I desire to depart and be with Christ." And so he died.

These good men had studied well the subject of Christ's burial, and had learned the lesson of comfort it was intended to teach us. And when we think of the burial of Christ, let us remember the lessons of which we have now spoken in connection with it. These are the lessons about the *certainty of his death:—the fulfillment of his word;—the working of his providence;—and the comfort we derive from his burial.*

The collect for Easter-even, is a very appropriate one with which to close this subject:— "Grant, O Lord, that as we are baptized into the death of thy blessed Son, our Saviour, Jesus Christ, so by continual mortifying our corrupt affections, we may be buried with him; and that through the grave and gate of death, we may pass to our joyful resurrection, for his merits, who died, and was buried, and rose again for us, thy Son, Jesus Christ our Lord. Amen."

THE RESURRECTION

THE rising of our blessed Lord from the dead was one of the most important events in the history of his life on earth.

Let us take an illustration of its importance. Suppose that we were living in England, and that we were well acquainted with Victoria—the good and gracious queen of that great kingdom. And suppose that it should please the queen to make us a present of one of the fine old castles of England, with all the lands and property belonging to it. In giving us this castle, or, as the lawyers say, in "*conveying* it to us," the queen would order a title deed to be made out. This deed would be necessary; because if any one else should claim that the castle belonged to him, we could then open the deed and show that the queen had really given it to us. A title deed, like this of which we are now speaking, is generally written on a sheet of parchment. In this deed would be found the name of the castle, with a full description of it, and all the property belonging to it. It would be stated here how many acres of land were connected with it; and then it would be written down that the queen had given it to us, and that it was to belong to us, and to our children, or heirs forever. But after all this had been written out, the deed would be good for nothing unless something more were done to it. It would be necessary for the queen to sign her own name to the deed—Victoria Regina—and then put the royal seal upon it. The property described in it could never become ours, unless the queen's signature and seal were added to it.

When Jesus came down from heaven to earth, his great object was to secure for his people a home in heaven,—a mansion in the skies. When he hung upon the cross, we may well say that he was writing out the title deed to those mansions, in his own blood. But, after this deed had thus been written, it was necessary for his Father in heaven to show that he approved of what had been done. When Jesus died and was buried, we may say that he took with him the title deed to our heavenly home, to get his Father to sign it and seal it. And when the resurrection of Jesus took place it showed that this was done. Then God the Father did, as it were, say—"I approve of what my beloved son has done. I sign and seal the title deed which he has written out to secure a home in heaven for all who love and serve him."

This shows us how very important the resurrection of Jesus was. And because it is so important, we may well feel a great interest in studying the subject of Christ's resurrection. And in doing this there are two things for us carefully to consider. These are—*The proof of the resurrection of Christ; and the lessons we are taught by it.*

Let us begin by considering—*the proof of the resurrection of Christ.* We have great cause for thankfulness that the proof given us on this subject is so clear and strong. There is no fact of history supported by stronger proof than is the fact of Christ's resurrection. We believe that there was such a person as Napoleon Bonaparte; that he was emperor of France; and that he died a prisoner on the island of St. Helena. We believe that there was such a person as George Washington; that he was the leader of our armies during the revolutionary war; and that, after the war, he was the first president of the United States. We believe that there was such a person as Julius Cæsar; that he was a successful general of the Roman armies; and that he met his death in the Senate chamber from the daggers of the Roman senators. No one doubts these facts. They are matters of history. And yet the proof we have of the resurrection of Christ is clearer and stronger than the proof we have for what we believe respecting Julius Cæsar, or George Washington, or Napoleon Bonaparte. Nothing that we read of in history is more sure than this, that Jesus did rise from the dead.

Many years ago, there was an infidel club in England. It was composed of learned and distinguished men. At the meetings of the club, its members were in the habit of ridiculing the Bible and of trying to show it was not worthy of being believed. On one occasion a member of this club was appointed to examine the subject of the resurrection of Christ and to write an essay for the purpose of showing that there was no satisfactory proof that he ever rose from the dead.

He examined carefully what is said on this subject in the New Testament. And the end

The Resurrection

of it was, that he became fully convinced of the fact that Christ did rise from the dead. And, instead of writing an article for that infidel club to show that what Christians believe about the resurrection of Christ is not true, he wrote one of the best books that ever has been written, to prove, beyond all doubt, that the resurrection of Christ is true. He became an earnest Christian. And that which led to this great change was the convincing proof he found in the New Testament of the truth of the resurrection of Christ. He saw it was true that Jesus did rise from the dead. And when he became satisfied that this was true, he was obliged to admit that all the other teachings of the New Testament respecting Christ must be true also. The resurrection of Christ is the foundation stone on which the religion of the Bible is built up. If that falls, this must fall. But if that stands firm and sure, then this must stand firm and sure also.

And in examining the proof of the resurrection of Christ the most important thing to notice is—*the number and character of the witnesses.*

The first person who saw our blessed Lord, after he rose from the dead, was Mary Magdalene. We read about this in St. Mark xi: 9.

St. John xx: 11-18. After this he appeared to certain other women, who were returning from the sepulchre. St. Matt. xxviii: 9, 10. Then he appeared to Simon Peter, alone. St. Luke xxiv: 34, I. Cor. xv: 5. His next appearance was to two of his disciples, as they were walking together from Jerusalem to a village called Emmaus. He had a long talk with them and stopped and ate bread with them. St. Luke xxiv: 13-32. The fifth appearance of the risen Saviour was to ten of his disciples, Thomas being the only one of them who was not there. This was at Jerusalem, on the evening of the first glad Easter day. St. John xx: 19-32. After this we hear nothing of him for a week. But on the evening of "the first Sunday after Easter," he made his sixth appearance. On this occasion the eleven disciples were all together. Thomas was with them now. They were sitting in a room, with the door closed, and no doubt fastened, for fear of the Jews. Only one subject could occupy their thoughts—and that was the resurrection of their wonderful Master. Suddenly Jesus himself stood in the midst of them, and said, "Peace be unto you." In spite of all that he had heard from the other disciples, Thomas declared he could not believe it possible that Jesus had risen from the dead. When his brethren told him that it was true, he said, "Except I shall see in his hands the print of the nails, and put my finger into the print of the nails, and thrust my hand into his side, I will not believe." But on this occasion the loving and gracious Saviour met his doubting disciple in the very way in which he had desired to be met. For we read: "Then saith he to Thomas, reach hither thy finger, and behold my hands: and reach hither thy hand, and thrust it into my side; and be not faithless, but believing." St. John xx: 26-29.

The seventh appearance of the risen Saviour, was on the shore of the sea of Galilee. A number of the apostles were together on this occasion. It was one of the most touching and impressive of all his interviews with them. The deeply interesting account of what took place at this time is given in full in the twenty-first chapter of St. John's gospel; but we cannot enlarge on the subject now.

The eighth time that Jesus was seen after his resurrection was by the eleven disciples again. We read in St. Matt. xxviii: 16—"Then the eleven disciples went away into Galilee, into a mountain where Jesus had appointed them."

This refers to St. Matt. xxvi: 32, when as they were partaking together of the Lord's Supper for the first time, after referring to his death he said, "But after I am risen again, I will go before you into Galilee." We are not told where this meeting was held, or what took place on that occasion.

The ninth appearance of the risen Lord, is that of which St. Paul speaks in I. Cor. xv: 7, where he tells us that "he appeared to above four hundred brethren at once." The place here referred to is not mentioned, and so cannot be known. It was probably in Galilee. Jesus had spent most of his public life in that part of the country. He had made most of his disciples there. It was proper, therefore, that those disciples, who would, of course, hear of his death, should have some public proof given them of the fact of his resurrection. No doubt the eleven disciples went to Galilee after Jesus rose. They would spread the news that he had risen, and that he was about to show himself to his friends on a certain mountain. Nothing more would be necessary anywhere to draw together a great concourse of people than a report that one who was dead had come to life again, and was about to show himself; and in this case where they greatly loved him, and where, no doubt, many believed he would rise, they would naturally come together in great numbers to see him once more.

The tenth appearance of Christ after his resurrection was to the apostle James. This is told us by St. Paul, who says I. Cor. xv: 7. "After that he was seen of James." This is not mentioned in any of the gospels. But as Jesus was on earth for forty days after his resurrection, it is most likely that he appeared often to his disciples, and that only enough of the more prominent appearances were mentioned, to prove the fact that he had risen.

The eleventh occasion on which Jesus was seen after his resurrection was on the Mount of Olives, just before his ascension into heaven. On this occasion all the eleven apostles were present, and no doubt great numbers of his other disciples.

And then there was one other occasion on which Jesus appeared, making twelve in all. This was after his ascension into heaven. To this the apostle Paul refers, when he says, "And last of all he was seen of me also." I. Cor. xv: 8. This was when he had that wonderful vision near Damascus. Then the great apostle to the

Gentiles, saw the same Lord Jesus, in the same body which had been seen by others. Unless it were so, this would be no proof that Jesus was risen from the dead. It was not a *fancy* therefore that he had seen him. It was not *revealed* to him, that Jesus was risen. "Last of all he was *seen* of me." With his bodily eyes, St. Paul actually saw, in a bodily form, that same Jesus who had died upon the cross; who had been buried in that rocky sepulchre; who had risen from the dead and had ascended into heaven. Such were the witnesses of the resurrection, as to their number.

And now look at the *character* of these witnesses. They were *sensible* men. They knew what they were doing. They could not be mistaken about the fact of Christ's resurrection. They had seen him put to death upon the cross. They had seen him buried. On the third day after his burial they had found his tomb empty. His body was gone. Then they saw him alive. They could not be mistaken about his person. They knew him too well for this. They had seen the print of the nails in his hands. This made the proof of his resurrection perfect.

And then they were *honest* men. They had no motive for preaching the resurrection of

Christ but the sincere belief that it was true. If they could have made money or gained honor by preaching the resurrection, that would have been a reason for their doing so even if it had not been true. But the very opposite of this was the case. Preaching the resurrection brought on them the loss of all they had in the world. It caused them to be persecuted, imprisoned, and put to death. And yet they went on preaching that Christ had risen. And they would have been guilty of the greatest folly if they had done this without being thoroughly convinced that it was true. But they were perfectly satisfied of the truth of what they preached, and *this* was the reason why they went on preaching it.

And then, if Christ had not risen from the dead, it would have been the easiest thing in the world for the enemies of his cause to have denied it. That would have ended the matter. *But they never did this.* And the only reason why they did not do so, was that they knew it was true that Christ had risen. They could not deny the fact. And when we put these things all together, we see how perfectly convincing is the proof of the resurrection of Christ.

And now let us look at some of the lessons taught us by our Lord's resurrection.

The first lesson we may learn from this great fact is about—THE POWER OF CHRIST.

We know of nothing that is harder to do than to bring the dead back to life. Men can do many things, but this is one thing which they cannot do. All the men in the world and all the angels in heaven could never, by their own strength, restore life to the dead. When the blood stops flowing through the veins, and the heart stands still, there is nothing but the power of God that can make the heart begin to beat, and the blood begin to flow again. But Jesus had the power to do this. He raised Lazarus to life after he had lain in the grave four days. And he did the same to the widow's son, and to the daughter of Jairus. And what he did for others in this matter, he did for himself also. And he did it by his own power. On one occasion, when speaking to his disciples about his death, or, as he called it, laying down his life, he said, "I lay it down of myself; *I have power to lay it down, and I have power to take it again.*" And he did this on the morning of the resurrection. He exercised his own power to give new life to his dead body. Here we have a grand lesson about the power of Christ. And it is very comforting to know how great the power of Jesus is, because we so often need to have him exercise that power to help us when we are in trouble. And he is exercising his power in this way continually.

Let us look at some of the ways in which he does this.

"The Power of Christ to Save." A young man, the son of a pious mother, was wandering away from the paths in which he had been trained to walk. He had given up going to church, and in the summer time generally spent his Sundays in sailing on the river in a boat with his gay companions. One Sunday the boat upset. He could not swim and he went down in the deep water. As he rose to the surface for the last time, he was seized and his cold and apparently lifeless body was brought to the shore. He was carried home. Everything possible was done for his recovery, but for a long time it seemed uncertain whether he would come back to life. There was a feeble flutter about the wrist, just enough to keep hope alive.

His mother knelt by his bedside, and prayed in her agony that he might be spared at least till he could seek and find pardon. As she thus prayed, the cold hand held in hers gave a feeble pressure. The eyelids quivered a little, but did not open. After a while he looked at his mother, and said, in a low whisper, "Mother I am saved." Supposing that he meant saved from drowning, she replied, "Yes, dear, thank God you are saved." And then in broken sentences, with long intervals between them, he gave this remarkable experience:

"Mother, I heard you praying: if I had died you would have thought me lost: but I am saved. When I let go my hold upon the boat, the thought flashed across my mind—I am lost. I am going into eternity with all my sins unpardoned. I lifted up my heart to heaven, and said, 'God be merciful to me a sinner. Lord save me!' I seemed to hear a voice distinctly saying, 'I will save thee, trust me.' I am sure it was the voice of Jesus. All my fear was gone. But after that I knew nothing until I heard you praying for me. You would have mourned for me as lost; but mother I am saved."

And the result proved that he was right. As soon as he recovered his health and strength, he gave up all his wicked ways, and lived the life of an earnest and devoted Christian. How wonderful is the power of Jesus to save!

"The Power of Jesus to Provide." A Christian widow was dying. She was very poor, and had four young children to leave helpless and alone in the world. As she took leave of her little ones, Nettie, the oldest girl, about fourteen years of age, said amidst heart-breaking sobs and tears, "O, mother dear, what shall we do when you are gone?"

"Nettie, darling," said the mother, "God's hand will help you. It is an omnipotent hand. Never let go of it."

The mother died and was buried. Towards evening of the next day, little Dick, the youngest of the children, came to Nettie and said, "Nettie, Dick's awful hungry. Isn't there a bit of crust anywhere?" "Poor Dick," said Nettie, "what shall we do?" And then, remembering what her dying mother had said about the Omnipotent hand, she dropped on her knees, and said, "O God, our God, and our mother's God, look on these hungry little ones, left in my care, and send them some food for Christ's sake. Amen."

A rich merchant of the town was going home that evening. He was a widower, but had no children. Without knowing why, he took a different way home from the one ordinarily taken. As he walked slowly along he happened to be just under the open window when Nettie made that prayer for bread. The tone of deep sadness in it touched his heart. He stopped. He knocked at the door. Nettie opened it, and asked him in. He found out the sad condition of those helpless orphans. He gave them money to get what they needed. He continued to visit them, and finally became so much interested in them that he took them to live with him in his own home. Nettie felt the blessedness of holding on to the Omnipotent hand. Here we see the power of Jesus to provide.

One other illustration shows us—"The Power of Jesus to Protect."

A young Christian woman, whose family were very well off, was confined to her sick bed for many years. She seldom had any one in the room with her at night. On one occasion she lay awake about midnight. The family were all asleep and the house was very still, when the door of her chamber opened and a man walked softly in. He came towards her bed and then stopped a moment. Her little night lamp was shining on them both, from the stand by her bedside. She did not scream, or cry. The robber looked at this lovely girl, as she gazed on him with perfect calmness. Lifting her finger, and pointing solemnly towards heaven, she said, "Do you know that God sees you?" The man waited a moment, but made no reply. Then he turned and walked quietly away. He had opened no other doors than the street door and the door of her chamber. The omnipotent hand was there, too. What a blessed thing it is to hold on to that hand! Here we see the power of Jesus to protect. The power he had to raise himself from the dead, he has still, to use for the help and comfort of his people.

The second lesson to be learned from the resurrection is a lesson about—THE TENDERNESS OF CHRIST.

We learn this lesson from two little incidents connected with the resurrection.

You remember that on the night of our Saviour's trial, though all the disciples forsook him, yet Peter was the only one of them who denied him. In the very presence of Jesus, he declared with oaths and curses, that he did not know him. How painful this must have been to the blessed Saviour! It might have been expected that when he met Peter again, for the first time after this, he would have had some sharp rebuke to give him. But it was not so. Instead of this, we find that when the angels at the empty tomb met the women who had come early to anoint the body of Jesus, they told them that he had risen from the dead, and then charged them to go and tell the good news to "his disciples, *and Peter.*" He was the only one of all the disciples who was mentioned by name in this message of the angels. "Tell his disciples, *and Peter!*" How strange this was! The angels did not do it of their own accord. No doubt Jesus had told them to say this. And why did he do so? What led him to do it? It was the tenderness of his loving heart. He knew how badly Peter had been feeling about his shameful denial of him. He knew what bitter tears he had been shedding over his sin. And he wished to let him know that, notwithstanding what he had done, his injured Master had no unkind feeling in his heart towards him. And so he told the angels to say to the women that they should—"go tell his disciples, *and Peter,*" that their Lord was risen. Here we see the tenderness of Jesus.

And then there was another incident connected with the resurrection of Jesus which shows his tenderness still more touchingly. He arranged matters so that Peter might have a private interview with him, early in the day on which he rose from the dead. St. Luke tells us, Ch. xxiv: 34, that Jesus "appeared unto Simon." And St. Paul says that—"he was seen of Cephas." I. Cor. xv: 5. This was a meeting that Peter had with the Master whom he had denied, *all by himself.* We are not told what took place at this meeting. Peter never said a word about it; and it was too sacred for any one else to intrude upon. But we can very well imagine what was said and done. We can imagine how the poor penitent disciple would sob, as if his heart were breaking, when he saw his injured Master. We can fancy we see him throwing himself at the feet of Jesus and bathing them with bitter, burning tears, as he begged to be forgiven. And then we can think of the kind and gentle words that Jesus would speak to him. How tenderly he would assure him of his free forgiveness! How he would tell him that he loved him still! and how willing he was to put him back in his old place as a disciple, and let him go and preach salvation for lost sinners through his death and resurrection! How kind it was in Jesus thus to give Peter an opportunity of making up with him, when they were all alone by themselves!

Let us never forget the tenderness of Jesus, as shown by these two incidents. And let us try, like him, to be loving and gentle and kind to all. See how much good may be done by those who imitate the example of Christ in this respect.

"The Power of Kindness." An English merchant had taken passage on board a Turkish vessel, on the Mediterranean Sea. During the voyage his attention was called to an interesting man on the vessel, who was a slave belonging to the captain. He had frequent conversations with him and found him to be a kind-hearted, active, and intelligent person. In the course of their conversations together, he learned that the man had been born free, but had been taken captive in war, and was now a slave for life.

The merchant felt a great sympathy for the poor captive and had a desire to get him released. He inquired what it would cost to purchase his freedom. The sum named was more than the whole profit of his voyage. Still he could not give up the thought. He offered the captain a price for his slave. The offer was accepted. The slave overheard this conversation. He supposed the merchant was going to purchase him, that he might keep him as his own slave. This made him very angry. He sprang forward and said, with great excitement, "You call yourself a lover of freedom, an enemy to slavery, wherever found, and yet you are purchasing me!"

The merchant turned and looked kindly on him, as he calmly said, *"My friend, I have bought you to set you at liberty. Now you are a free man."*

In a moment the storm of passion was stilled. The slave burst into tears; and falling at the feet of his deliverer, he exclaimed, *"You have taken my heart captive! I am your servant forever!"*

Few of us may have the opportunity of showing kindness as this merchant did. But every boy and girl in the land may follow the example of the noble lad whose kindness to the aged is told in these simple lines:

SOMEBODY'S MOTHER.

"The woman was old, and ragged and gray,
And bent with the chill of the winter's day;
The street was wet with recent snow,
And the woman's feet were aged and slow.
She stood at the crossing, and waited long,
Alone, uncared for, amid the throng
Of human beings who passed her by,
None heeded the glance of her anxious eye.

"Down the street, with laughter and shout,
 Glad in the freedom of 'school let out,'
 Came the boys, like a flock of sheep,
 Hailing the snow piled white and deep.
 Past the woman so old and gray,
 Hastened the children on their way,
 Nor offered a helping hand to her
 So meek, so timid, afraid to stir

"Lest the carriage-wheels, or the horses' feet
 Should crowd her down in the slippery street.
 At last came one of the merry troop,
 The gayest laddie of the group;
 He paused beside her and whispered low
 'I'll help you across if you wish to go.'
 Her aged hand on his strong young arm
 She placed, and so, without hurt, or harm,

"He guided the trembling feet along,
 Glad that his own were firm and strong.
 Then back again to his friends he went,
 His young heart happy and well content.
 'She's somebody's mother, you know,
 Altho' she is aged, and poor, and slow;
 And I hope some fellow will lend a hand
 To help my mother, you understand,

"If ever she's poor, and old, and gray,
 When her own dear boy is far away.'
 And 'somebody's mother' bowed low her head
 In her home that night, and the prayer she said
 Was, 'God be kind to that noble boy,
 Who is somebody's son, and pride, and joy!'"

Let us never forget the lesson of tenderness which Jesus taught on the morning of his resurrection.

The Resurrection

The only other lesson, in connection with the resurrection of Christ, of which we would now speak is about—THE WAY OF SHOWING OUR LOVE TO HIM.

This lesson was taught on the shore of the Sea of Galilee. Some of the disciples of Jesus had gone back to their old trade of fishing. On one occasion they had been out all night, but had caught nothing. The next morning, Jesus stood on the shore of the lake, but they did not know him. He asked them if they had anything to eat. They said no. He told them to cast the net on the right side of the ship, and they would find plenty of fish. They did so, and their nets were filled at once. Then John, the loving disciple, was the first to find out who it was. He said to Peter, "It is the Lord." As soon as Peter heard this, he fastened his fishing coat about him, plunged into the sea, and swam to the shore. The other disciples rowed to land in their boat. As soon as they landed, they found a fire of coals, with fish and bread all ready for eating. Jesus invited them to come and dine with him. They did so, and when the dinner was over, he had a long conversation with them. As they were talking together, he said to Peter, "Simon, son of Jonas, lovest thou me?" He saith unto him, "Yea, Lord; Thou knowest that I love thee." He saith unto him, "Feed my lambs." This question was repeated by Jesus the second and the third time. Peter gave the same answer each time. The reply of Jesus was—"Feed my sheep." The lambs of Christ's flock mean the children, or young members of his church. The sheep of Christ mean the older members of his church. By feeding his lambs and his sheep, Jesus meant teaching his people, both young an old, about himself, and what he has done for their salvation. And by what Jesus said on this occasion, he meant to teach Peter, and you and me, and all his people, that if we really love him, the way in which he wishes us to show that love, is by being kind to others— by teaching them about him, and by trying to get them to love and serve him, too.

This is a good lesson for ministers to learn; for parents, for teachers, and for all who love Jesus. When we have found what a faithful friend, what a loving Saviour, what a kind and tender comforter we have in him, then he wishes us to do all we can to help others to know him, and love him, and serve him. This is what we should all be trying to do.

Let us look at some of the ways in which we may do this.

"The Unexpected Friend." The Rev. Mr. Moffatt,—the missionary to Southern Africa, tells an interesting story which illustrates very strikingly this part of our subject. "In one of my early journeys in this land," he says, "I came, with my companions, to a heathen village on the banks of a river. We had travelled far, and were hungry and thirsty and very weary. The people of the village would not let us come near them. We asked for water and they would not give us any. We offered to buy milk, but they refused to sell us any. We had no prospect but that of spending the night without anything to eat, or to drink. But at the close of the day a woman came to us from the village. She bore on her head a bundle of wood, and had a vessel of milk in her hand. Without saying a word, she handed us the milk. She laid down the wood and returned to the village. Presently she came again with a cooking vessel on her head, with a leg of mutton in one hand and a vessel of water in the other. Silently she kindled the fire and put on the meat. Again and again we asked her who she was and why she was doing all this for us strangers. At last she said that years before there had been a missionary in her neighborhood. He had gone away a long while ago; but from him she had learned to know the Saviour. 'I love him,' she said, 'whose servants you are, and I wish to show my love to him by doing what I can to help you.' 'I asked her,' said Mr. Moffatt, 'how she, alone in that dark land, without a minister, without a church, and without any Christian friends, had kept up the light of God in her heart?' She drew from her bosom a soiled and worn copy of the New Testament, which the missionary had given her. 'This,' she said, 'is the fountain from which I drink; this is the oil that makes my lamp burn.'"

"How a Boy Showed his Love for Christ." Some time ago a dreadful accident took place on the river Thames, in England. A steamer, called the *Princess Alice*, when crowded with passengers, on an excursion, was run into by another vessel and sunk. Fearful screams filled the air as the great crowd of people were plunged into the water. Among those who were drawn to the spot was a good Christian boy, about sixteen years of age, who worked in the neighborhood. Being a good swimmer, he at once plunged into the water, took hold of the first struggler he met with, and bore him away in safety to the shore. He did the same the second time, and then the third. As he was nearing the shore the third time he saw a small bundle floating on the water, which he thought must be a baby. He caught it with his teeth, and thus was the means of saving four lives on that terrible occasion. By the time he had done this, his strength was exhausted, and he was unable to venture again among the drowning ones. But he carried the baby home to his mother's humble dwelling, and placing the little orphan in her arms, he said, "Here, mother, *suppose you nurse this baby for our blessed Saviour; and I will work for its support as long as I live.*"

A noble boy that was! and a beautiful illustration he gave of the way in which we should show our love to Jesus, by feeding and taking care of his lambs, and doing good to his people.

I never saw the lesson now before us better expressed than in the following simple lines:

SHINING FOR JESUS.

"Are you *shining* for Jesus children? You have given your hearts to Him;
But is the light strong within them, or is it but pale and dim?
Can *everybody* see it—that Jesus is all for you?
That your love to Him is burning with radiance warm and true?
Is the seal upon your forehead, so that it must be known
That you are 'all for Jesus,' that your hearts are all His own?

"Are you shining for Jesus children, so that the holy light
May enter the hearts of others, and make them glad and bright?
Have you spoken a word for Jesus, and told to some around—
Who do not care about Him,—what a Saviour you have found?
Have you lifted the lamp for others, that has guided your own glad feet?
Have you echoed the loving message, that seemed to you so sweet?

"Are you shining for Jesus, children, shining just everywhere?
Not only in easy places, not only just here or there?
Shining in happy gatherings, where all are loved and known?
Shining where all are strangers,—shining when quite alone?
Shining at home, and making true sunshine all around?
Shining at school, and faithful—perhaps among faithless—found?

"Oh! rise, and 'watching daily,' ask Him your lamps to trim,
With the fresh oil which He giveth, that they may not burn dim.
Yes, rise and shine for Jesus! Be brave, and bright and true,
To the true and loving Saviour, who gave Himself for you.
Oh! shine for Jesus children! and henceforth be your way
Bright with the light that shineth unto the perfect day!"

THE ASCENSION

WE come now to the last event in the history of our Saviour's life on earth. His work is done. His teachings are finished. His sufferings are ended. Nothing remains for him to do but to return to heaven, from whence he came, and take his seat at the right hand of God. And this is the subject we are now to consider—*The Ascension of Christ.*

And in considering it, the first thing for us to notice is—*the time of the Ascension.*

And in all the New Testament there is only one place in which anything is said about the time of the ascension. Indeed it is surprising that so little is said about it altogether. Two of the gospels, that of St. Matthew and St. John, have not a word to say on the subject. And the other two do not say much. All that St. Mark says about it is in a single verse. We read thus in Chap. xvi: 19:—"So, then, after that the Lord had spoken unto them, he was received up into heaven, and sat on the right hand of God." There are two verses in St. Luke in which the ascension is spoken of. In Ch. xxiv: 50, 51, we find the ascension thus described: "And he led them out as far as to Bethany; and he lifted up his hands and blessed them. And it came to pass, while he blessed them, he was parted from them, and carried up into heaven."

The most particular account of the ascension that we have in the New Testament is given in the "Acts of the Apostles." In the first chapter of this book we are told that the ascension took place "forty days after the resurrection." We are told of the "many infallible proofs" that he had risen, and how he spoke to them "of the things pertaining to the kingdom of heaven." And he "commanded them not to depart from Jerusalem," until they should "be baptized with the Holy Ghost," which was to take place "not many days" after his ascension. "Ye shall receive power," said he, "after that the Holy Ghost is come upon you." Then he told them how "they should be witnesses for him, both in Jerusalem and in all Judea, and unto the uttermost parts of the earth." "And when he had spoken these things, while they beheld, he was taken up; and a cloud received him out of their sight."

And then we read about the two angels who appeared to the disciples and told them that "this same Jesus, which was taken up from you into heaven, shall so come, in like manner, as ye have seen him go into heaven."

In the third verse of this chapter we have the only information which the whole Bible gives us about the *time* of the ascension. Here we learn that this great event took place on the *fortieth* day after his resurrection. We are not told why the ascension was delayed so long after Jesus had risen from the dead. But, no doubt, there were good reasons for it. And it may be that we shall know all about these reasons hereafter, though we do not know them now.

If we begin and count the forty days from Easter Sunday, the fortieth day will always come on the Thursday in the fifth week after Easter. And this day is always kept in the Church of England, in the Protestant Episcopal Church in this country, and in some other churches in memory of the important event we are now considering. It is called Ascension

Day, or Holy Thursday; and the portions of Scripture read on that day all have reference to the ascension of our blessed Lord. And this is all that need be said about the *time* of the ascension.

The *place* where the ascension occurred is the next thing to notice.

From what we read in the gospel of St. Luke, we might suppose it was from Bethany that Jesus made his ascension. Here it says, "He led them out as far as to Bethany, and he lifted up his hands and blessed them. And it came to pass, while he blessed them, he was parted from them, and carried up into heaven." St. Luke xxiv: 50, 51. But in the first chapter of the Acts of the Apostles, after describing his ascension, we read that the disciples "returned unto Jerusalem from the Mount called Olivet." Acts i: 12. But there is no contradiction here; for Bethany, the home of Lazarus and his sisters, was on the Mount of Olives. It was situated just below the top of the Mount, on the other side from Jerusalem. And so we know that it was either from the village of Bethany, or from some spot between that and the summit of the Mount, that Jesus made his ascension. When he was here on earth he often went to the Mount of Olives. It was from this mountain that "Jesus beheld the city and wept over it," when he used that beautiful illustration, "how often would I have gathered thy children together, even as a hen gathereth her chickens under her wings, and ye would not!" It was on this mountain that he sat with his disciples when he gave that wonderful prophecy about the destruction of Jerusalem, and his coming again into our world, of which we read in the twenty-fourth chapter of St. Matthew.

The Mount of Olives was the last spot of this earth on which the feet of the blessed Saviour stood before he went up to heaven. And when he comes again into our world he will return to the place from which he ascended. This we are told by the prophet Zechariah. For it is when he is speaking of the return of Jesus from heaven that he says—"And his feet shall stand at that day on the Mount of Olives." Ch. xiv: 4. This thought very naturally makes Olivet an interesting place to visit.

I remember, when at Jerusalem, a very pleasant visit we made to this sacred Mount. It was at the close of a Sunday afternoon. The sun went down as we stood there. And there was something very sweet and solemn in the thought that Jesus, our glorious Lord, had once stood on that Mount, near where we then were. It was from there that his disciples saw him go into heaven. And when he comes back from heaven, his feet will stand again upon the Mount of Olives. And so, when we think of our Saviour going back to heaven, we may always remember that some spot on or near the top of the Mount of Olives was the place of the ascension.

The Manner of the Ascension—is the third thing of which to speak.

It was a *visible* ascension. There are only two other persons spoken of in the Bible as having gone up from earth to heaven in a bodily form. One of them was "Enoch, the seventh from Adam." His ascension was not visible. No one saw him go. It took place in secret. We are told in one place that "he was not, for God took him." In another place it is said, "he was translated." This is all we know about the translation of Enoch.

The other case mentioned in the Bible is that of the prophet Elijah. His ascension was visible, indeed, but it was only seen by one person, and that was the prophet Elisha. But it was different with the ascension of Christ.

This did not take place in secret, but in public. It was not only visible, but was witnessed by a crowd of people. All the eleven disciples were there to see it. And there can be no doubt that a great many others, besides the apostles, were there too. And they all saw him, as he rose from the midst of them, and went up to heaven. It was a *visible* ascension.

It was a *calm and tranquil* ascension. It was not done in a hurry. Solomon tells us, when speaking of God's doings, that his "judgments are not executed speedily." This means they are not done in haste. God never works in a hurry. After he gave to Adam the first promise, of a future deliverer from the effects of sin, he waited more than four thousand years before he sent him into the world. And, after Christ had risen from the dead, he was not in haste to leave the world, and go back to heaven. We might have expected that he would just have shown himself once or twice to his disciples, so as to make them sure of his resurrection, and would have left immediately for heaven. But it was not so. Instead of this he remained here for forty days. He did not spend all this time in the company of his disciples. He only showed himself to them from time to time, and talked with them "of things pertaining to the kingdom of God." And when at last these days were over, and the time came for him to go, still there was no haste about it.. He did not go up with a rush, as a rocket goes up. That would not have been like him. But, as he stood on the Mount of Olives talking to his disciples, who were standing round him, he began to rise slowly and silently towards heaven. And as he began, so he went on. Slowly and silently he continued to rise. Upwards he went, higher—and higher,—till at last a cloud received him out of their sight. That cloud became, as it were, the chariot in which he was carried up in triumph to heaven. It was a *calm* and *tranquil* ascension.

It was a *blessed* ascension. You know how it is at the close of a service in church. The minister lifts up his hands to bless the people, or as we say, to pronounce the benediction. And this was what Jesus was doing at the very moment of his ascension. He knew that the time had come for him to go. He knew that he was about to be separated from his disciples, and that they would see him no more in this world. So he lifted up his hands to bless them; and, while he was in the act of speaking those words of blessing, the ascension took place. As his hands were stretched out to bless his disciples, he rose calmly in the midst of them and went back to heaven, from whence he came.

It was said of him before he came into our world, that—"men should be blessed in him:" Ps. lxxii: 17. He was the promised seed of Abraham, in whom it was declared that "all the nations of the earth should be blessed." Gen. xxii: 18. The blessing of the world was wrapped up in Jesus. When he came into the world, he came to bless it. And when he began his public ministry in the Sermon on the Mount, the first thing of which he had to speak was the blessings he came to bring. We read, "And when he was set, his disciples came to him, and he opened his mouth and taught them, saying, Blessed are the poor in spirit, &c. Blessed are they that mourn, &c. Blessed are the meek, &c. Blessed are the merciful, &c. Blessed are the pure in heart, &c." He began his work in blessing; he continued it in blessing; and he ended it in blessing. But the work of blessing in which he had been engaged here did not cease when he ascended into heaven. He has been carrying on the work of blessing men ever since he ascended. He went to heaven to procure for his people the best of all possible blessings. He told his disciples that it was necessary for him to leave them and go to heaven; because if he did not go the Holy Ghost would not come to them; but that when he went to heaven he would send the Spirit to be their helper and comforter. It is the Holy Spirit who helps us to understand the Scriptures and who teaches us how to love and serve God. And whatever helps us to do this is the best thing—the greatest blessing for us. And when we know that Jesus went to heaven to obtain for us the help of God's grace and Spirit, we may well say that the ascension of Christ was a blessed ascension.

The only other thing we have to say about the ascension of Christ is that it was a *wonderful* ascension. There were two wonderful things connected with it. It was wonderful to think *where* he went. He did not go simply to join the company of the angels, who have always lived in heaven, and of the good people who went there when they died. No; but he went where no one else had ever gone before, and where no one else could go. When he arrived in heaven, he rose above all the company that was there, and took his seat at the right hand of the throne of God. This was wonderful, indeed. When Jesus was on earth, he was so poor that he "had not where to lay his head." He was despised and persecuted; "a man of sorrows and acquainted with grief." He was put to death as a criminal, by being crucified between two thieves. But when he ascended into heaven it was to take his place "far above all principalities and powers." And so his ascension was wonderful when we think—*where* he went.

And it was wonderful, too, when we think *how* he went there. If he had left his human body behind him, and had ascended to heaven simply in his divine nature, as God, it would not have been so wonderful. But he did not do this. He took his human body with him. The body that was nailed to the cross and laid in the grave, he took with him to heaven. He ascended, indeed, as the Son of God. But that was not all. No, for he ascended as the Son of man, too. It was Jesus Christ who ascended into heaven. But it was our human nature, as well as the divine nature which helped to make up the person of Jesus Christ. And so when he ascended into heaven, and sat down at the right hand of the throne of God, he took our human nature with him. He took a body like yours and mine, up to that high and glorious place. And he is sitting there now, on the throne of God, as our brother. *This* is the most surprising thing connected with the great event we are now considering. This shows us how wonderful the ascension of Christ was.

And so, in studying this subject, these are the things about it that we have noticed, viz.: the *time* of the ascension—forty days after the resurrection; the *place* of the ascension—the Mount of Olives; the *manner* of the ascension—*visible —calm and tranquil—blessed—and wonderful.*

There are several lessons that may be learned from the ascension of our Saviour, but we can only speak of one. This is *the lesson of obedience to the command of Christ.*

Just before he went up to heaven, Jesus said to his disciples—"Go ye into all the world, and preach the gospel to every creature." St. Mark xvi: 15. This is the last command he gave to his people. He kept it till now because he wished it to be especially remembered. When we lose a father, or mother, or a friend whom we love very much, we listen attentively to the words spoken by that friend as we gather round the dying bed. We may forget some things spoken by him in the days of his health and strength, but those last words that were spoken just before he died, we always remember. They seem very sacred to us, and we pay particular attention to them. And no doubt this was the reason why Jesus kept this command about the missionary work he wishes his people to engage in, till now. He had finished his work for them. He had died for them. He had done all that was necessary for them to be saved, and to be happy with him forever in heaven. He knew how much they ought to love him for all this. And he knew that those who really did love him would wish to show their love by doing what he had told them to do. And so he kept this—the most important of all his commands—to the last. He wished it to be connected with the thought of his leaving the world and going back to heaven. And as they gathered round him, to see him and hear him for the last time on earth, he spoke these words: —"Go, ye, into all the world, and preach the gospel to every creature." He did not speak them for the apostles or the early Christians only. No; but he spoke them for you, and for me, and for all his people, till the end of time. He intended his church to be a missionary church. He intended that all the members of that church should feel an interest in the missionary work, and that they should do all they can to help it on. This command is very broad. It takes in "all the world," and "every creature." We have no right to make the field for this work narrower than Jesus made it. And, until the gospel has been preached in "all the world," and until "every creature" has heard it, this command of Christ is binding upon all his loving people. If we do not have the missionary spirit which these words require us to have, that is, if we are not trying all we can to bring "every creature," in "all the world," to be the friend and servant of Jesus and to be saved by him, then, it is clear, either that we are not loving Jesus as we ought to love him; or else, we are not showing our love for him in the way in which he wishes us to show it. He says, "If ye love me, keep my commandments." And this is his last and most solemn command for us to remember, and keep.

When he says—"Go ye into all the world and preach," he does not mean that all his people must leave their homes and go out as ordained ministers. What he means is that whether we go out as missionaries, or not, we must have the missionary spirit, and must do all we can to help the missionaries in their work. We must try to get those around us to know, and love, and serve Jesus. And the important question for us all to consider here is —how can we do this? In answering this question, let me point out *four* ways in which this may be done.

We can be missionaries, and help to preach the gospel, *by our example.*

A little boy named Ernest had begun to love the Lord Jesus Christ and to be a Christian. One day he said to his aunt, "Now I want to grow up a big man, and then I will be a minister and preach to lots of people about Jesus."

His aunt told him that he need not wait till he was a man before he began to preach. "Try now, every day, to learn your lessons well," said his aunt; "to be kind, and gentle to all, and try by God's help to overcome your bad temper, and so, by your example you may be preaching Jesus every day."

"The Children's Service." A little girl went to a Children's service one Sunday afternoon. On going home she told her mother about it. "What led you to go, Mary?" asked the mother.

"I went, mamma," she said, "because I was invited to come by a kind boy that I met in the street yesterday. I saw him stop and stroke a donkey that was frightened by a cruel boy. Then he kindly picked up my ball that was rolling away and returned it to me. As he did this he handed me a paper about the children's service, and invited me to come. I knew he was a good boy because he was so kind and had such a happy face. He said he was sure I would like the services; and I did like them. And I mean to go every time."

"A Young Hero." Thirty years ago a boy had given his heart to the Saviour. He had been confirmed and joined the church. The next day he went to school. Some of the wild boys of the school heard that he had joined the church, and they made up their minds to have some fun with him about it. At recess time they formed a ring about him, and cried out:

"Oh! here is the good boy, Charley! He is going to be a Christian!"

And what did Charley do? Did he feel ashamed and try to steal away? Did he get angry, and hit, or kick, or speak cross to them? No. But he calmly looked the rude boys in the face, and said, in a manly way: "Yes, boys,

I am trying to be a Christian. And isn't that right?"

The boys' consciences told them he was right. They felt ashamed. The ring was broken up at once, and Charley had no more trouble.

He was preaching by his example.

"A Beautiful Illustration." Mary Duncan was a little girl, only four years old, who was trying to be a Christian. This incident shows us that even at that early age she was beginning to preach, and do good by her example.

One day she was playing with her little brother. In a fit of anger he struck her in the face. But instead of screaming out, or striking him back, she quietly turned to him the other cheek; and said, "There Corie, now strike that!" The uplifted hand was dropped. The tears came into her brother's eyes. He kissed her, and said—"Forgive me, sister, and I'll never strike you again."

When Mary was asked what led her to do so, her reply was that she had heard her papa read out of the Bible, at prayers that morning, what Jesus had said about it.

And so if we try to be like Jesus, we may be helping to keep his last command, and to preach the gospel—by our example.

Another way in which we may do this is—*by our efforts*. This means by what we say and do to show that we love him, and to try to bring others to do so too. We find many illustrations of the way in which this may be done.

"Preaching in the Hayfield." A good, earnest minister of the gospel was riding one day past a hayfield. A sudden shower was coming up. He saw a farmer, who never went to church, sending off in haste for a horse to draw his hay in before the rain came. The minister stopped and offered his horse to do the work. It was declined; but the minister insisted, and pulling off his coat, unhitched his horse and went to work helping the farmer to load the hay. They got in several loads, and when the last load was in the barn, and the rain came pouring down, the farmer drew out his pocket book, and said:

"How much do I owe you, sir, for your help?"

"Oh, nothing," said he, "nothing at all."

But the farmer insisted on paying him for his work.

"Well, my friend," said the minister, "did you ever hear an Irishman preach?"

"No," said the farmer.

"Well, you come next Sunday, and hear me preach, and we'll call it even."

The farmer agreed to do it, and for the first time in many years was present in the house of prayer. He found out that the man who could load the hay could preach the gospel too. He believed it. He obeyed it. That hour's work, helping him to save his hay from the rain, was the means of leading him to Jesus, and of saving his soul.

"The Lost Diamond." An elegantly dressed lady, as she stepped one day from her carriage, in the city of Washington, missed her valuable diamond ring. It had slipped from her finger in some way, as she left the carriage, and had fallen into the gutter, where it was speedily buried in the filth that flowed toward the sewer. She looked with dismay on that muddy stream, and offered a policeman five dollars to put his hand into the gutter and find the ring. He hesitated awhile, but finally agreed, and reached down into the filth and spent some time in groping about the gutter But he failed to find the lost jewel. At length he gave up the search and told the lady that it had probably been washed along, and gone down the sewer. She paid him the five dollars, and he went away. But the lady stood there still, looking sadly down at the place where her lost gem had disappeared. She could not bear to give it up. She lingered and hesitated; and finally, taking off her glove, and pushing back her silks and ruffles and laces, she bared her arm for the work, put her fair hand down into the reeking filth, and after searching patiently in every direction, she found the precious jewel, and carried it away in triumph.

Now there are lost souls all about us, souls for whom Christ died, ten thousand times more precious than that lady's gem. They are lost in the mire of filth and sin. But they may be found and brought to Christ, by such earnest, persevering efforts as she made for that lost jewel. And if we put forth such loving, personal efforts for them, they may be saved. And those who make such efforts are obeying the Saviour's command to preach the gospel to every creature.

"It's All I Can Do." Bessie King was a bright child about fourteen years old. She was a serious, thoughtful girl, who wanted to make herself useful. One summer afternoon she went into her father's garden and gathered a bunch of flowers. While doing so, she wondered if she could not make some one happy by the gift of these flowers. All at once she thought of her young friend, Nellie Vance. Nellie was sick with consumption. She had been confined to her room for months, and was not expected to live very long. Her mother was a poor widow, and unable to do much for her sick child. But Nellie was trying to be a Christian, and the thought of the loving Saviour made her cheerful and happy.

Bessie was very fond of Nellie and loved to visit her whenever she could. So she gathered some of the loveliest flowers in the garden and hastened with them to her friend Nellie's humble home. As she entered her chamber, she said—"Nellie, dear, I've come to bring you a bit of my summer," and she laid the flowers down by Nellie, who was lying on a couch near the window. Nellie's delight at seeing the flowers was an abundant reward to Bessie for bringing them. It was touching to see the sick child as she lay there, with the bright flowers around her. She handled them so tenderly, one by one, almost forgetting, in the pleasure they gave her, the weary, aching pain, she was always feeling.

"I am so glad you came this afternoon, Bessie dear," said Nellie, when the flowers were arranged. "I have something so happy to tell you." Bessie looked at her with surprise, wondering what happiness poor suffering Nellie could have left to her.

"I have been thinking for a long time," said Nellie, "how little I have done for the Lord Jesus. I have been shut out from people so long, that I'm afraid no one knows I love him; and I can't bear to go away from earth without a word *out loud* for him. So Bessie, I am going to be confirmed. That will be standing up for Jesus, and it's all I can do."

"But, Nellie dear, how can *you* be confirmed? You hav'n't been out of your room for months, and church is more than two miles away."

"I can do it for Jesus," she said firmly. "Mr. Gray has promised to take me in his carriage, and to carry me up in the church."

Bessie could say no more. Her heart was full, and she threw her arms round Nellie's neck and wept.

"I want you to come with me, Bessie dear," said Nellie. But Bessie could not speak. So Nellie went on, and said: "You have your whole life to live for him, so you ought to begin right off. But mine is so nearly ended, that I must come now, or I never can come. It's all I can do. But Bessie I want you to come with me."

And they did both come. Bessie held back at first, afraid of herself, but Nellie talked so sweetly to her that she had to yield. "When Jesus called the little child to him, Bessie," said her friend, "don't you think he would have felt hurt if he had held back, and refused to come to him? Suppose he had said he wasn't good enough, or old enough! Jesus wanted him, just as he was. He had plenty of grown up people. He wanted a little child then, and he wants us now."

It was a touching sight when the sick child was carried up the aisle, to join her young companions at the chancel; and when the bishop laid his hands on her head, and his voice trembled there was not a dry eye in the church.

Not long after, Nellie was carried again into the church. Yet this time it was not Nellie herself, but only the poor worn body that had suffered so long, and was now at rest Her sufferings were now over, and her work was done. Her spirit was with her Saviour she had loved, to be forever happy in his presence.

Nellie was faithfully carrying out the last command of Jesus, when she tried so lovingly to get her friend Bessie to stand with her and confess him before men. By our efforts to bring those around us to Jesus, we may help to carry out that last command of his.

We can do this also—*by our gifts*. There is no better use to make of our money than to give it to help in sending the gospel of Jesus to those who do not know him. And the smallest sums are often very useful when given for this purpose. Here is a story of a poor little orphan girl who had earned six cents by running errands, and of the great good that was done by her gift. Her name was Dixey, and we may call the story:

"Dixey's Six Cents." One day, a pale-faced little girl walked hurriedly into a book store in Boston, and said to the man at the counter: "Please sir, I want a book that's got, 'Suffer little children to come unto me,' in it; and how much is it sir? and I'm in a great hurry."

The bookseller wiped his spectacles, and looking down at the poor child, he took her thin little hand in his, and said: "What do you want the book for my child? and why are you in such a hurry?"

"Well, sir, you see, I went to Sunday-school, last Sunday, when Mrs. West, the woman who takes care of me, was away; and the teacher read about a Good Shepherd, who loves little children, and who said these words. And the teacher told us about a beautiful place where he takes care of his children and makes them all happy, and I want to go there.

"I'm so tired of being where there's nobody to care for a girl like me, only Mrs. West who says I'd better be dead than alive."

"But why are you in such a hurry, my child?"

"My cough's getting so bad now, sir, and I want to know about him before I die; it would be so strange to see him and not know him. Besides, if Mrs. West knew I was here she'd take away the six cents I've saved from running errands, to buy the book with, so I'm in a hurry to get served."

The bookseller wiped his spectacles again, and taking a book from the shelf, he said, "I'll find the words you want, my child; listen while I read them." Then he turned to St. Luke xviii: 16, and read to her the sweet words of the loving Saviour. After reading them he told her about the Good Shepherd; how he came down from heaven to seek and save the lost sheep; how he suffered and died for us that we might live; and about the bright and beautiful home in heaven, which he has prepared for all who love and serve him.

"Oh, how sweet that is!" said the earnest and almost breathless little listener. "He says—'Come.' I'll go to him. How long do you think it'll be sir, before I see him?"

"Not long, I think, said the bookseller, turning away his head to hide the tears that were running down his cheeks. "Now you can keep the six cents and come here every day, and I will read to you some more out of this Book."

The little girl thanked him and hurried away. The next day, and the next, and many days passed away, but the poor child never came to hear about Jesus again. Some time after this a rough-looking woman came into the bookstore, and said in a loud voice, "Dixey's dead! She died rambling about some Good Shepherd, and she said you were to have these six cents for the mission-box at school. I don't like to keep dead people's money, so here it is," and throwing the six cents down on the counter, she hurried out of the store.

The six cents were put into the missionary box on the next Sunday, and when the story of Dixey was told it touched so many hearts and led so many to follow her example with their pennies that by the end of the year "Dixey's cents," as they were called, had brought in money enough to send out a missionary to China, to help in finding out the lost sheep and bringing them to Jesus. And if little Dixey, in her feebleness and poverty, could help to carry out our Saviour's last command, then we may all do so.

But there are other things than money that may be given to the work of saving lost souls. We see this illustrated in the following story. It may be called:

"The Rescue." "O my child, my child!" cried an almost heart-broken mother, as she met a party of gentlemen, among the hills of Scotland.

"What's the matter?" they asked.

"A few hours ago I left the house and my baby-boy in charge of his sister. Being a fine day, he was lying in the cradle, outside the cottage-door, prattling away in the sunshine. After awhile, baby fell asleep, and my little girl being hungry, went in-doors to get some food. While she was lingering there, I returned, but only in time to see an eagle bearing away my child in his talons. O sirs! pity me, help me, recover my darling child."

The mother's loving eye had watched the flight of the eagle; and with these gentlemen she went to the edge of the cliff, and looking over the precipice they could see, far down its steep sides, the nest of the eagles, to which the child had been carried. The distress of the mother touched the heart of one of the gentleman who was a Scotch nobleman. He resolved, by God's help, to try and snatch the child from the terrible death that awaited it.

Ropes were procured, and at his own request, the nobleman was lowered down over the rugged cliff. The two eagles fluttered round, as if daring the intruder to approach their nest; but a brave heart was beating beneath that Scotch plaid. Fearlessly the heroic Scotchman approached the nest. He took the child from among the young eagles. He bound it to his bosom, and gave the signal to be pulled up. Gently, but steadily, he was raised in safety to the top of the cliff; and with a glad heart he gave back the recovered child to the arms of its grateful and rejoicing mother.

This story illustrates what Jesus has done for us; but, at the same time it shows what we should do for those whose souls have been carried away by Satan the great enemy, and who are in danger of perishing forever. If we feel for them, as this good nobleman felt for that lost child, it will lead us to give, not our money only, but our sympathy, and everything in our power, to bring them to Jesus, that they may be saved through him forever. And so we see how by our gifts, we may help to carry out the great command which Jesus left for his people, just before his ascension into heaven.

And then, there is one other way in which we may help to do this, and that is by—*our prayers.*

There is a wonderful power in prayer. It is a power which all may use, and which will reach all around the world. We see this strikingly illustrated in the case of the Syro-Phœnician woman mentioned in St. Matt. xv: 20-28. Her prayers caused the casting out of the devil from her daughter. When Jesus was on earth he said to his disciples—"All things whatsoever ye shall ask in prayer, believing, ye shall receive." St. Matt. xxi: 22. This is God's promise to you and to me and to all his people. And so when we pray for ministers and missionaries; when we pray for the conversion of the heathen, and for others who do not not love and serve God, we are helping on the good work which Jesus left for his people to do when he said—"Go ye into all the world and preach the gospel to every creature." It would be easy enough to fill a volume with incidents which illustrate the power of prayer. But we have only room for a single illustration.

"Saved by Prayer." Some years ago, a boy left his home in Indiana for Chicago. He was not there long before he fell into bad company, and was led astray. A friend of his father's, who lived in the same town, happening to visit Chicago, saw that boy on the street one night drunk.

On returning home, he thought at first that he would not say anything to the father about what he had seen; but afterwards he felt that it was his duty to tell him. So meeting him one day in the crowded street of their little town, he took him aside and told him what he had seen in Chicago. It was a terrible blow to him.

On returning home that night, before going to bed, he told his wife what he had heard. They were both so much distressed that they could not sleep. They spent the greater part of the night in earnest prayer for their poor boy. Before morning the mother said, "I don't know how it is, but God has given me faith to believe that our son will be saved and not be allowed to fill a drunkard's grave."

Not long after this, that boy left Chicago. He could not tell why, but an unseen power seemed to lead him to his mother's home. On entering the house the first thing he said was: "Mother I have come home to ask you to pray for me." She prayed with him, and for him, and he soon became a sincere and earnest Christian. Here we see the power of prayer. Let us all use this power, and we shall be helping on the preaching of the gospel in all the world, and to every creature.

And so, when we think of the ascension of Christ, let us always remember the great work that Jesus commanded his people to do; and let us try to help on that work in the four ways of which we have spoken,—by our *examples*—by our *efforts*—by our *gifts*—and by our *prayers*.

The Collect for Ascension Day is a very suitable one with which to close this subject:

"Grant, we beseech thee, Almighty God, that like as we do believe thy only-begotten Son, our Lord Jesus Christ, to have ascended into the heavens; so we may also in heart and mind thither ascend, and with him continually dwell, who liveth and reigneth, with thee and the Holy Ghost, One God, world without end. Amen."

THE DAY OF PENTECOST

JESUS has finished his work on earth and gone back to heaven. We have now, in bringing this history to a close, to consider how the work was carried on, after he was gone.

After the ascension of Christ there was a pause. For some days everything stood still in connection with the great cause for which Jesus had lived and died. This pause continued until the day of Pentecost. Then the Holy Ghost was sent down from heaven. He took up the work where Jesus had left it, and has been engaged in carrying it on from that day to this. Nothing could be done till he came. No sermons were preached. No lessons were taught. No souls were converted till the Holy Ghost came. This shows us how important his presence and help are in all the work which the church of Christ has to do for the glory of God and for the salvation of men. Take an illustration.

Here is a locomotive, standing on a railway, with a train of cars attached to it. The engine is new and beautiful. Every wheel and crank and pin is in its proper place. It is complete; it is perfect. The boiler is full of water. The tender, attached to the locomotive, is full of fuel. The passengers are all waiting; but yet the engine stands still. Nothing moves. What is the matter? Simply this: there is no steam in the boiler. And what is wanting to make the steam? Why a fire in the furnace. Can nothing take the place of this? Nothing in the world. This is absolutely necessary. Everything depends on this. But now see, the fire is kindled. There is steam in the boiler. The wheels begin to move, and away goes the train.

When Jesus went to heaven, the church he left on earth might well be compared to such an engine. He had built it well. Its machinery was all complete; but it stood still. The power was wanting to put it in motion. The Holy Spirit alone could give this power. When he came the fire was kindled: the steam was generated; and the train was started, which was to run around the world, and carry countless numbers of ransomed souls to heaven.

The Day of Pentecost 213

And in speaking about the coming of the Spirit, there are three things for us to notice. These are—*the time of the Spirit's coming: the manner of the Spirit's coming; and the purpose of the Spirit's coming.*

The time of the Spirit's coming is pointed out in the name of the day when he came. It was on the day of Pentecost. This word means the *fiftieth:* whether it be a day, or a number, or anything else to which it may be applied. The Jews used this word as the name of one of the three great feasts which they were commanded to keep every year. This one was called "the feast of Pentecost," because it was kept on the fiftieth day after the feast of the Passover. It was sometimes called also—"the feast of Weeks." This name was given to it, because the forty-nine days, which came in between these two feasts, just made up seven weeks.

It pleased God to connect with this day of Pentecost the most important event that has ever taken place in the history of the church or of the world since the ascension of Jesus into heaven—and that was—the coming of the Holy Ghost.

And this great event has always been remembered with interest by the Christian church. In the early days of the church, the day kept in memory of the coming of the Holy Ghost was set apart as one of the solemn seasons for baptizing persons who wished to be received into the church. The candidates for baptism on these occasions were clothed in white garments, to denote the purity which should mark those who received baptism properly, by truly repenting of their sins, and having their souls washed in the blood of Christ. And for this reason, the Sunday on which the day of Pentecost was thus celebrated, was called Whit-Sunday, or Whit-Suntide.

In the Episcopal Church in this country, in the Church of England, and in some other branches of the Church of Christ, this Whit-Suntide festival is still kept with great interest. The scriptures read on this day refer to the coming of the Spirit and to the importance of his work; and the sermons preached at this season generally have reference to the same subject. And when we remember how the success of the great work in which the Church of Christ is engaged depends upon the help which the Holy Spirit gives, we see how important it is that we should be constantly reminded of the necessity of having his presence and power with us in all our efforts to do good to the souls of men. And so, when we think of the time of the Spirit's coming, we may bear in mind that it was on the day of Pentecost, or on the fiftieth day after the death of Christ.

And now, we may go on to speak of—*the* MANNER *of the Spirit's coming.*

It was an *expected* coming. Jesus had told his disciples about the coming of the Spirit and had given them a promise that he should come. He said to them on one occasion: "It is expedient for you that I go away; for if I go not away, the Comforter will not come to you; but if I depart, I will send him unto you." St. John xvi: 7.

And then, just before his ascension into heaven, he repeated this promise, commanding them "not to depart from Jerusalem, but to wait for the promise of the Father:" again he said, "ye shall be baptized with the Holy Ghost not many days hence;" and again, "ye shall receive power after that the Holy Ghost is come upon you." Acts i: 4, 5, 8.

And, according to these promises, we find that the apostles were waiting for the coming of the Holy Spirit and expecting it when the day of

Pentecost arrived. They had not been told how long they were to wait. All that had been said about the time of his coming was that it would be "not many days hence." After Jesus left them and went to heaven, they seem to have met together every day, engaging in prayer and praise. No doubt they read the scriptures on these occasions, and talked together about their ascended Lord and the fulfilment of the promise he had left them. Day after day, they had met for this purpose, waiting for the Holy Spirit. But one day passed by after another and the Spirit did not come. Still they felt sure that he would come. They were waiting for his coming: and when at last he came, we may well say of it, that it was an *expected* coming.

It was a *sudden* coming. We know how often it happens that something we have been expecting for a long time comes suddenly at last. And it was so with the disciples on this occasion. They had met once more for their daily worship. As they came together, on the day of Pentecost, there was no more sign of the coming of the Spirit on that day than there had been on any of the previous days; but he came at last. We are not told whether it was at the beginning, or the middle, or the close of their meeting, that he came. The Holy Spirit did not send a messenger before him, to tell of his coming, as kings and great men in the East were in the habit of doing. No trumpet was sounded. No signal was given. But, all at once, the promise of the Father was fulfilled; the expectation of the disciples was met—the Holy Ghost came down from heaven. But it was a *sudden* coming. Acts i: 2.

In the next place it was—a startling coming. The *sound* connected with it made it such for one thing. We read that "there came a *sound* as of a rushing, mighty wind." We are not told that there *was* a wind on this occasion; but only that the sound which attended the coming of the Spirit was *like* that of a mighty wind. The Spirit might have come to the disciples on this occasion as "the still, small voice" of God came to the prophet Elijah, on Mount Horeb. But it was not so. On the contrary, he chose that his coming should be attended with a loud noise. We read that "it," that is the sound, "filled all the house where they were sitting." We are not told what this sounding noise was for. It may have been to arouse the attention of the disciples and make them fully awake to the important event that was then taking place. And, no doubt, another reason why this rushing sound attended the Spirit's coming was to indicate to them what great power would attend the Spirit in the work he was to carry on in the church and in the world. The wind, when it goes rushing on, in the form of a tempest, is one of the most powerful agents that we know of. It can lash the ocean into foam and fury. It can dash to pieces the noblest works of men, whether on the land, or on the sea. It can tear up the giant oak by its roots and lay it prostrate on the ground. And the sound of that "rushing, mighty wind" with which the Spirit came was intended, it may be, to make the disciples feel how great was the power he was able to give them in the important work they had to do. "The sound, as of a rushing, mighty wind," seemed to tell of this.

But again, we are always startled by that which is *unusual*. And there were several things about this coming of the Holy Spirit which were unusual, and so calculated to startle the waiting disciples. There was, for instance, the *direction* of this sound. It came "*down from heaven.*" The winds, with whose sound we are familiar, never act in this direction.

The Day of Pentecost

From whatever point of the compass they come, they always blow around, or over the earth. A wind blowing *"down from heaven,"* directly towards the earth, as was the case with that sound which the disciples heard, was something unusual, and so calculated to startle them.

Another unusual thing about this sound was, that it was a sound *like* that of a wind, but yet without any wind at all. They heard that sound. It reminded them of the wind. But there was no motion there, such as the wind produces when it blows. Nothing stirred in that upper chamber. A feather would not have been moved. So far as motion was concerned— all was calm, and still there. And yet there was that mighty sound. How startling this must have been!

And then, what accompanied this sound was startling, as well as the sound itself. There were those "cloven tongues, like as of fire." Little long pieces of flame were seen in the air of that chamber. There were about a hundred and twenty persons present there. And a hundred and twenty of these fiery tongues were seen. How strange it must have been to look on such a number of these marvellous appearances, and to see one of them come down and rest on the head of each person present! But, the Holy Spirit was come; and these things must have made it a startling coming.

And then it was—an *abiding* coming. When the Holy Spirit came down upon the Church of Christ, on the day of Pentecost, he did not come to remain for a little while, and then go back to heaven. No! but he came to *stay*. When Jesus spoke to the disciples about the coming of the Holy Ghost, he used these words: "And I will pray the Father, and he shall give you another Comforter, that he may *abide with you forever.*" St. John xiv: 16.

It was not for the help and comfort of the apostles and early Christians only that the Holy Spirit came. No; but it was for the help and comfort of all the people of Christ, down to the end of the world. The coming of the Spirit, which took place on the day of Pentecost was intended to be an abiding coming. He has never left the church from that day. But he may be present, without putting forth his power and making his presence felt. What we need to pray for is not that the Holy Spirit may *come* into our churches; for he is there; but that he may make his power and presence felt. What we want above all things, in our hearts, in our homes, in our Sunday Schools, and in our churches, is to feel the power and presence of that Spirit, who came on the day of Pentecost, and whose coming was to be an abiding coming.

And so, when we would show the manner of the Spirit's coming to the early church, we may say that it was an *expected* coming—a *sudden* coming—a *startling* coming—and an *abiding* coming.

And now, the only other thing to notice, is —*The*—PURPOSE—*of the Spirit's coming.*

And if we wish to understand clearly the meaning of this part of the subject, there are these two things for us to consider; viz., *what the Holy Spirit is; and what the Holy Spirit does.*

And in order to understand satisfactorily what the Holy Spirit is—we must find out what the scriptures call him; and how the scriptures speak of him. Here are some of the titles given to the Holy Spirit in the scriptures, or the names by which he is called.

The great names, Jehovah, Lord, and God are all given to the Spirit. He is called—the Most High—the Holy Spirit—the Holy Ghost—the Free Spirit—the Good Spirit—the Spirit of Life —the Spirit of Truth—the Spirit of Grace—the

Spirit of Adoption—the Spirit of Wisdom—the Spirit of Counsel—the Spirit of Might—the Spirit of Knowledge—the Spirit of the fear of the Lord—the Spirit of Promise—the Eternal Spirit—the Power of the Highest—the Comforter—the Guide—the Teacher.

And the giving of such names as these to the Holy Spirit proves two things about him, one is that he is a real person; and the other is that he is God. He is a divine person, equal to God the Father and to God the Son.

And this is proved, not only by the names given to him, but also by *the way in which the scriptures speak of him.* Let us look at one or two illustrations of the way in which they do this. When the prophet Isaiah is speaking of Christ, the Messiah, he represents him, as saying of himself—"And now, the Lord God and his Spirit hath sent me." Is. xlviii: 16. Here we see the three persons of the Holy Trinity—God the Father—God the Son—and God the Holy Spirit are spoken of as all working together. God the Son is sent, and God the Father and God the Spirit are the ones who send him.

We see them uniting together again, in the same way, on the occasion of our Saviour's baptism. Thus we read, "And Jesus, when he was baptized, went up straightway out of the water, and lo, the heavens were opened unto him, and he saw the Spirit of God descending like a dove, and lighting upon him; And lo, a voice from heaven saying, This is my beloved Son, in whom I am well pleased." St. Matt. iii: 16, 17. Here we see the three Persons of the blessed Trinity acting together. God the Son has taken our nature upon him, and is baptized, as a man, in the river Jordan. God the Spirit comes down from heaven in the form of a dove, and rests upon him; while God the Father speaks from heaven, in a voice that was heard by those who were attending that baptism. This proves to us that there are three Persons, in the One God whom we worship; and that the Holy Spirit, who came down upon the church on the day of Pentecost, is the third Person in this Trinity. He is a divine Person, equal to the Father and the Son. It is impossible to explain, satisfactorily, what took place at the baptism of our Saviour in any other way. And in this way, we get a clear view of the first thing, important for us to know, in order to understand the meaning of the Spirit's coming. We see now *what the Holy Spirit is*. He is a divine Person—united with the Father and the Son in the great work of our salvation, and equal to them both.

And then there is another thing that we must understand clearly, if we would know the purpose of the Spirit's coming on the day of Pentecost—and that is—*what the Spirit does.* This refers to the work which the Holy Spirit has to do in the Church of Christ. It takes in both what he had to do in the church when he first came and also what he has to do now. The work which the Spirit has to do for the souls of men is the same now that it was then. There were, indeed, works of wonder, great miracles, to be performed in the early church which are not done now.

But, apart from this, there is no difference. The work of the Holy Spirit has always been the same. How important his work was to the church at first, we see in the fact that nothing was done till the Spirit came. After Jesus had ascended to heaven there was, as we have already said, a long pause before anything else was done. This pause lasted for ten days. Jesus had left a great work for his disciples to carry on in the world; but during those days nobody moved a step or lifted a finger towards doing that work. Everything stood still. And the reason for this long pause was that nothing could be properly done in carrying on this work till the Spirit came. The disciples had been distinctly told to wait for his coming. They waited till the day of Pentecost. Then, this Spirit came. Then the work began—the work of saving souls from death. The work has never ceased. It has been going on to the present day; and it will continue to go on till Jesus comes again.

Now there are four things that must be done for every soul that is to be saved through Jesus Christ. And none but the Holy Spirit can do these things.

The first thing that the Holy Spirit has to do for every soul is to—CONVERT—*it.*

He began this work at once when he came. He set the apostles to preaching Jesus Christ, and the result of the first day's preaching was—that *three thousand souls* were converted.

The conversion of the soul refers to the great change which takes place when a person becomes a Christian. The word conversion is only one of several words applied to this subject in the Scriptures. Sometimes it is called being quickened, or made alive; and at other times it is called being "born again." This was the way in which our Saviour spoke of the great change we are now considering, in his interesting conversation with Nicodemus. And he spoke of the Holy Spirit as the One who is to work out this change in every case when he said—*"Except a man be born of water and of the Spirit, he cannot enter into the kingdom of God."* St. John iii: 5. To be "born of the Spirit," is the same as to be converted, or to have the heart changed, and to be made a new creature in Christ Jesus. Good people differ much in their opinions about what our Saviour means by "water" here. Some think it means the truth of God's word, which is spoken of as the means employed in the conversion of souls; while others think that the word "water" here refers to baptism; but we cannot stop to argue the point now.

Some souls are converted, or born again, before they are old enough to understand the truth that God has taught us in his holy word. We have two cases of this kind mentioned in the Bible. One is the prophet Jeremiah, chap. i: 5, and the other John the Baptist, St. Luke i: 15. When it says of one of these that he was "sanctified;" and of the other that he was "filled with the Holy Ghost" from the time he was born, it means that the great change, of which we are now speaking, was made in them both, by the Holy Spirit, at that early time. And so it may be now with children, even while they are very young, especially if they have Christian parents to pray for them. But, if they are not converted, or born again, till they grow up to be boys and girls, or men and women, then the word or truth of God is that which the Holy Spirit makes use of in causing them to be converted, or born again. Here is an illustration of one, out of many ways, in which the Spirit does this:

"How a Christmas Card Saved a Soul." There was a merchant in one of our large cities who had failed in business. He had lost everything that he had. He was not a Christian, and did not know where to go for comfort. His troubles and disappointments made him gloomy and sad. He saw no way in which he could get out of his troubles; and after thinking over them a long time, he finally made up his mind to go to the river and drown himself. He was not married, and had no family of his own; but there were a number of children in the house where he lived.

This happened on a Christmas day. The children had just come home from their Sunday-school festival. In passing through the entry, one of them dropped a beautifully illuminated card, with a text of scripture on it. As the poor man was going out on his sad errand, his eye rested on this card, lying on the entry floor. He stooped down and picked it up, and read on it these sweet words—"Casting all your care on him, for he careth for you." I. Peter v: 7. Reading these words had a strange effect upon him. Instead of going out to drown himself, he went back to his room, got his Bible, found the passage there, and meditated on it. He thought of the great sin he had just been going to commit in taking away his own life. Then he thought of all his other sins. This filled him with great distress. The burden of his sins soon grew to be heavier than the burden of his losses and cares. He kneeled to pray. With many tears and cries he asked for the pardon of his sins and for grace to make him a Christian. His prayer was heard. His sins were pardoned. His burdens were lifted off. He became a Christian. He was converted by God's blessing on that text of scripture. And it might truly be said of him that he was "born of water and of the Spirit."

One part of the work which the Holy Spirit has to do for men is to convert them. And this is a fair illustration of one of the ways in which he does it.

*But another part of the Spirit's work is to—*TEACH—*men, as well as to convert them.*

When Jesus was speaking to the disciples of the Spirit whom he promised to send, he said, "He shall *teach you all things.*" St. John xiv: 26. But, when our Lord spoke of the Spirit teaching us "*all* things," he did not mean those things which we can find out ourselves by diligence in study. We do not need the help of the Holy Spirit to teach us spelling, or reading, or history, or geography. He meant "all things" about himself and the work he has done for our salvation. Sin has closed the eyes of our souls. It has made us blind to spiritual things. One part of the Spirit's work is to open our eyes so that we may see. David was seeking the Spirit's help in this matter when he offered the prayer, "Open thou mine eyes, that I may behold wondrous things out of thy law." We may be very learned in the things that are taught in our schools and colleges. We may know a great deal about different languages; about botany, and chemistry, and mathematics, and astronomy, and other studies of that kind. But all this will not help us to understand the things taught in the Bible about Christ, and the way to heaven. The knowledge of other things is sometimes a *hindrance*, rather than a help, in trying to understand the Bible. In learning what is here taught, none but the Spirit of God can help us.

Suppose we take a blind man into a large gallery, filled with fine paintings and beautiful statuary. It is a clear day. The sun is shining through the windows, and there is plenty of light there. But that is no help to our blind friend. We point to one after another of the beautiful paintings before us, and describe them to him. But still he cannot see one of them. And then, suppose that we had the power to open the blind man's eyes, so that he could see them all for himself; what a wonderful change that would make to him! And this is what the Holy Spirit does for us. The Bible is like a great gallery. It is full of beautiful pictures, such as none but God can make. But our eyes are blinded, and we cannot see them. The Spirit's work is to open these blind eyes so that we may see.

And the great end of all the Spirit's teaching is to help us to see Jesus, as our Saviour, and the one in whom we must trust for everything necessary to our salvation. Here is an illustration of what I mean. We may call it:

"Jesus Only." A lady had been trying for some time to be a Christian, but she could find no comfort. The minister of the church which she attended called to see her. Finding that though she went regularly to church, and read her Bible at home, and prayed every day, she yet found no peace; he said to her, "My friend, do you expect to be saved because you are doing these things?"

"Certainly I do," was the answer.

"Well this is your mistake. You are putting these in the place of Jesus. There is no peace, or comfort, or salvation anywhere but in Jesus only. Now let me give you one verse to think about, and act upon. Jesus said—'Come unto me—*and I will give you rest.*' Have you gone to Jesus only for rest and peace and salvation?"

She looked amazed. She thought awhile of what had been said to her, and then burst into tears. New light shone in upon her. It was like opening the eyes that had been blind. She saw that it was Jesus, and *Jesus only*, that she needed. She came to him; that is she trusted or believed in him, and here she found rest and peace and salvation.

When Jesus was speaking to his disciples about the coming of the Holy Spirit, he said—"he shall *testify to me*." This was what the Spirit did in the case just mentioned. And this is what he is doing all the time. The end of all his teaching is to show us that "Jesus only" can give rest and peace and salvation to poor lost sinners.

Another part of the Spirit's work is to—SANCTIFY—*or make holy—all the people of Christ.*

He is called—the *Holy* Spirit—not only because he is holy himself, but because his work is to make his people holy. And this is what we all need to make us fit for heaven. The great law of that blessed world, the law that is written, as it were, over the gate of heaven, is this—"*without holiness no man shall see the Lord.*" And Jesus pointed out the way in which this holiness or sanctification is to be secured when he was praying for his disciples, and said, "Sanctify them through thy truth." The truth here spoken of, means "the truth as it is in Jesus"; or the things that the Bible tells us about him. This truth is the instrument, or means, which the Spirit employs in making us holy. The best definition of holiness is to say that it means being made *like Jesus*. He is the example, or model, we have set before us, which we must try to imitate. We must ask ourselves what would Jesus think, or feel, or say, or do, if he were in our position? and then we must try to think, and feel, and speak, and act as much like him as possible. And so you see how important it is for us to know "the truth," or what the Bible teaches us about him, because it is only in this way that we can ever hope to become like him, or to be made holy.

There was a famous artist in Italy many years ago, whose name was Michael Angelo. He was a great painter and a great sculptor. And when he was occupied on any work he always took the greatest pains to finish it as finely as possible. He was once engaged in making the statue of an angel out of a block of white marble. At last it was nearly done; but still, he lingered over it, trying to improve it in every possible way. He was a firm believer in the old proverb, that "whatever is worth doing, is worth doing well." A person who had been in his studio and had seen him at work upon this statue came back, several days after, and found him busy with it still. "Why," said he, "I don't see that you have done anything since I was here before."

"O, yes, I have," said the great artist." It was too full here, and I have reduced it somewhat. I have brought that muscle out better. I have rounded off this arm. I have improved the lip here; and the chin there, and I have put more expression into the face."

"Well, but these are mere trifles," said the visitor.

"They help to make my work perfect; and *perfection is no trifle,*" was the great man's wise reply.

And this shows us exactly what the Spirit's work is in making us holy. It is trying to make us more and more like the model of perfection we have set before us in Jesus. But there is one point of difference between Michael Angelo's work on his marble statue and the Spirit's work upon us. That block of marble was a dead stone. It could do nothing at all to help the sculptor in his work upon it. But we are living stones, in the hands of the heavenly Artist. We can and must take hold, and help in the great work which the Holy Spirit is carrying on, in trying to make us more holy, or more like Jesus. And as we yield ourselves to the blessed

THE DAY OF PENTECOST 235

influences of the Spirit, we should be lifting up our hearts to Jesus in the prayer:

> "Make us, by transforming grace,
> Dear Saviour, *daily more like thee!*"

And then there is one other thing the Holy Spirit has to do in carrying on his great work, and that is to—HELP AND COMFORT—*us.*
The work we have to do, as the followers of Christ, is what we never can do of ourselves. We need the help of the Holy Spirit here all the time. It is only he who can, in the language of one of our beautiful Collects, help us to "*think* those things that are good, and then enable us to *perform* the same." But he can, as another of the Collects says, both "put into our hearts good desires, and give us grace to bring the same to good effect." The Spirit is given for this purpose. And if we seek and secure his help, we shall not only be able to do all that God requires, but we shall find comfort in doing it. The work of the Spirit is to give help and comfort to those who are trying to serve the blessed Saviour. And it is because he does this that he is so often called the Comforter. How many illustrations we find of the way in which the Spirit

does this part of his work! But we have only room for one.

"Blind Robert." Robert's mother was a poor widow. She had a large family of children. Robert was the youngest. His mother took in washing. His brothers and sisters all helped to support the family by working in one way or other. But poor blind Robert could not work. The only way in which he could help his mother was by carrying home the clothes for her when the washing and ironing were over. And it was a touching sight to see him with a large basket on his arm, full of clothes, and groping his way slowly and carefully along. But Robert had been taught by the Spirit to know and love the Saviour; and what help and comfort he found in him appears in the following conversation, between him and a gentleman who met him on the road one day.

After talking with him for a while about his mother and family, the gentleman asked him if it did not make him unhappy to think of being blind. For a moment, he looked sad; then he smiled, and said: "Sometimes I think it hard to have to creep about so. I should so like to look at the bright sun that warms me; and the sweet birds that sing for me; and the beautiful flowers that feel so soft as I touch them. But God made me blind, and I know that it is best for me. I am glad that he did not make me deaf and dumb, too. I am glad that he gave me such a good mother. But, above all, I am so glad that he has taught me to know and love the blessed Saviour; for I find it such a help and comfort to think about him."

"And how does the Saviour help you?"

"Oh, sir, I pray to him; and then I seem to hear him say, 'I forgive you Robert; I love you, poor, blind boy! I will take away your evil heart and give you a new one!' And then I feel so happy; it seems to me as if I could almost hear the angels singing up in heaven."

"I am glad to hear this, Robert. And do you ever expect to see the angels?"

"Oh, yes, sir! When I die, my spirit will not be blind. *It is only my clay house that has no windows.* I can see with my mind now; and that, mother tells me, is the way they see in heaven. I heard mother reading in the Bible the other day, where it tells about heaven, and it said there is 'no night there.' But *here*, it is night to blind people all the time. Oh! sir, when I feel bad because I can't see, I think of Jesus and heaven, and that helps and comforts me."

This is a beautiful illustration of this part of the work of the Holy Spirit. It shows us how the Spirit helps and comforts us. It is by testifying of Jesus, or by teaching us to know what a precious Saviour he is and what glorious things he does for those who love him.

And now we have considered the three things about the coming of the Holy Spirit, mentioned at the beginning of this chapter. We have spoken of the *time* of his coming—on the day of Pentecost; the *manner* of his coming—*expected—sudden—startling*—and *abiding;* and we have spoken of the *purpose* of his coming; this led us to show *what the Spirit is*—he is a divine Person—one of the three Persons in the blessed Trinity; and *what the Spirit does.* His work is to *convert*—to *teach*—to *sanctify*, or make holy, —and *help and comfort* all the people of Christ.

Jesus left the great work to be done for his church, and by his church, in good hands, when he left it with the Holy Spirit.

Let us pray God to give us a larger measure of the Holy Spirit's presence and power in our hearts, and then we shall be holy and useful and happy!

THE APOSTLE PETER

IN our last chapter, we saw how the Spirit of God came down from heaven to carry on the work which Jesus left for his people to do after his ascension. And now, before leaving this subject, it is necessary to show what the Holy Spirit did to build up the Church on the foundation which Jesus had laid for it; and to make known to a world of lost sinners, the great salvation which he had prepared for them. The best way of doing this, would be to give a sketch of the lives and labors of the twelve apostles whom our Lord had chosen, and left behind him, to carry on the important work begun by him. But this would take more room than we can spare. There are only two numbers now remaining to finish this work. All that can be done, therefore, is to make choice of three of the principal apostles, and take their histories as fair specimens of the way in which the work of building up the Church was carried on by them and their companions after Jesus, their great Master, had ascended into heaven.

The three selected for this purpose are the apostle Peter, the apostle John, and the apostle Paul. All will agree in regarding these as among "the very chief of the apostles." We begin then with

THE APOSTLE PETER.

And in considering the life of this great and good man, the two points of view from which we may look at it are *the facts of his history;* and *the lessons which it teaches.*

We begin then, with considering the facts of St. Peter's history, as mentioned in the New Testament. We shall not attempt to give all the facts woven into this history. It will be enough for our present purpose if the principal facts are stated. The first fact to notice about this good man is that he was a native of the city of Bethsaida, on the northern coast of the Sea of Galilee, and that his father's name was Jonas, or Jonah. The next thing known of him is that his occupation was that of a fisherman. It is a fact that he was first brought to Jesus by his brother Andrew, who had been one of the disciples of John the Baptist. Jesus spoke kindly to him, and told him that his name should be changed from Simon, as he was then called, to Cephas, which is the Greek word for a rock, or a stone. The Latin word, that means the same thing, is the word Petrus. And so Cephas, or Peter, is the name by which he was afterwards called. St. John i: 41, 42; St. Matt. xvi: 18. It is a fact that he did not continue to follow Jesus, as one of his disciples, immediately after this first interview with him, but went back, for a while, to his old employment as a fisherman.

It is a fact that some time after this he was called by Jesus to be one of his disciples. It happened in this way:—One day, Jesus was standing on the shore of the Sea of Galilee. A crowd of people were pressing around him, to hear him preach. He wanted a convenient place from which to speak to them. Peter was near at hand, in his fishing-boat. Jesus stepped on board the boat, and asked Peter to push it out a little way from the land. He did so; and Jesus made a pulpit of that boat, and preached to the people, as they stood upon the shore of the lake. When the sermon was ended, Jesus told Peter to push the boat out into deep water and let down the net, and he would catch a fine lot of fish. Peter said they had been fishing all night and had caught nothing. Still, he did as Jesus told him; and immediately they found more fish than their net would hold. This showed Peter the wonderful knowledge and power of Jesus. He felt afraid of him, and fell down at his feet, saying, "Depart from me, for I am a sinful man, O Lord!" Jesus said unto him, "Fear not; from henceforth thou shalt catch men." St. Luke vi: 1-11. St. Matthew tells us that on this occasion Jesus said to Peter and his brother Andrew, "Follow me; and I will make you fishers of men." St. Matt. iv: 18, 19.

It is a fact that some time after this, Jesus chose out from the rest of his disciples Peter and eleven others, to be his twelve apostles. They were to be with him at all times, to hear his teachings, in private, as well as in public; to witness his miracles; and be prepared, in this way, to take up and carry on his work when he should return to heaven. We have the account of this in St. Matt. x: 2-4; St. Mark iii: 13-19; and St. Luke vi: 13-17.

It is a fact that in these different lists of the apostles, the name of Peter always stands first.

We are not told why this was so. One thing is certain, however, it was not because he was set above the rest of the apostles, or had any power or authority superior to what was given to the others. It was, probably, only because he was quicker to speak and more ready to act than his brethren were. Two occasions are mentioned in the gospels on which he did this. One of them was when some of the followers of Jesus were offended at his preaching. They went away and would not hear him any more. Then Jesus turned to his chosen twelve and said: "Will ye also go away?" Peter, speaking for the rest, immediately replied: "Lord, to whom shall we go? Thou hast the words of eternal life." St. John vi: 66-69.

The other occasion was when the disciples had returned from one of the missionary tours on which they had been sent. Jesus asked them what men said about him. Different answers were given to this question; but none of them were correct. Then he asked them what they thought about him. Peter at once, answering for the rest, said: "Thou art the Christ, the Son of the living God." This was a noble confession. It showed that Peter had very clear views of the character of Jesus and of the work he came on earth to do. Jesus pronounced a blessing on him for this, and said: "Thou art Peter; and upon this rock I will build my Church, and the gates of hell shall not prevail against it." St. Matt. xvi: 18. There has been great difference of opinion among good Christian people about the meaning of these words of our Saviour. They cannot mean that Peter, in his person or in his office as an apostle, was to be the rock, or foundation, on which the Church of Christ was to be built. This is certain; because St. Paul tells us that there is only one foundation on which this Church is built, and that is Christ himself. I. Cor. iii: 11. There can be no doubt, I think, that what Jesus meant here was that the noble confession which Peter made on this occasion was the truth on which his Church was to be built. And this we know is the case.

It is a fact that Peter, with James and John, was present to see and hear what Jesus said, and did, and suffered, on several occasions when the other disciples were not present. One of these occasions was when he raised the daughter of Jairus from the dead. Another occasion was when Jesus appeared in such wondrous glory on the Mount of Transfiguration. And, in striking contrast to this, when he sank to the earth, amidst the gloomy shades of Gethsemane, overwhelmed by the "agony and bloody sweat," Peter was one of the three chosen witnesses of that awful scene.

It is a fact that when he saw his Master walking on the water, he asked permission to come and meet him, by walking over the surface of the sea. Jesus gave him leave to come. He got out of the ship, and began that watery walk. But, when he saw the rough waves rising and swelling against him, his heart sank, his faith failed, and he was beginning to sink, when Jesus stretched forth his hand and saved him.

It is a fact that, on one occasion, Jesus sent Peter to the seaside with a fishing-line to catch a fish, in whose mouth he was to find the money required to pay the taxes due to the government for himself and his Master.

It is a fact that the night before the crucifixion of our Lord, Peter solemnly declared that he would never forsake his Master, though all the rest of his followers should do so; and, even though he should have to die for clinging to him. It is a fact, nevertheless, that he did forsake him that very night, and three times deny that he knew him; yea, even with oaths and curses. It is a fact that, notwithstanding this, Peter was freely forgiven, on the morning of the resurrection, and restored to the place which he had forfeited, as one of the twelve apostles.

It is a fact that after the ascension of Jesus into heaven, Peter was the first to propose the election of another apostle to fill the place which had been left vacant by the death of the traitor Judas.

It is a fact that when the Holy Ghost came down on the day of Pentecost, Peter was the first of all the apostles to preach the gospel; and that three thousand souls were converted, as the result of one day's labor; and that, in all the work done in the earliest history of the new church, he was the principal preacher.

It is a fact that the first miracle of which we read in the history of the new church was performed by Peter. It was the miracle of healing the lame man, who was sitting at "the gate of the temple called Beautiful," when Peter and John were entering the temple, at the hour for evening prayer. Acts iii: 1-9.

It is a fact that when the apostles were forbidden by the Jewish rulers to preach in the name of Jesus, Peter was the first boldly to tell them to their faces, that they must "obey God, rather than men"; and that, in spite of all that might be said, or done, to hinder them, they would go on, and preach "Jesus Christ, and him crucified." Acts iv: 13-23.

It is a fact that as the first miracle of mercy in the early church was performed by this apostle, so was the first miracle of judgment. We read about this in Acts v: 1-10. It was before him that Ananias and Sapphira were struck dead for the sin of lying and cheating.

It is a fact that the miraculous power of Peter was so great and so well-known that people laid their sick friends down in the streets along which he was walking, that his shadow might fall upon them, and heal them. Acts v: 15.

It is a fact that the first missionary journey undertaken, in the early church, was by this apostle.

It is a fact that in the course of this journey he healed a lame man, who had been confined to his bed eight years, with palsy. He also raised to life a good Christian woman, named Tabitha, or Dorcas. She lived at Joppa, and had spent her time in making garments for the poor. She was the founder of the first Dorcas society of which we have ever heard; and her name has been connected with these excellent charities since then, all over the world. Acts ix: 32-43.

It is a fact that when the time came for the opening of the kingdom of heaven to the Gentiles, it was the apostle Peter who had the honor of performing this important act. He was the first minister of Christ who ever preached the gospel to a Gentile, and made to him the offer of eternal life. He did this when he preached to Cornelius, the Roman centurion, and received him into the church by baptism. We read about this great event in the tenth chapter of the Acts.

It is a fact that, after this, Peter was put in prison by Herod, who was persecuting the Christians. He had just put the apostle James to death and intended to do the same with Peter. But his friends united in earnest prayer to God for him; and God sent an angel, who struck off his chains, opened the prison door, and set him free. Acts xii: 1-20.

After this we have no clear account of the ministry of St. Peter. We only know that he spent the rest of his life in going about from place to place, preaching the blessed gospel of the great Master whom he loved so well.

It is a fact, however, that he wrote the two epistles which bear his name and which have been such a comfort and blessing to the church for more than eighteen centuries. And then, the last fact in his history is that he suffered martyrdom, by crucifixion, in the city of Rome. We have no definite information about the time when this event took place, or about the particulars connected with it. It is generally believed that the death of St. Peter occurred about the same time as that of the apostle Paul; and, that they both took place during the persecution that arose under the cruel and bloody emperor Nero. The tradition is that when St. Peter came to the place of execution, he requested to be crucified with his head downwards, because he felt that he was not worthy to suffer in the same way in which his great Master was put to death.

Here we have woven together more than twenty facts that make up the history of the apostle Peter.

The next thing for us to do is to notice some of the more important lessons taught us by this history.

The first lesson we may learn from the history of this apostle is, about—THE DANGER OF SELF-CONFIDENCE.

Solomon says, "He that trusteth in his own heart is a fool." Prov. xxviii: 26. By a man trusting in his own heart, he means, having too much self-confidence. And the folly of this sort of trust is seen in this, that it keeps us from seeking the help of God; and without this help, we are not able to resist temptation when it overtakes us; and then we are sure to fall. We see a striking illustration of this in the case of Peter. When Jesus told the disciples that they would all forsake him, Peter had such trust in his own heart—such confidence in himself,—that he said, "Though all men forsake thee, yet will I never forsake thee." And, when Jesus told him that, on that very night, he would deny him thrice, Peter, confidently, declared: "Though I should die with thee, yet will I not deny thee." And, no doubt, he was perfectly honest in saying this. He meant just what he said. The trouble with him was that he did not know himself. He trusted too much in his own heart. His confidence in himself led him to neglect praying for the help and strength he would need when the temptation to deny his Master came before him.

And so, that very night, when Jesus was delivered into the hands of his enemies, and some of those about him said to Peter,—"Thou art one of this man's disciples," his courage failed him. He not only denied that he was a follower of Jesus, but even declared, with oaths and curses, that he did not know him. Here we see the folly of self-confidence, of which Solomon speaks.

And how many illustrations of this self-confidence we meet with!

"The Folly of a Soldier's Self-Confidence." When the English commander, General Braddock, in the early history of this country, was leading his little army through Pennsylvania to attack the French fort DuQuesne, where Pittsburgh now stands, George Washington, then a colonel, was an officer in the general's staff. The French had enlisted the Indians on their side. Washington understood the mode of fighting which the Indians adopted. He knew their custom was to hide themselves in trees and fire upon their enemies without being seen.

As the English army was pursuing its march, not far from the fort they were to attack, they came to a dense forest through which they had to make their way. Washington knew that it was in just such a woody region that they might expect to find the Indians. He told General Braddock what he feared and suggested that he should command the army to halt, and send forward some scouts to examine the woods and find out if there were any Indians there before marching through. But the general had so much confidence in himself and in his own way of managing his army that he refused to listen to Washington's advice.

The army entered the forest; but they had not gone far before they were fired upon from every side. The firing was kept up. The soldiers were falling to the ground, killed, or wounded; but no enemy was in sight, and no one could see where the firing came from. General Braddock and his chief officers were killed. The army was defeated; and Washington, the principal officer left alive, gathered their shattered ranks together; led them out from the woods and marched them back to the place from which they had started. The failure of that military enterprise, stands out on the page of history as a striking illustration of the folly of self-confidence.

"The Folly of a Sailor's Self-Confidence." The captain of a ship had brought his vessel to the entrance of the channel that leads to the harbor of one of the principal seaport towns of Scotland. He had often sailed in and out of that harbor. He felt confident that he could take the vessel in himself. When the pilot came and offered his services, he said: "No, I'll be my own pilot. I know every rock in the channel. I am sure I can take the ship safely in."

He started on his way. It was blowing a gale at the time. But he had not got far before the ship was dashed against a hidden rock of which he did not know. The vessel went to pieces, almost in sight of the harbor, and the captain and his crew were all lost. Here we see the folly of self-confidence.

But we often see this folly even when it does not lead to such fatal results as followed in the illustrations already given. This is clearly shown in the following fable:

"The Owl That Thought He Could Sing." "What in the world can bring so many people into the grove to hear the nightingales sing?" said a young owl to his mother.

The old owl didn't know and didn't care—she was busy watching a bat.

"I am sure I have as fine a voice as any nightingale and a good deal stronger."

"Stronger, certainly, my son," said the owl, blinking her eyes, for the bat had escaped.

"I shall go into the grove to-night, and give them a song," said the self-confident young owl.

The old owl opened her round eyes very wide, but said nothing.

So, when night came, and the hour for the sweet singing of the birds drew near, he flew heavily along and placed himself in a part of the grove where he could be seen and heard to the best advantage.

But the nightingales did not like the prospect either of his company or his help in their concert; so those of them who were going to sing flew away to another grove, while those who were to be quiet for the night kept snugly at roost.

"Where can the nightingales be?" said one of the people who had come to hear them.

Then the self-confident young owl set up a hoot so long and loud that it startled the people.

"That horrid creature has frightened them all away," said one. "Where's my gun? I'll soon fix him." The owl took the hint and without waiting till the gun appeared hastened back home.

"Your feathers are ruffled, my son," said the old owl. "Have you been singing?"

Then the foolish young owl told about his disgrace and his narrow escape from death.

"It is just what I expected," said his mother, "and I'm glad you are safe back."

"Then why did you let me go?" he asked.

"Because I saw you wouldn't mind what I said, and that nothing but experience would teach you the folly of thinking too much of yourself."

That young owl had reason to feel thankful that he had learned this lesson without any greater harm or loss to himself.

The first lesson from the history of this apostle is about the danger of self-confidence.

The second lesson from this history is about— DELIVERANCE FROM TEMPTATION.

When we rise in the morning we can never tell what will happen to us before evening. But Jesus knows all about things before they come to pass. At the beginning of a day, or week, or month, or year, he has a clear view of all that can happen to the end of it. Early in the evening of the night on which he was betrayed, Jesus said to Peter: "Simon, Simon, Satan hath desired to have you, that he may sift you as wheat; but I have prayed for thee, that thy faith fail not." St. Luke xxii: 31, 32. Looking forward through that sad and solemn night Jesus saw that Satan, the great enemy of souls, had laid a snare or prepared a temptation for Peter which, he thought, would ruin his soul forever. He had arranged things in such a way that Peter would be tempted to deny his Master, and would be most likely to yield to the temptation; and this was so great a sin that it would seem sure to prevent him from being one of the apostles, and cause him to lose his soul. And such would have been the result, no doubt, if Jesus had not seen this temptation coming, and had not prepared a way of escape in the very midst of it. He prayed for Peter, "that his faith might not fail." *And it was this prayer of Jesus that saved Peter.* For we read in the gospel that as soon as he had committed his great sin he was sorry for it. *"He went out and wept bitterly."* And it was just here that the prayer of Jesus secured to Peter the grace that led him to true repentance; *and this was what saved him.* It was in this way that he was brought out of his temptation. We do not wonder, therefore, to find St. Peter using these comforting words in one of his epistles: "The Lord knoweth how to deliver the godly out of temptation." II. Peter ii: 9. He knew very well about this. He could speak from his own experience here. His history affords a beautiful illustration of this passage from his epistle. And as we are all exposed to temptation it will be a great help and comfort to us to remember that what Jesus did for Peter he can do for us.

"An Illustration from History." In an old English history, called "The Chronicles of Froissart," there is an account given of the escape of the garrison from a besieged citadel, which illustrates very well this part of our subject. An enemy's army had encamped before this citadel, for the purpose of taking it. They had completely surrounded it. It was impossible for anyone to go in or out of the place. The day was fixed for storming the fortifications and putting the garrison to death. The assault was made. The walls were mounted and the gates forced open; but no one was found within. What had become of them? On examining the place, it was found that through the solid rock, on which the fortress was built, a secret passage-way had been made. It led down under the walls, far away from the besieged citadel, out into the beautiful country beyond it. Thus the soldiers and inhabitants of that fortress found "a way of escape" from the power of their enemies.

"An Illustration from Daily Life." A gentleman who lived in a small country town in England obtained a situation for his son, a promising young man, in one of the banks in the city of London. His father took him up to London and introduced him to the president of the bank and the other officers. On taking leave of his son, the father said: "Harry, my boy, you must be obedient, obliging, civil, and respectful; be attentive to your business and trustworthy. Above all things, never forget these four words—"*Thou, God, seest me.*" Harry promised his father, solemnly, to do as he had said. And he did so for awhile. He gained the confidence of all about him, and rose, by degrees, till he held one of the most responsible positions in the bank. Thousands of pounds passed through his hands every day. At last, temptation overtook him. The thought came into his mind how easy it would be to make himself rich by quietly taking some of this gold and silver, without anyone knowing it. He was frightened when this idea first entered his mind, and tried to put it away. But still it would come back to him, again and again, till he ceased to be alarmed at it. Finally, it seemed to take full possession of him. He made up his mind to do it.

One evening, when all the others had left the bank, he remained behind, under pretence of finishing some business. He went to the vault and put in the keys. The heavy door flew open. But, just as he had reached out his hands, and grasped the money, his father's words—"Thou, God, seest me"—came into his mind. The money dropped from his hands, as if it had been red-hot iron. He fell on his knees and cried,—"O, God, save me from this temptation!" And God did save him. He put the money back, and closed the vault. Then he went to the president, and, with bitter cries and tears, confessed his fault and offered to resign his situation.

The president was a wise and good man. He said he would keep the secret to himself; and not allow him to give up his situation in the bank. But he told him to seek every day the help of that God who had delivered him from this great temptation.

He went back to his duties, feeling that he had no strength in himself, but firmly relying on the grace of God to "deliver him from evil," and remembering the great truth—"Thou, God, seest me."

Let us always remember this lesson from the history of St. Peter, about deliverance from temptation.

The third lesson we learn from this history is about—OVERCOMING PREJUDICE.

The word prejudice is made up of two Latin words. One of these means, to judge, or to form an opinion, or to make up our minds on any subject; and the other means, beforehand. And a person who has a prejudice, is one who has made up his mind about something before he understands it. When Nathanael first heard our Saviour spoken of as "Jesus of Nazareth," he asked: "Can any good thing come out of Nazareth?" He had a prejudice against it. He had made up his mind that nothing good could come out of it, before he really knew the place. And so the Jews and the Samaritans had a very great prejudice against each other. The Jews thought it impossible that there should be any good Samaritans, and the Samaritans thought it impossible that there should be any good Jews. But they were both mistaken. They had made up their minds on this subject before they understood it.

But perhaps there never was a stronger prejudice than that which the Jews had toward the Gentiles. They thought it was impossible for them to be saved; and they would never share any of their religious privileges with them. And as the apostle Peter was a Jew, he had this strong prejudice against the Gentiles. And how strong this prejudice was, we see from the great trouble taken to overcome it. When God wished to have Peter go and preach the gospel to the Gentiles, his prejudice against them was so strong, that three miracles had to be performed before that prejudice could be overcome and he be willing to obey God's command in this matter. We read about this in the tenth chapter of the Acts of the Apostles.

Peter was at Joppa, at this time, staying at the house of Simon the tanner, by the seaside. Here he had a vision. In the vision, he saw a great sheet, fastened by the four corners, and let down from heaven. In this sheet were all manner of four-footed beasts, and creeping things, and fowls of the air. As he gazed on them, he heard a voice saying, "Rise, Peter, slay and eat." But many of these creatures were such as the Jews thought unclean. So Peter declined to do this, for he said that "nothing common, or unclean, had ever entered his mouth." The same voice told him not to call anything unclean that God had cleansed. This was done three times; and all was taken up to heaven. Here was the first miracle performed to overcome the prejudice of Peter.

Just as this vision ended, three men came to the house of Simon, inquiring for Peter. They were sent by Cornelius, a Roman centurion, who lived at Cæsarea, on the seacoast, more than a day's journey from Joppa. Cornelius was trying to find out the way of salvation. He had prayed earnestly to God for direction. God had sent an angel to tell him to send to Joppa, and ask Simon Peter to come and preach the gospel to him, or to tell him how he was to be saved. This was the second miracle wrought on purpose to overcome the prejudice of Peter.

And while these men were inquiring for Peter, the Spirit of God spoke to him and told him to go with the men and do what they wanted him to do, because he had sent them. This was the third miracle that took place on this occasion. And thus the strong prejudice of Peter was overcome. He went with these men. He preached the gospel to a company of Gentiles. And when he saw the Holy Ghost come down on them, in a visible form, as it had come down on the apostles, on the day of Pentecost, he baptized them, and received them into the church. And thus Peter had the honor of being the first minister of Christ who preached the gospel to the Gentiles. He first opened the door of the Christian church to them. The prejudice of Peter, if it had not been overcome, would have prevented him from being useful in this way.

And if we wish to be useful, and do the work God has for us to do, we must try to overcome our prejudices.

"A Lesson from a Pair of Shoes." There was a minister of the gospel once, who had a member of his church who was a shoemaker. He thought no one could be a Christian who did not think and feel just as he did. This interfered with his usefulness. His minister had often talked with him on the subject, but in vain. At last, he concluded to give him a lesson from his own trade, which he would not be likely to forget, and which he hoped would do him good. He did it in this way:

He sent for the shoemaker one day, and when he came in, he said, "I wish you to take my measure for a pair of shoes."

"I will do so with pleasure; please take off your boot."

The minister did so; and the shoemaker took his measure, put down the figures in his notebook, and was going away, when the minister said to him, "I want a pair of boots also for my son."

"Very good, sir. Can I take the young man's measure?"

"That is not necessary," said the pastor, "you can make my boots and his from the same last."

"Please, your reverence, that will never do," said the shoemaker, with a smile of surprise.

"O yes, it will do very well. Make my shoes and my son's on the same last."

"That cannot be, your reverence. If a shoe is to fit it must be made on a last that is just the size of the person's foot who is to wear it."

"Is that so?" said the minister. "You say every pair of shoes must be made on their own last or they will not fit. And yet you think that God must make all Christians on *your* last; and if they do not think and feel just as you do you think they are not true Christians."

"I thank your reverence for this lesson," said the shoemaker. "I will try and remember it, and pray God to help me to overcome my prejudices."

This is a good lesson for us all to learn.

The last lesson of which we may speak, as taught us by the history of this apostle, is about—THE BENEFIT OF TRIALS.

When Jesus foresaw the great trial that was coming on Peter, during the night of his betrayal, he could easily have saved him from it if he had thought it best and wisest to do so. Before leaving the upper chamber in Jerusalem where he kept the Passover for the last time with his disciples, he could have sent Peter on some errand or could have given him something to do that would have occupied him till the next day. Then he would not have been exposed to the temptation of denying his Master. This could easily have been done. But Jesus did not do this. And the reason was he knew very well that though the trial would be very painful to Peter, and would cause him to shed many bitter and sorrowful tears, yet it would be useful to him in the end, and would help to make him a better minister than he could have been without it. It would show him his own weakness, and teach him how to sympathize with others in their troubles and to be kind and tender in his dealings with them. And this is what Jesus meant when he said to Peter after telling him about this coming trial:

"And when thou art converted, *strengthen thy brethren.*"

And no doubt Peter had this sorrowful event in his mind, and the benefit he had derived from it, when, in one of his epistles, he compares the trials through which God causes us to pass to the fire into which the jeweler puts his gold when he desires to have it purified. I. Peter i: 17. He was a more useful minister for having passed through this trial than he ever could have been without it. The benefit of it followed him through all his life. And this was the reason why Jesus did not save him *from* that trial, but saved him *in* it.

And in the same way God intends to do us good by all the trials through which he causes us to pass. It is not for *his* pleasure, but for our profit that these trials are allowed to come upon us; and the profit will surely follow if, as Paul says, we are rightly "exercised thereby."

It would be easy enough to give many illustrations of this important lesson, but there is room for only one. We may call it:

"The Marble-Block; or, The Sculptor's Lesson." "One of my scholars," says a Sunday-school teacher, "had a little sister who was lame. Her name was Annie. I often called to see her, and pitied her as I saw her sitting by the window watching the other children on the playground. In addition to her lameness she was sometimes so sick that she could not sit at the window. One bright spring day I bought for her some oranges and candies and a pretty picture-book, and hoped to comfort her with these. I gave her the oranges and candies, and read to her from the little book; but still she seemed sad.

"'Why are you so sad to-day, Annie, dear?' I said.

"'Oh, ma'am,' she replied, 'I don't see why God should afflict me, and yet let other children be so well and happy. But if I only knew that God was not angry with me I shouldn't care so much.'

"I asked her to take a little walk with me. In the course of our walk I took her into the room of a sculptor whom I knew. Here were a number of beautiful marble figures and some blocks of rough marble. The artist was at work on one of these, and Annie and I watched him with great interest. Presently I pointed to a great rough, dark block of marble that stood in the middle of the room, and said: 'Do you like that, Annie?'

"'Oh, no,' she said, 'why did they bring such an ugly block here?'

"'That block,' said the artist, 'I shall begin to work upon to-morrow. Come in and see it again.'

"The next day Annie and I went in again. The artist spent most of that day in simply knocking off the rough places. Day after day we watched him; and every day the block seemed to grow less ugly. The sharp chisel cut here, and there, and everywhere. As we watched him we often thought if the block was alive and could feel how much it would suffer from the blows of that chisel!

"After a while the artist sent us an invitation to come to his studio. I took my little friend and went. As we entered, he said: 'I have something to show Annie.' Then he drew aside a thin, white veil, and behold! there stood before us, white as the driven snow, the beautiful image of an angel, that had been made out of that rough marble block. Annie shouted with joy when she saw it.

"'Now, Annie, dear," I said, 'do you think the sculptor hated that rough block of marble when he gave it so many hard knocks?'

"'Oh, no,' said she, 'he loved it; and every blow he gave showed his love for it.'

"'And so, my dear child,' said I, 'does God love us. And the trials which he sends on us are the proofs of his love. As the sculptor was trying to make this image of an angel out of the marble block, by every blow he gave it, so God, by all the afflictions of this life, is fitting us to be like the angels in the heavenly kingdom.'

"'Now, I shall never feel sad on account of my lameness,' said Annie. 'To think that this is a proof of God's love will always make me happy.'"

Let us remember these four lessons when we think of the history of the apostle Peter. The lesson about *self-confidence*—about *deliverance from temptation*—about *overcoming prejudice*—and about *the benefit of trials*.

We may close this subject with the Collect for All Saints' Day: "O Almighty God, who hast knit together thine elect in one communion and fellowship, in the mystical body of thy Son Christ, our Lord: grant us grace so to follow thy blessed saints, in all virtuous and godly living, that we may come to those unspeakable joys which thou hast prepared for those who unfeignedly love thee; through Jesus Christ, our Lord. Amen."

ST. JOHN AND ST. PAUL

IN the original plan of this work, it was intended to have a separate chapter for each of these two noble workers in the cause of Christ. But room for this fails. All that can be done is to give a brief sketch of each in this closing chapter.

We have now to speak of the apostle John. Most of the pictures that have been made of this apostle, represent him as looking more like a woman than a man. But we shall find that there was no authority for this when we come to see what his real character was.

He is supposed to have been born in Bethsaida, the city of Andrew and Peter. This town was situated on the western shore of the sea of Galilee, or the lake of Tiberias, at the upper part of the lake. His father's name was Zebedee, and his mother's, Salome. We know nothing more of Zebedee than that he was a fisherman, the husband of Salome, and the father of James and John. Salome, the mother of John, we often read of afterwards, as one of those good women who followed our Lord through the different scenes of his ministry, and were a great help and comfort to him. John is supposed to have been younger than his brother James, who is generally mentioned first when they are spoken of together. They are referred to, as "James and John, the sons of Zebedee." John was probably the youngest of all the apostles. It is said, that he was younger than the Saviour himself, having been born in the year four, Anno Domini, or when Jesus was four years old.

The family of this apostle is supposed to have been better off in regard to property than any of the other apostles. This is evident from several things mentioned about him and his family. One thing which shows this is that when John and his brother James were called from their business as fishermen, to follow Christ, we are told that "they left their father Zebedee in the ship with the *hired servants.*" St. Mark i: 20. Andrew and Peter were too poor to have hired servants. They had to do all their own work. But Zebedee could afford to hire help for himself and sons. And then, at the time of our Saviour's trial, the servants who kept the door of the judgment hall, in which the trial took place, allowed John to enter the hall, because they knew he was acquainted with the high priest. St. John xviii: 16. And then when Jesus left his mother in the charge of John, while hanging on the cross, we are told, that from that day, "he took her to his own home." St. John xix: 27. John had a home of his own at Jerusalem. From all this, it seems clear that the family of this apostle were better off in worldly things than were the families of the other apostles.

Now we may just glance at *what John's character was by nature*, or before he was a Christian; and *what it was by grace, or after he became a Christian.*

From what we read of this apostle in the gospel history, we see that there were three things in John's natural character which show that he was not the weak, womanly sort of man he is represented to have been in most of the pictures that have been made of him.

For one thing, it is clear that John was naturally *an ambitious man.* This is evident from the request to Jesus by John and his brother James, through their mother, that they might have the highest places in his kingdom. St. Matt. xx: 20-23. Their mother made the request. But she probably consulted them about it first. And if they had not agreed in it, she would not be likely to have done it. This shows that they were all ambitious together. And so we are right in saying that John was ambitious. He wanted the best place in Christ's kingdom for himself, without thinking whether others might not be better fitted for it. Our Saviour's reply shows that he was wrong in giving way to this ambitious feeling. But then this shows that there was a good deal of strength in John's natural character. He was ambitious.

And then he was *narrow-minded*, as well as ambitious in his natural character.

Persons of this character are accustomed to think that all those who think, or feel, or act differently from what they do, must certainly be wrong. And this was the way John felt when he first became a disciple of Christ. He came to Jesus one day and said, "Master, we saw one casting out devils in thy name, and we forbade him, because he followeth not us." Jesus rebuked him for giving way to his narrow-mindedness, or bigotry, or uncharitableness. It was wrong for him to think that no one could be doing good, or be serving God acceptably, unless it was done in just the same way in which he was doing it. This was a wrong feeling to have, but it shows there was a good deal of decision and strength about John's natural character.

And then another thing about John before he became a Christian, was that he was *an angry, or passionate man.* As Jesus was going up to Jerusalem on one occasion, in the company of his disciples, they came to a Samaritan village.

When the Samaritans in the village found that he was going to Jerusalem, it stirred up all their prejudice against the Jews, and they refused to receive him. They would not let him stop for rest or refreshment. This made the disciples very angry, and John and his brother James showed their anger by saying, "Lord, wilt thou that we call down fire from heaven, to consume them, as Elias did?" St. Luke ix: 51-57. But Jesus rebuked them, and showed them that this was not the right spirit for his disciples to have.

These traits of John's natural character, although they are not to be approved or admired, yet show that he was a man of a good deal of force of character, and very different from what his pictures represent him to have been. But when we turn from considering what he was by nature, or before he became a Christian, and think of what he was by grace, or after he became a Christian, we see a wonderful change. The apostle Paul tells us, "that if any man be in Christ, he is a new creature; old things have passed away, and all things have become new." And it was so with this apostle. When he learned to know and love Christ, the old things about his character passed away, and all things became new. After this we see no more of his ambition, of his narrow-mindedness, or of his passion.

The one thing that marked his character as a Christian was *love*. He seemed to get nearer to Jesus than any of the other disciples. And it is always the case, that the nearer we get to Jesus and the more we learn to know him, the more we shall love him. John's love to Christ seemed to take entire possession of him. It filled his whole soul. And so we think of him as the *apostle of love*. He is spoken of particularly as "the disciple whom Jesus loved." It was he who sat nearest to his Lord and leaned on his bosom at the last Passover. Peter was great for his readiness in serving Christ; Paul was great for the learning and the labor with which he served his Master; but John was great in the love for that Master, which ran through all he did. And this great love made him useful both *in his life* and *in his writings*.

It made him useful in his life. There is nothing that will lead to such earnest and devoted labor as this principle of love. We know but little of the life of this loving apostle after the ascension of Christ. We have no report of his missionary journeys, as we have in the case of the apostles Peter and Paul. But we know he was so earnest in the cause of his Master that he was sent a prisoner to the island of Patmos to stop his labor, but in vain. He was willing to be an exile, a prisoner, and, as some say, a laborer in the mines, but he was not willing to give up working for his Master. Tradition tells us that he had to take his choice between stopping his work for Jesus and being thrown into a cauldron of boiling oil. He could not cease from his work. He was thrown into the boiling oil; but came out uninjured and kept on with that work which his love constrained him to do. He lived the longest of all the apostles, and was the only one of them who died a natural death. And in the closing days of his life, when too feeble to do anything else, we are told that he used to be carried into the church at Ephesus, where his latest labors had been performed, and, standing up in the midst of the congregation, would stretch forth his trembling hands and say, "Little children, love one another." What a beautiful close to the life of this loving apostle! Truly his love made him *useful in his life.*

And then it made him *useful in his writings, too.* Think of the gospel of St. John. How different it is from all the others! John's love for Jesus seemed to bring him nearer to his great heart of love than the rest of the brethren. We are not surprised, therefore, to see that love speaking out more clearly and fully in his writings than it does anywhere else. It is only John who gives us that wondrous statement, that glorious, golden epitome of the gospel which is found in the sixteenth verse of his third chapter—"God so loved the world that he gave his only begotten Son; that whosoever believeth in him should not perish, but have everlasting life." And then think of the marvellous discourses of our Saviour found in the fourteenth, fifteenth, and sixteenth chapters of this gospel;

and of that most sublime and wonderful prayer of Jesus, for all his people, found in the seventeenth chapter. O, no one can tell what an unspeakable loss the Church of Christ would have sustained if this loving apostle had not written his precious gospel!

And then how useful he has been in his epistles, too, as well as in his gospel! Love is the golden thread that runs through them all. Look at the opening words of the third chapter of his first epistle. How the very heart of the loving disciple seems to be speaking out when he exclaims: "Behold, what manner of love the Father hath bestowed upon us, that we should be called the sons of God!" It is remarkable that the two shortest verses in the whole Bible, and yet two among those that most melt, and stir our hearts, were written by this apostle. One of these is in his gospel and contains only two words—"*Jesus wept.*" The other is in one of his epistles and contains only three words—"*God is love.*" If he had never written anything else than these two verses, how well it might be said that he was useful in his writings!

And then think of that marvellous book with which the Bible closes. We call it "The Revelation of St. John the Divine." For, although it is true that there is much in this book that we cannot understand, yet its opening and closing chapters have been an unspeakable blessing to the Church in all ages. When St. John closes the Bible with those last two chapters of the Revelations, it seems as if he had been permitted to leave the gates of heaven ajar on purpose that we might gaze through them in wondering awe. Those jewelled walls; those pearly gates; those golden streets; that river of the water of life, clear as crystal; and all the sparkling imagery employed by this loving apostle in what he here tells us about heaven, how can we sufficiently thank God for permitting his servant John to write such glorious things for us? Truly we may say that his love made him useful in his life and useful in his writings!

I know not how better to close this brief sketch of the life of St. John the Evangelist than by quoting here the words of that beautiful Collect which our Church uses on the day with which his memory is connected:

"Merciful Lord, we beseech thee to cast thy bright beams of light upon thy church, that it, being instructed by the doctrine of thy blessed Apostle and Evangelist, St. John, may so walk in the light of thy truth, that it may at length attain to everlasting life, through Jesus Christ our Lord. Amen."

> "Praise, for the loved disciple, exile on Patmos' shore;
> Praise for the faithful record he to thy Godhead bore;
> Praise for the mystic vision, through him to us revealed;
> May we, in patience waiting, with thine elect be sealed."

THE APOSTLE PAUL.

It would require a large volume to consider fully and properly the character and work of this apostle. We have only space to take a hasty glance at the subject. But even this, it is hoped, may prove useful to those who read it.

St. Paul spoke of himself as "the least of all the apostles." I. Cor. xv: 9. It was natural and proper enough for him to think lowly of himself. But he stands alone in this opinion. Nobody agrees with him here. We all love to think and speak of him as—"the *great* apostle of the Gentiles." When first converted, he began his ministry by preaching to his own countrymen, the Jews. But finding their prejudices against "Jesus of Nazareth," were so strong that they would not listen to him, he changed his course and turned to the Gentiles. And well he may be called—"the great apostle."

He was great in every view we can take of him. Let us notice now, as briefly as we can, some of the elements of greatness about this apostle.

In the first place, he was *great in the natural talents* that it pleased God to give him. He had a stronger, clearer mind than any other of the apostles. He could take hold of the greatest subjects brought before him and handle them and master them with wonderful power. He had great reasoning powers. He could argue and reason about anything in the grandest way. And then he had great powers as a speaker. He was marvellously eloquent. See what an illustration we have of this in his famous speech on the top of Mar's Hill, in the city of Athens, as we read it in Acts xvii: 16-32. We have another illustration of this in his speech before Agrippa, in Acts, twenty-sixth chapter. I would gladly give anything I have in the world to have enjoyed the privilege of hearing Paul deliver that speech. When Agrippa interrupted him by saying, "Almost thou persuadest me to be a Christian;" only think how touching it must have been to see Paul lift up his chained hands towards heaven and say with the tenderest feeling—"I would to God, that not only *thou*, but also all that hear me this day, were both almost, and altogether such as I am; except these bonds!"

He was great in *his early opportunities*. He was born at Tarsus, and had a better education than any of the other apostles. His family were well off. It is no argument against this to say that he was a tent-maker by trade. For it was customary among the Jews, even with the richest families, to teach their sons some useful trade. Paul went through the best schools that were to be had then. He had studied all about history, and philosophy, and poetry. And he was learned also in all matters concerning the religion of the Jews. He tells us himself that he was "brought up at the feet of Gamaliel"— who was, at that time, the most famous of all their teachers.

He was *great* in his *prejudices*. He was a real Jew in this respect. They all had very strong prejudices against people who differed from them in their religion. But Paul was stronger in his prejudices than even his countrymen were. We see this in the first mention that is made of him in the New Testament. This was at the death of the first martyr, St. Stephen. The wicked men who stoned him, we are told, "laid down their clothes at the feet of a young man whose name was Saul." And then we see the strength of his prejudice in the fierceness of the persecution which he carried on against the followers of Jesus. He "breathed out threatenings and slaughter" against them. He was "exceeding mad against them." Not content with imprisoning and putting to death those who lived in Jerusalem, he "persecuted them even unto strange cities." Furnished with letters from the chief priests, he went as far as Damascus, that he might seize and bring bound to Jerusalem any of the followers of Jesus found there. How unlikely it seemed that one who was so very strong in his prejudices should ever, himself, become a follower and an apostle of Jesus!

But he was *great in his conversion*. It was impossible for him to be converted as other men were. It is hearing about Jesus which leads to the conversion of men. But Paul would not listen to the preaching of the gospel. He would allow no one to speak to him about Jesus of Nazareth. He believed that he was a wicked impostor, and he hated him most bitterly. And so it pleased God to work a miracle for his conversion. He had gone on his journey, till he had nearly reached Damascus, when a marvellous scene occurred. Suddenly the heavens seemed to open above him. A light shone around him above the brightness of the sun. A strange voice was heard speaking to him. It came from heaven. The words it spoke were—"Saul, Saul, why persecutest thou me!" He gave one look at the opening heavens and then fell overpowered to the earth. "Who art thou, Lord!" was his astonished inquiry. And the answer, more astonishing still, was—"I am *Jesus* whom thou persecutest!" What a revelation that was to him! How overwhelming was his amazement! No wonder that he was converted by that vision. It was indeed a great conversion. He was baptized by Ananias at Damascus, and began at once to preach that gospel which he had gone there hoping to destroy. Such was the commencement of Paul's life as a Christian and his labors as an apostle. Everything about it was great.

And then he was *great in his privileges.* He saw the risen and ascended Lord amidst the glories of the heavenly world. What a privilege this was! It was a privilege which none of the other apostles enjoyed except St. John. We have an account of his vision of the glorious Saviour in the first chapter of the Revelation, verses 10-20. And then afterwards, St. Paul was taken up into the third heavens, or into Paradise, and saw and heard things of which it is not lawful or possible to speak. He had broader and fuller and clearer views of the great doctrines of our holy religion than any of the apostles. And this is one of the greatest privileges we can have in this world. We see the proof of Paul's privileges in this respect in all the blessed teachings he has given us in his epistles about Christ and his salvation.

He was *great in his labors.* When he found out the great mistake he had made respecting Christ, and learned to know and love him as the one, only glorious Saviour of lost sinners, the love for Christ kindled in his soul by this discovery constrained him to give himself a living sacrifice to him. And the burning zeal with which he began to work for his Saviour never grew cold. The apostles were all earnest in their labors for Jesus; but Paul was the most earnest and the most untiring of them all. In his case, it was indeed true, that the last became first. No one city or country was large enough to be the field of his labors. He went from city to city, and from country to country, till he had gone all over the world as it was then known. And when he had gone all over the earth once, preaching the gospel, he was not satisfied. When one missionary journey was ended, he began another; and then another, and so on to the end of his days. Then he sealed his life's labors with his blood, and died a martyr's death at Rome by order of the cruel emperor Nero. The tradition is that he was beheaded outside of the walls of that great city. And on the spot which is said to be the place of his death, there stands a beautiful church, called after him, and which is a monument to his memory.

How well it may be said of him that he was great in his labors. And yet the Saviour, whom he served so faithfully, had done nothing for him which he has not done for you and me. He bore the same cross, and shed the same precious blood for us, that he did for Paul. Then, in our labors for Jesus, let us try to follow Paul, as he followed Christ. If we try to catch Paul's spirit, whoever we are, or wherever we may be, we shall find it easy and pleasant to work for our blessed Master. Here is an illustration of what I mean. We may call it:

"Paul's Spirit in a Child." A little girl had great dislike for sewing. She had commenced making a bed-quilt, but was not likely to finish it soon. One day she came home from Sabbath-school. They had been having a missionary-meeting there, and she was full of zeal in the missionary cause. "Mamma," she asked, "can't I do some work to earn money for our missionary box?"

"Well, Lizzie, darling," said her mother, "if you will finish one block for the quilt, every other day, I will gladly pay you for it, and you can give this as your own offering to the missionary cause."

Poor Lizzie's face grew sad on hearing this; for she disliked this kind of work very much. It seemed as if her missionary spirit was likely to die out at once. But, after thinking over it a little while, her face brightened up and she said, "Well, mamma, I'll piece blocks, or do anything else you wish me to do, for Jesus' sake. Amen." That quilt was soon finished, and there is now an earnest, active little worker for missions in that home. This was Paul's spirit in a child. And if we get that spirit, it will make us all, like Paul, great in our labors for Christ.

But Paul was *great in his sufferings,* too, as well as in his labors.

Before he became a Christian he had the prospect of rising to a position of great honor and great profit in connection with the Jewish church. But he gave this all up at the time of his conversion. He tells us that, "what things were gain to me, those I counted loss for Christ. Yea, doubtless, and I count all things but loss for the excellency of the knowledge of Christ Jesus, my Lord." Phil. iii: 7, 8. There is something very touching in the record which this great apostle has left us of his sufferings for Christ. He speaks of himself as having been—"In labors more abundant, in stripes above measure, in prisons more frequent, in deaths oft. Of the Jews five times received I forty stripes save one. Thrice I was beaten with rods, once was I stoned, thrice I suffered shipwreck, a night and a day I have been in the deep. In journeyings often, in perils of water, in perils of robbers, in perils by mine own countrymen, in perils by the heathen, in perils in the city, in perils in the wilderness, in perils in the sea, in perils among false brethren. In weariness and painfulness, in watchings often, in hunger and thirst, in fastings often, in cold and nakedness." II. Cor. xi: 23-28. What a marvellous record of sufferings we have here! There is perhaps nothing like it to be found in the whole history of the Church of Christ. And yet the apostle never had a word of complaint to make. The spirit in which he bore his sufferings for Christ is beautifully illustrated in the glimpse we have of him in the prison at Philippi. His back had been torn with cruel scourges. His feet were made fast in the stocks. We might have expected that he would spend that night in sighing and crying. But, instead of this, we read that—"At midnight, Paul and Silas,"—his companion in labor and suffering—"prayed, and sang praises to God." Acts xvi: 25. Surely this should make us ashamed of complaining on account of any trifling suffering we may have to bear in the cause of our great Master. And Paul had no relief from these sufferings. He went on bearing them cheerfully to the very close of his life. How was he able to do this? There is only one answer to give to this question. It was his love for Jesus that made him so willing to labor and to suffer for him. And if we love Jesus, we should be willing to suffer for him, too.

Here is a striking illustration of the way in which real love will make one willing to suffer even for a friend or fellow-creature. We may call it:

"Love Triumphing Over Suffering." Some years ago a fine church was built in one of the towns in Belgium. It was all finished at last, except the fastening of the weather-vane on the top of the steeple. The scaffolding was not high enough to reach it. There was no way in which the work could be done, but for one workman to stand on the highest part of the scaffolding and let the other workman stand on his shoulders, while he put the vane on the steeple, and soldered it in its place. A bravehearted, broad-shouldered workman agreed to stand there for this purpose. He took his position, holding on to a piece of scaffolding. His companion climbed up and stood on his shoulders. The vane and vessel of melted lead were handed up to him. It was a perilous thing to do. A crowd of spectators below watched the operation almost breathless with anxiety. The moments seem like hours, as the work goes on. At last it is done. The men come down amidst the shouts of the multitude. But, when the brave man who had borne his friend on his shoulders reached the bottom of the ladder, he fell exhausted to the earth, and had to be carried home. Then it was found that the poor fellow's back was in a dreadful state.

While the man was doing his work on the vane, some of the melted lead had dropped down on the friend who was supporting him. But he stood bravely still. He would not move an inch, for that would have caused the death of his companion. Here was love triumphing over suffering. And if that brave man was willing to bear all this for his earthly friend, what should we not be willing to bear for Christ, "the friend who sticketh closer than a brother?"

In the next place the apostle Paul was *great in his influence.* Suppose we could have a history written of all the persons who were converted by the preaching of this apostle during his life; and then of all who were converted by them, and so on, from one generation to another, down to our own times, what a wonderfully interesting history that would be! Or suppose we could trace out, in the same way, all the good that has been done by the writings of this apostle; the persons who have been brought to Jesus by reading the truths found in those writings, or who have been instructed, or guided, or comforted, encouraged, and helped by the same—how surprising it would be! Then we should see, indeed, how great this influence has been!

There are twenty-one epistles in the New Testament. Of these the apostle Paul wrote fourteen. They form a large part of the New Testament. Now, suppose we could take these epistles of St. Paul, chapter by chapter, and follow every verse in each chapter as it has gone round the world from age to age, and find out every case where good has been done to any soul, what a history we should have! No one could write such a history now. But I suppose we shall have such a history set before us when we get to heaven. Then, we shall understand better than we can do now how great the apostle Paul was, in the influence for good which he exerted. But, though none of us can be compared at all with this great man, yet, if we are trying, like him, to love and serve the blessed Saviour, we may all, even to the youngest, be exerting influence for good that will last forever. Here is an illustration of what I mean. We may call it:

"A Child's Influence for Good." Bessie was a sweet little girl who was trying to love the Saviour. The nursery in which she slept was on the first floor of the house adjoining the street. It was summer time when the incident here referred to took place. Her mother was sitting near the open window one evening, when Bessie knelt down by her side to say her evening prayer. She first repeated, after her mother, the words that she taught her to use in prayer. After this she was in the habit of offering up little prayers of her own for anything she wished to ask from her Father in heaven. She did so on this occasion; and these were the last words she had to offer: "God help everybody to love Jesus. Amen." While Bessie was saying her prayers that evening her mother heard the steps of some one passing. He lingered a moment under the window and listened to the words of the dear child. It happened that this was a neighbor of theirs, an infidel, whose name was Jones. The closing words of Bessie's prayer made a deep impression on his mind. After this he manifested the greatest interest in her, though he always said that what she prayed for never could take place; for he was certain that *he*, for one, never could be a Christian.

Not long after this Mr. Jones was taken sick. He had a long and severe spell of illness. As he was living in a boarding house, and had no family of his own, Bessie's mother used to send the dear child in every day to inquire how he was and to take him little things that he might need. He would allow no one to speak to him on the subject of religion; but Bessie's father and mother hoped that her gentle ways and simple loving words might do him good.

A week or two had passed away, and one night, as Bessie's mother was putting her to bed—she said: "Mamma, Mr. Jones loves Jesus now."

A few days after this they heard that their sick neighbor was near his end. Taking her little one by the hand the kind mother went in to see him. They found that he was dying. As Bessie sat on her mother's lap, by the side of his bed, the sick man died; but just before his spirit passed away, these were the last words heard from his lips: "God, help everybody to love Jesus—*everybody.*"

And so dear Bessie's words were the means which God employed to save a soul from death. And if a little child can exert such an influence as this, then we see how, by loving and serving Jesus, we may all make ourselves useful. We may so live that every act and word may be a good seed sown that will yield fruit unto everlasting life.

"Not ourselves, but the truths that in life we have spoken,
   Not ourselves, but the seed that in life we have sown,
  May pass on for ages—all about us forgotten,
   Save the truth we have spoken, the things we have done.

"So let our living be—so be our dying;
   So let our names lie, unblazoned, unknown;
  Unpraised, and unmissed, we shall yet be remembered;
   But only remembered by what we have done."

The apostle Paul was great in his influence. And then, as the only other point to speak of, he was *great in his reward.*

This is true of all God's people who serve him faithfully. David, when speaking of God's words, or commandments, tells us that "in keeping of them there is *great reward.*" Ps. xix: 11. When St. Paul had reached the close of his life, he paused to look back upon the past, and then forward to the future; and as he did so, these are the words that he used: "I am now ready to be offered, and the time of my departure is at hand. I have fought a good fight, I have finished my course, I have kept the faith; henceforth there is laid up for me a crown of righteousness, which the Lord, the righteous judge, will give me at that day; and not to me only, but unto all them also that love his appearing." II. Tim. iv: 6-9. We learn from this passage that there is a crown in heaven prepared for every follower of Jesus. These crowns are procured or purchased by what Jesus did and suffered for us. But they will be very different in the number and character of the jewels that are to sparkle in them. And how many jewels, and what kind of jewels your crown, or my crown, will have must depend upon how much we do for Jesus. I suppose the apostle Paul will have the most beautiful crown that any of the servants of Jesus will wear. He was greater in his labors, in his sufferings, and in his influence for good than others—and his reward will be greater. He will have more jewels in his crown than will be found in any other; and they will sparkle with more brightness and beauty. But none will envy him. We shall all feel that he is worthy of it, and we shall rejoice to see him wear it.

But let us remember that every work we do for Jesus, and every sacrifice we make for him, will put another jewel in our crown. Then let us try to serve him faithfully with all our hearts, and we may be sure that we shall receive a great reward. I close with just one little incident, to show how we may add jewels to our crowns. We may call it:

"A Star in the Crown." A young lady was standing before a large mirror, preparing to go to a ball. She had just placed a light crown on her head, ornamented with silver stars. While she stood there, looking at herself in the glass, her little sister, about five years old, climbed upon a chair, and putting out her tiny fingers, tried to touch the beautiful crown. "What are you doing, Nellie, darling? You mustn't touch my crown," said her sister.

"I was *looking* at that and *thinking* of something else," was the little one's reply.

"Pray tell me, Nellie, what you were thinking about?"

"I was remembering what my teacher said last Sunday. She told us that if we brought sinners to Jesus by our influence, we should win stars for our crown in heaven; and when I saw those stars in your crown, I wished I could save some soul."

These simple words that Nellie spoke took a strong hold of her sister's feelings. She went to the ball that night, but felt little interest in it. She had no heart for the music or the dancing, and was truly glad when all was over.

On reaching home she went to Nellie's room. There she lay, sleeping sweetly. She stooped and kissed her loving lips; and then, kneeling down by the side of her bed, she asked God to forgive her for the giddy, careless life she had been living. She gave herself to Jesus then and there, and prayed for grace to live henceforth for him and for heaven.

Then she kissed Nellie again and said, "Precious darling, you have won one star for your crown!" God help us all to win many stars for our crowns!

Thus we have taken a hasty view of this great apostle. We have seen that he was great in his natural talents; great in his opportunities; great in his prejudices; great in his conversion; great in his privileges; great in his labors; great in his sufferings; great in his influence; and great in his reward.

And now this work is done. I thank God, with all my heart, for permitting me to engage in it, and for helping me to get through with it. It humbles me in the dust to think how utterly unworthy it is of the glorious Saviour to whom it refers. But I know he is pleased to work by feeble means. He puts the treasure of the gospel in earthen vessels, on purpose that "the excellency of the power may be of God, and not of us." My earnest prayer is that he will graciously accept it as a tribute of grateful love from one of the least and most unworthy of his followers; that he will pardon all the mistakes and imperfections connected with it; and bless it, notwithstanding, and make it useful. And if it shall prove helpful to Christian parents and teachers in training their children for Jesus; and if the young who read these pages shall find anything here to aid and encourage them in trying to know and love and serve the blessed Saviour, I shall feel that the time and labor spent upon this work have not been in vain! AMEN!

ANALYTICAL INDEX

OF

FACTS, LESSONS, ILLUSTRATIVE ANECDOTES, AND BIBLE STORIES

	VOL.	PAGE
ACORN, The	iii	195
Adam and Eve	i	1
" "	ii	113
A just God and Saviour	ii	118
All for the best	i	249
Androcles and the lion	iii	80
Angel in the stone	iii	207
Angelo, Michael	iv	233
Antidote, The	ii	293
Apostles Chosen	iii	1
" The Men	iii	5
" The Work	iii	12
" The Help	iii	18
" The Lesson	iii	23
Ark, Noah's	i	27
" Size of	i	32
" Occupants of	i	33
" Jesus the true	i	34
" Supplies of	i	35
" Safety of	i	40
" The blessings of, and how secured	i	45
Ascension, The	iv	179
" Time of	iv	179
" Place of	iv	182
" Manner of	iv	184
" Lesson from :—Obedience to the Command of Christ	iv	190

	VOL.	PAGE
Ashamed to tell mother	iv	102
Assyrian call to prayer	iii	27
Augustine, Saint	iii	164
Aunt Lucy	iii	14
Awakened at the bottom of the sea	ii	7
B APTISM of Christ	ii	244
" A very Strange	ii	245
" A very Wonderful	ii	247
" A very Instructive	ii	251
" Instructive, Because it teaches us to think of Jesus as the Pleasing Son	ii	251
" " Because it leads us to think of Jesus as the Gentle Dove	ii	257
" " Because it leads us to think of Jesus as the Atoning Lamb	ii	263
Baptized pocket-book	ii	198
"Be"	iii	66
Beetle an object of worship and interest	i	131
Being loved back again	iii	193
Believing saves	ii	133
Best time for doing this	iii	210
Bible, One for seven hundred men	i	155
Bickersteth, Rev. Mr.	iii	211
Birth of Christ	ii	89
" Time of	ii	90
" Place of	ii	97
" Bethlehem	ii	99
" Circumstances of	ii	103
" " Strange Neglect	ii	103
" " Strange Attention	ii	103
" " Strange Poverty	ii	105
" " Strange Wealth	ii	106
" " Strange Humiliation	ii	107
" " Strange Glory	ii	107
" Lessons taught by	ii	109
Blessed are they that mourn	ii	207
Blesses (Jesus) By giving riches to the poor	i	58
" By giving comfort to the sorrowing	i	62
" By giving liberty to the captives	i	70
" By giving sight to the blind	i	73
Blessing of guidance	i	146
Blessing of the world, Christ the	i	53

ANALYTICAL INDEX

	VOL.	PAGE
Blessings owed to Jesus	i	80
Blind beggar of London	i	74
Blind boy and the Welsh woman	i	196
Blind man	ii	186
Blind Robert	iv	236
Blue sky inside	i	65
Boy, Christ the	ii	209
" " Poor	ii	217
" " Thoughtful	ii	219
" " Obedient	ii	227
" " Patient	ii	234
Boy's influence, A	iii	87
Boy with the spirit of Christ	iv	24
Brave Charlie	iv	68
British man-of-war	i	155
Brought in by a smile	iii	8
Bullfinch, The	iv	134
Burial, The	iv	121
" Lessons taught by the certainty of Christ's death	iv	128
" " " fulfilment of Christ's word	iv	131
" " " working of his providence	iv	138
" A lesson of comfort	iv	144
Captain's experience, The	ii	45
Charcoal carrier, The	iii	15
Children, Christ and the little	iii	187
" His great love for	iii	191
" His great wisdom	iii	195
" His great encouragement	iii	201
" Great lessons	iii	206
Children in Africa	iii	190
Children, Why they were thrown into the river Nile	i	113
Children's service, The	iv	193
Child, How the heart of a princess was made tender by the crying of	i	118
Child's gospel, The	iii	43
Child's influence for good	iv	293
Child's preservation, A	ii	16
Chinaman and the minister	ii	7
Christ and the dying thief	ii	36
Christ in the Old Testament, The earliest shadow of	i	28
Christ, Naming of	ii	121
" Importance of the name of	ii	123
" Wonderful authority of the	ii	125

		VOL.	PAGE
Christ, Wonderful comfort of the		ii	127
" " salvation in the		ii	131
" " glory of the		ii	138
" " stability in the		ii	142
Christ the blessing of the world		i	53
Christ, What he was sent into the world to do		i	112
Christian miner, The		i	51
Christ in the temple		ii	223
Clara's obstinacy		iv	46
Cleansing fountain, The		iv	106
Coachman and his prayer		iii	29
Coleridge		iii	38
Comforter, The meaning of a		i	12
Cottage on fire		ii	187
Collect		ii	240
"		ii	300
Congleton (Lord) and his servants		i	47
Covenant, Christ the messenger of the		ii	29
Cross, The		iii	69
Crucifixion, The		iv	89
" Place of		iv	90
" Time of		iv	91
" Manner of		iv	93
" Wonders of		iv	95
" Words spoken by Jesus at time of		iv	96
" Lesson of Forgiveness from		iv	97
" " on Duty to parents from		iv	100
" " from the power and willingness of Jesus to save		iv	105
" " from the depth of his sufferings		iv	109
" " from the wonders of his love		iv	112
Curse of the granted prayer		iv	18
Curtius, Marcus		ii	265
DANGER of self-confidence		iv	249
David, Christ the king like		i	227
" Because he was a chosen king		i	230
" Because he was a prepared king		i	234
" David as a shepherd and a soldier		i	236
" Christ prepared by obedience and suffering		i	238
" Because he was a victorious king		i	239
" David and Goliath		i	240
Dead raven		iii	99
Deaf and dumb boy		iv	12

Analytical Index

	VOL.	PAGE
Death of the first-born	i	140
Debt paid, The	ii	267
Delay, The sad result of	i	46
Delivered by a dog	iv	141
Desertion, The betrayal and	iv	29
" Things taught about Jesus:—		
" The loneliness of his sufferings	iv	35
" His willingness to suffer	iv	38
Dixey's six cents	iv	202
Doesn't he love to save?	iii	203
Doing good by sympathy	iii	50
Drive the nail	iii	31
Dying girl, The	iii	37
ETHIOPIAN, The	ii	195
Every talent useful	iii	268
Example of forgiveness	iii	84
" "	iv	98
FABLE of the oak and the violet	iii	172
Faith and how it helped the miner to be saved	i	51
Faith, Lack of, causes a serious loss	i	47
Faithful soldier and his reward	iii	270
Farragut, Admiral	ii	73
Fiery serpents	i	156
Fisherman's mistake, The	iii	175
Fletcher's disappointment	i	148
Flood, The story of the	i	29
Folly of a sailor's self-confidence	iv	252
Folly of a soldier's self-confidence	iv	251
For Charlie's sake	i	107
Forgiveness, How a bishop taught	iv	99
Forgiving boy	iv	98
For thine is the power	iii	19
Fragments, The use of	iii	16
Frog a sacred animal	i	130
Frogs, The plague of	i	129
GABRIEL, The angel	ii	35
Gethsemane, Jesus in	iv	1
" The facts of	iv	3
" Lesson of Prayer	iv	6
" " Sin	iv	11

	VOL.	PAGE
Gethsemane, Lesson of Submission	iv	16
" " Tenderness	iv	20
Girard, Stephen	ii	80
Girl from the jungle	ii	174
Giving, God's way for getting	ii	201
God cares for the hungry	i	163
God leads us to do good	i	36
God loves bad children	ii	117
God loves me	ii	116
God's work is perfect	i	31
Golden rule and the new commandment	i	144
Good for evil	iii	84
Good friends	iii	262
Good Samaritan	iii	78
Good that children do	iii	197
Gospel can do for us, What the	i	59
Gospel in a kiss, The	ii	260
Grasshopper, The	ii	284
Great harvest from a little seed	iii	271
Greek word for day and night	i	278
Growth of lying	iv	51

	VOL.	PAGE
HAPPY deaf mute	i	64
Havelock (Genl.) and his boy	ii	253
Heber's (Bishop) prayer	i	149
Hebrew children	i	117
Hebrew nurse	i	118
Help of feeling Jesus near	iv	38
Helper, Promise of the	i	6
" A human	i	9
" A suffering	i	14
" A successful	i	20
He loved me	iii	74
Henry the Eighth	i	13
Herod the king of the Jews	i	119
Herod, Why he wanted to kill Jesus	i	119
Holy Spirit, His names	iv	221
Home duties, Importance of	ii	215
Honey shield	iii	79
Hope for the lost	iv	115
Hope of glory	iii	300
How a bishop taught	iv	99

Analytical Index 307

	VOL.	PAGE
How a boy may serve God	iii	258
How a boy showed his love for Christ	iv	176
How a Christmas card saved a soul	iv	227
How a wonderful hymn was written	ii	136
How Christ should be honored	iii	234
How God feels toward sin	ii	113
How God loves sinners	ii	115
How hard it is to make people understand	i	46
How little God thinks of earthly riches	ii	110
How little God thinks of places	ii	109
How to become a willing servant of Jesus	iii	255
How to get the angels out	iii	209
How to learn patience	iv	77
How to serve God	iii	257
How to walk straight	iii	239
How we know there is a heaven	iii	231
Humble (The) king	iv	82
Humility, Christ teaching	iii	157
" " By his command	iii	160
" " By his example	iii	165
" The comfort we find in it	iii	169
" The usefulness connected with it	iii	174
" The blessing attending it	iii	180
" Examples of	iv	81
Humility proving a blessing	iii	184
Hushed tempest	iii	111
ICE in summer	iii	105
I feel it pull	i	217
I have seen Jesus	ii	157
I like your Jesus	iii	49
Imitating Christ's humility	iii	167
Infidel club	iv	154
Infidel converted by a flower	i	242
Influence of the love of Christ	iv	113
Influence of the spiritual Christian woman	iv	22
Instead of me	ii	268
Irish minister	ii	121
I so happy	ii	130
It is certain that God loves you	ii	43
It's all I can do	iv	198
It's for me	iii	43

	VOL.	PAGE
JACOB'S dream	ii	54
Janeway, Rev. Wm.	iv	148
Jesus a better helper than an angel	i	11
Jesus blesses men	i	70
Jesus care over us	i	43
Jesus makes everything right	iii	66
Jesus only	iv	231
Jesus on the Sea of Galilee	ii	49
Jesus the bread of life	i	163
Jesus the healer	i	159
Jesus washes feet of disciples	iii	158
Jesus, why he was sent into the world	i	93
Job	ii	290
John and the postage stamp	ii	286
John, the Apostle, Character by nature	iv	273
" " Character by grace	iv	276
John, the Forerunner	ii	59
" the Baptist	ii	61
" " Facts and lessons of his life	ii	61
" " His coming foretold	ii	61
" " Gabriel sent to announce his coming	ii	62
" " His dwelling in the wilderness	ii	63
" " His preaching	ii	64
" " His baptism	ii	66
" " In prison	ii	67
" " Lessons taught by these	ii	69
" " Lesson of temperance	ii	71
" " Lesson of humility	ii	75
" " Lesson of obedience	ii	79
" " Lesson of courage	ii	82
John White's hymn	i	223
Johnny and the cow	ii	298
Jonah and Jesus contrasted and compared	i	257
" " Contrasted because Jonah was an unwilling preacher	i	259
" " Contrasted because Jonah was a successful preacher	i	264
" " Contrasted because Jonah was a selfish preacher	i	271
" " Compared because Jonah was ready to die for the sake of others	i	273
" " Compared because of the length of time Jonah was buried	i	275
Joseph and Jesus compared	i	83
" Like Jesus because he was the sent one	i	85
" Like Jesus because he was sent to show his father's love	i	89

Analytical Index

	VOL.	PAGE
Joseph Like Jesus because his mission brought him into trouble, being sold by his brethren	i	94
" Like Jesus because he received great honor	i	99
" Like Jesus because he used his power for good	i	104
" In Egypt	i	100
" The story of	i	80
Judas	iv	29
Judas. Things taught about the power of sin	iv	44
KAZAINAK, the robber chief	iv	14
Keep away from the wheels	ii	18
King Ptolemy and his light-house	ii	145
LAMB of God I look to thee	iii	213
Lazarus	i	63
Learning to love Jesus	iii	202
Learn to stoop	iii	171
Leaving it all with Jesus	iii	70
Lesson from a pair of shoes	iv	263
Lesson of kindness	iii	82
Liberality, Christ teaching	iii	125
" Lesson of	iii	126
" (Illustrations of this lesson), Elijah	iii	133
" " The Saviour's gift of himself	iii	137
" " Sowing the grain	iii	138
" " The ocean	iii	139
Life in the midst of danger	iii	237
Light in the valley	ii	163
Lily, The	iii	221
Little blind boy	i	192
Little child	i	280
Little girl's patience	ii	237
Little loaf	iii	182
Little Mary	i	160
Little spring, The	iii	196
Little substitute	i	19
Lord's Supper	i	139
Lost diamond	iv	196
Lost horse found	iii	45
Love leads to love	iii	204
" stronger than death	iii	294
" The power of	iv	115
" triumphing over suffering	iv	291

	VOL.	PAGE
MAGGIE'S secret	iii	75
Manna	i	162
Martyr's joy	ii	129
Matthew the publican	iii	56
Melchizedek, Christ like, Because he was to teach	i	203
" " Because he was to atone	i	208
" " Because he was to intercede	i	213
" " Because he was to bless	i	220
" Mention of	i	199
" Christ a priest like	i	199
Messenger, Christ the	ii	29
" Christ a swift	ii	33
" Christ a loving	ii	38
" Christ an ever-present	ii	44
" Christ an able	ii	47
" Christ a faithful	ii	53
Minister in the robber's vault	i	281
Minister, Story of the poor rich	i	60
Miracles, Christ teaching by	iii	93
" Teach us that he has power to help	iii	96
" Teach us that he has power to comfort	iii	102
" Teach us that he has power to encourage	iii	107
" Teach us that he has power to protect	iii	112
" Teach us that he has power to pardon	iii	119
Miser and the hungry children	iii	151
Mite song, The	iii	11
Montgomery's hymn	ii	144
Morrison, Dr.	ii	77
Moses—Christ the prophet like	i	111
" In the danger attending his birth	i	113
" In his preparation for his work	i	120
" Preparation of privilege	i	120
" Preparation of trial	i	122
" On account of his miracles	i	124
" Because he gave the people laws or commandments	i	143
" Because of the blessings he obtained for his people	i	145
" Blessing of shelter	i	152
" Blessing of healing	i	156
" Blessing of bread	i	161
" Blessing of water	i	165
" Commandments given to	i	143
" His mother is hired to take care of him	i	118
" How he got into trouble in Egypt	i	123

Analytical Index

	VOL.	PAGE
Moses' rod	i	124
" turned to a serpent	i	126
Muckle Bess	iv	107

NAZARETH, Description of	ii	214
"Neither do I condemn thee"	ii	260
New England minister	iv	19
Niagara, Falls of	ii	244
Nile, Why the Egyptians worshiped the	i	128
Nineveh, Description and history of	i	264
Noble boy, A	iii	263
None but Jesus	ii	129
No pardon but from Jesus	iii	121
Not all the blood of beasts	i	76
Not alone	iv	37

OBEDIENCE, Noah's safety the result of	i	46
Obedient, We must be, to be saved	i	46
Obey him, Why we are God's and why expected to	i	7
Obeying mother pleasantly	ii	255
Officer and the soldier	iii	144
Old man's struggles	ii	285
Old Patch	ii	84
Olivet, Lessons from	iii	245
" Lesson about the master	iii	248
" Lesson about the talents	iii	258
" Lesson about the rewards	iii	268
One died for all	ii	22
One drop of evil	iv	47
One talent improved	iii	260
One neglected child	iii	198
One worm did it	iv	48
Orphan provided for	ii	11
Owl (The) that thought he could sing	iv	253
O yes, I will try	ii	234

PAPER, Where we get our word	i	115
Parables, Christ teaching by	iii	61
" Meaning of the word	iii	61
" Lessons illustrated by the value of religion	iii	65

	VOL.	PAGE
Parables, Lessons illustrated by Christ's love for sinners	iii	71
" " " The duty of kindness	iii	77
" " " The duty of forgiveness	iii	82
" " " The influence of good example	iii	86
Pardon and peace	iii	122
Passover, Feast of the	i	127
" Method of keeping the	i	136
" Reasons why the Israelites were commanded to keep	i	137
" " Relating to the past	i	137
" " Relating to the future	i	137
Paul, the Apostle	i	23
Paul, St.	iv	281
" Great in natural talents	iv	282
" " His early opportunities	iv	183
" " His prejudice	iv	283
" " His conversion	iv	284
" " His privileges	iv	285
" " His labors	iv	286
" " His spirit in a child	iv	287
" " His influence	iv	292
" " His reward	iv	296
" " His sufferings	iv	288
Paul, St. John and St.	iv	271
Pentecost, Day of	iv	211
" Time of the Spirit's coming	iv	213
" Manner of the Spirit's coming	iv	215
" Purpose of the Spirit's coming	iv	221
" To convert the soul	iv	225
" To teach men	iv	229
" To sanctify	iv	232
" To help and comfort	iv	235
Perseverance rewarded	ii	191
Peter and the tax gatherer	iii	108
Peter, the Apostle	iii	82
" " His place among the apostles	iv	239
" " The facts of his history	iv	240
" " Lessons taught by his history	iv	249
" " Deliverance from temptation	iv	255
" " Overcoming prejudice	iv	260
" " The benefit of trials	iv	265
" " The message to	ii	41
Pharaoh's cruel law	i	113
Plague of the flies	i	130

ANALYTICAL INDEX

	VOL.	PAGE
Pilate, Story of	iv	67
Plague of the frogs	i	129
Plagues of the locusts and darkness	i	134
" of the murrain, boils, and hail	i	133
Polish prince	iv	101
Poor Caleb and the gentleman	i	164
" rich minister	i	60
Power of a kind word, The	ii	261
" of kindness	iv	170
" of love	iv	41
" of the cross	iii	227
" of the gospel	iii	85
Prayer, Answer to	i	38
Praying better than stealing	iv	9
" for a dinner	iii	27
" for bread	iii	109
Preaching in the hay field	iv	196
Presentation of Christ in the temple	ii	149
" What Simeon saw in the infant Jesus	ii	153
" Salvation	ii	153
" Light	ii	159
" Glory	ii	164
" The effect this sight had on Simeon	ii	168
" His readiness to depart	ii	168
Prisoner converted	i	247
" of Glatz	ii	49
Promise, The first	i	1
Prophet, What is a	i	112
Protection through prayer	ii	15
Providential deliverance	iii	115
Prussian nobleman	i	169
RAVEN of Winslade Quarry	iv	140
Reformed drunkard's story	i	71
Rescue, The	iv	205
Results of early choice	iii	199
Resurrection, The	iv	151
" Proof of	iv	153
" Lessons from :—		
" The power of Christ	iv	162
" Power of Christ to save	iv	163
" Power of Christ to provide	iv	165
" Power of Christ to protect	iv	166

	VOL.	PAGE
Resurrection, Tenderness of Christ	iv	167
" The way of showing our love to him	iv	173
Revelations, Meaning of the Book of	i	84
Revenge overcome	i	253
Reward of obedience	iii	242
Rich for a moment	ii	111
River turned into blood	i	127
Robber taught	i	205
Rochester, The Bishop of	iv	147
SACRIFICE for the first-born	ii	150
Sailor boy's belief	iii	101
Salvation	i	42
Saved by a rose	iii	57
" by prayer	iv	208
" from a lion	ii	154
Sampson	ii	71
Sculptor's (The) lesson	iv	266
Secret of comfort	iii	173
" of success	iii	146
" passage way	iv	257
Selden, John	iii	39
Shark of the Mediterranean	i	277
Sheba, Queen of	ii	154
Shelter, The need of	i	155
Shepherd, Christ the	ii	1
" " Because he seeks his sheep when lost	ii	4
" " Because he feeds and takes care of them	ii	9
" " Because he protects them	ii	14
" " Because he saves them	ii	19
" The, of Berne	ii	9
Shining in every window	iii	104
Sick sailor	i	186
Simeon	ii	153
Singing all the time	ii	204
Sin, How Jesus helps men break the bonds of	i	70
" in a life is like poison in a fountain	i	2
" like a whirlpool	iv	53
" Things taught about the growth of	iv	49
Smiting the rock	i	166
Snake and the spider	iv	52
Sodom and Gomorrah	ii	114

Analytical Index

	VOL.	PAGE
Soldier in the Crimea	i	168
Soldier's example of patience	iv	78
Solitary feast	i	66
Solomon, Christ the king like	i	246
" Because he was a wise king	i	246
" Because he was a peaceful king	i	251
" Choice of	i	246
Somebody's mother	iv	171
Soul compared to a fort	i	7
" saved by a tear	ii	156
Spirit of Christ in a little girl	iv	23
Star in the crown	iv	298
Steamboat captain and the soldier	iii	148
Story of the fort	i	7
Stream and the mill	iii	256
Substitute, The	i	212
Supper, the Lord's	iii	275
" " Account of	iii	275
" " Its connection with the word of command	iii	282
" " Its connection with the memory of his sufferings	iii	287
" " Its connection with the hope of his glory	iii	298
Swarm of bees worth hiving	iii	67
Swiss shepherd	ii	4
Sympathy with the poor	ii	219
Syro-Phœnician woman	ii	190

	VOL.	PAGE
TABERNACLE, Jewish, a figure of Christ	i	174
" What it was	i	174
Tabernacle, Enclosure	i	178
" The holy place	i	181
" What it taught	i	183
" That there would be a pardoning presence	i	184
" That there would be a purifying presence	i	188
" That there would be an enlightening presence	i	190
" That there would be a comforting presence	i	194
Taboo, Heathen custom called	i	81
Talent (A) for each	iii	259
Tartar chief	ii	161
Teacher, The Great	iii	33
" Because of the great Blessings	iii	35
" Because of the great Simplicity	iii	40
" Because of the great Tenderness	iii	44

		VOL.	PAGE
Teacher, The Great, Because of the great Knowledge		iii	51
" Because of the great Power		iii	56
Telegram, The		ii	21
Temptation of Christ, The		ii	271
" " Meaning of		ii	273
" " Place of		ii	274
" " Led into		ii	274
" " The tempter		ii	275
" " Time of		ii	277
" " To turn stones into bread		ii	278
" " To throw himself from the pinnacle		ii	279
" " To worship Satan		ii	282
" " Teaches us that we must expect temptation		ii	283
" " Teaches us there is no sin in being tempted		ii	288
" " Teaches us how to resist temptation		ii	292
" " Teaches us the reward of victory over temptation		ii	296
Ten Commandments		i	143
Thames Tunnel		iii	176
That's me		iii	162
The best that I can		iii	263
Themistocles		iii	197
There is that scattereth and yet increaseth		iii	156
There were ninety and nine		iii	48
The shilling Bible		iii	89
Thou God seest me		ii	294
" " "		iv	259
Thou shalt bruise his heel		i	15
Thou who once on mother's knee		i	11
Three jewels		ii	166
Tiny's work for God		iii	265
Train delayed		i	218
Transfiguration, The		iii	215
" Account of		iii	216
" Mount of		iii	217
" The wonderful change		iii	218
" The wonderful company		iii	222
" The wonderful conversation		iii	225
" The lesson of hope		iii	229
" The lesson of instruction		iii	232
" The lesson of duty		iii	236
Travellers in the desert		i	153
" in the snow		iii	143

Analytical Index

	VOL.	PAGE
Trial, The	iv	59
" History of	iv	60
" Lesson about the weak ruler	iv	65
" Lesson about the wicked priests	iv	70
" Lesson about the patience of Christ	iv	74
" Lesson about the humiliation of Christ	iv	79
" Lesson about the glory of Christ	iv	82
True hero, The	iv	85
Truthful and obedient	ii	230
Try it	iv	133
Two brothers	iv	73
UGLY Greg	iii	58
Unexpected (The) friend	iv	175
VISIT of the Wise men	ii	179
Von Zeiten, General	ii	85
WANDERER restored by the father's message	i	90
Wanted a boy	ii	255
Washington, How he taught his men that all should work	iii	178
" His humility	iii	178
" Prayer of	iv	8
Wasp's sting	ii	170
Was there ever gentlest shepherd?	iii	42
Water for cleansing	i	167
" for comfort	i	167
We cannot be our own masters	iii	251
Wellington, Duke of	i	21
" "	ii	79
Well-instructed boy	iii	54
Wesley (Charles) and the bird	ii	136
Wesley's, Mrs., patience	ii	237
Western sky, The	iii	221
Wet sand, The	ii	265
What a plant did	iii	7
Why didn't I mind my mother?	ii	232
Widow and the candles	ii	37
Widow of Nain	i	63
" "	ii	39

	VOL.	PAGE
Wilberforce	iii	39
Willie's heroism	iii	116
Wise men, Visit of	ii	179
" Earnest seekers of Jesus	ii	183
" Persevering seekers	ii	188
" Successful seekers	ii	193
" Liberal seekers	ii	196
" Happy seekers	ii	202
Woman of Samaria	iii	38
Working as well as praying	iii	28
Workingman's child	ii	56

YOUNG hero, A . . . . iv 194

INDEX OF POEMS

	VOL.	PAGE
ACCORDING to thy gracious word	iii	297
A dreary place would be this earth	iii	197
All hail the power of Jesus' name	iii	234
All is o'er, the pain, the sorrow	iv	127
A swarm of bees worth hiving	iii	67
CAN I Gethsemane forget?	iv	27
DARE to do right! dare to be true!	iv	70
Drive the nail aright, boys	iii	31
EVERY talent useful	iii	268
FATHER of mercies! in thy word	iii	91
From everything our Saviour saw	iii	53
GOD entrusts to all	iii	259
Great things are made of fragments small	iii	17
HE is a path, if any be misled	ii	131
How sweet is the gospel	ii	269
"I CANNOT do much," said a little star	iii	263
I have found the *Pearl of greatest price*	ii	203
I go to life and not to death	iv	146
I leave it all with Jesus	iii	71
Is thy cruse of comfort wasting?	iii	156
LAMB of God, I look to thee	iii	213
Light after darkness, gain after loss	iii	273

	VOL.	PAGE
MITE song, The	iii	11
My soul be on thy guard	iv	57
NO foot of land do I possess	i	61
None but Jesus	ii	129
Not all the blood of beasts	i	76
Not ourselves, but the truths in life we have spoken	iv	296
Numb and weary on the mountains	iii	144
ONCE in his arms the Saviour took	iii	206
Only a drop in the bucket	iii	11
Oppressed with noon-day's scorching heat	iii	228
O yes, I will try for the whole of the day	ii	234
PRAISE God from whom all blessings flow	iv	136
SEE the kind shepherd Jesus, stands	ii	26
Shining for Jesus	iv	177
Somebody's mother	iv	171
THE birds, without barn, or storehouse	iv	136
The reward of heaven	iii	273
There were ninety and nine	iii	48
Think kindly of the erring	iii	82
Thou art coming! at thy table	iii	303
Thou who once on mother's knee	i	11
Though little I bring	iii	268
UGLY Greg was the prisoner's name	iii	58
WAS there ever, gentlest Shepherd	iii	42
When I survey the wondrous cross	iv	119

Other Solid Ground Titles

In addition to *The Life of Jesus Christ for the Young* which you hold in your hand, Solid Ground Christian Books is honored to offer many other uncovered treasure, many for the first time in more than a century:

THE CHILD AT HOME by John S.C. Abbott
THE KING'S HIGHWAY: *The 10 Commandments for the Young* by Richard Newton
HEROES OF THE REFORMATION by Richard Newton
FEED MY LAMBS: *Lectures to Children on Vital Subjects* by John Todd
LET THE CANNON BLAZE AWAY by Joseph P. Thompson
THE STILL HOUR: *Communion with God in Prayer* by Austin Phelps
COLLECTED WORKS of James Henley Thornwell (4 vols.)
CALVINISM IN HISTORY by *Nathaniel S. McFetridge*
OPENING SCRIPTURE: *Hermeneutical Manual* by *Patrick Fairbairn*
THE ASSURANCE OF FAITH by *Louis Berkhof*
THE PASTOR IN THE SICK ROOM by *John D. Wells*
THE BUNYAN OF BROOKLYN: *Life & Sermons of I.S. Spencer*
THE NATIONAL PREACHER: *Sermons from 2nd Great Awakening*
FIRST THINGS: *First Lessons God Taught Mankind* Gardiner Spring
BIBLICAL & THEOLOGICAL STUDIES by *1912 Faculty of Princeton*
THE POWER OF GOD UNTO SALVATION by *B.B. Warfield*
THE LORD OF GLORY by *B.B. Warfield*
A GENTLEMAN & A SCHOLAR: *Memoir of J.P. Boyce* by *J. Broadus*
SERMONS TO THE NATURAL MAN by *W.G.T. Shedd*
SERMONS TO THE SPIRITUAL MAN by *W.G.T. Shedd*
HOMILETICS AND PASTORAL THEOLOGY by *W.G.T. Shedd*
A PASTOR'S SKETCHES 1 & 2 by *Ichabod S. Spencer*
THE PREACHER AND HIS MODELS by *James Stalker*
IMAGO CHRISTI: *The Example of Jesus Christ* by *James Stalker*
A HISTORY OF PREACHING by *Edwin C. Dargan*
LECTURES ON THE HISTORY OF PREACHING by *J. A. Broadus*
THE SCOTTISH PULPIT by *William Taylor*
THE SHORTER CATECHISM ILLUSTRATED by *John Whitecross*
THE CHURCH MEMBER'S GUIDE by *John Angell James*
THE SUNDAY SCHOOL TEACHER'S GUIDE by *John A. James*
CHRIST IN SONG: *Hymns of Immanuel from All Ages* by *Philip Schaff*
COME YE APART: *Daily Words from the Four Gospels* by *J.R. Miller*
DEVOTIONAL LIFE OF THE S.S. TEACHER by *J.R. Miller*

Call us Toll Free at 1-877-666-9469
Send us an e-mail at sgcb@charter.net
Visit us on line at solid-ground-books.com
Uncovering Buried Treasure to the Glory of God

Printed in the United States
73048LV00004B/4